Operation Big Ben

The anti-V2 Spitfire missions 1944–1945

What They Said

'9 September I received information from London that on the previous day the first V2 rockets had landed in England; it was suspected that they came from areas near Rotterdam and Amsterdam and I was asked when I could rope off those general areas.'
Memoirs of Field Marshal Montgomery

'After the V1, the V2, a far more formidable weapon. These were rockets, and travelled far faster than the V1s, and thus could not be destroyed in the air. They also carried more explosive. To give an idea of the havoc of these new terror weapons, the one which fell on 25 November scored a direct hit on Woolworth's store in New Cross, London: 160 people were killed and 135 injured.'
Fight for the Sky – The story of the Spitfire and Hurricane
Douglas Bader

'. . . Hitler's second secret weapon, the V2 fell on London. This new form of devilry continued until our armies captured The Hague, from which most of the rockets were launched, seven months later.'
The Memoirs of Lord Ismay

OPERATION BIG BEN

THE ANTI-V2
SPITFIRE MISSIONS 1944–1945

by

Craig Cabell and Graham A Thomas

Foreword by

Raymond Baxter

SPELLMOUNT
Staplehurst

British Library Cataloguing in Publication Data:
A catalogue record for this book is available
from the British Library

ISBN 1-86227-251-4

Published in the UK in 2004 by
Spellmount Limited
The Village Centre
Staplehurst
Kent TN12 0BJ

Tel: 01580 893730
Fax: 01580 893731
E-mail: enquiries@spellmount.com
Website: www.spellmount.com

1 3 5 7 9 8 6 4 2

Typeset in Palatino by MATS, Southend-on-Sea, Essex
Printed in Great Britain by
T.J. International Ltd
Padstow, Cornwall

Contents

For Raymond Baxter and the others who flew.
And to the lasting memory of RAF Coltishall.

About the Authors

Craig Cabell is the writer of four previous books including biography and military history. For five years he was an in-house reporter with *Focus – The House Journal of the Ministry of Defence*. However he has been a freelance reporter for over fifteen years, working most notably for *The Independent* newspaper. He lives in London with his wife and three children.

Graham Thomas is also a former reporter with *Focus* and is currently an Information Officer for the Government Information Communications Service at Media Ops in Salisbury. His work has taken him around the world, most notably to Russia and Iraq (after the latter he contributed to an official book on the Iraqi war published by the British Army). He has also published a military history of the Korean War for which Craig Cabell provided a Foreword.

Author's Note

The idea for this book came from a conversation I had with Raymond Baxter (veteran Spitfire pilot and original presenter of BBC TV's 'Tomorrow's World'). He told me about Operation Big Ben and his part in it. The thought of Mark IX, Mark XIV and Mark XVI Spitfires essentially dive-bombing V2 rocket sites during the last year of the Second World War seemed a fantastic one to me. Why had I not heard about this before? I asked a colleague at the Ministry of Defence about this – Graham A Thomas. He made a few enquiries but drew a blank. Individually, we did nothing about it for another year, however, we mentioned it occasionally over the odd drink, drawing the conclusion that the whole incident was still not in the public domain.

After completing my first book for a military history publisher (and assisting with a second), I decided to spend some time researching the operation myself. Graham had moved to Salisbury but we still managed to meet up for the odd drink and the conversation always turned to Operation Big Ben, or as we called it 'The Large One'. 'They had their wings clipped,' I told him. He took this in. What else had I found? 'They dive-bombed at night.' Impossible, was Graham's reaction (he wasn't far wrong there).

In short, the more we found out about the operation, the more impossible it seemed. This was fast becoming the stuff big budget Hollywood movies were based upon: V2 rockets, specially constructed Spitfires, secret and highly dangerous missions.

The first breakthrough came with the possession of a document entitled 'Vol. 6 (formerly Vol. 7) Air Defence of Great Britain', its sub-heading 'The Flying Bomb and Rocket Campaigns 1944–1945'. This paper gave us the official spur we needed: over fifty pages of well documented evidence, complete with facts and figures, of the length and breadth of Operation Big Ben and its success rate. This document would become the bare bones to which both Graham and I would soon add flesh.

Through official squadron histories, log-books and interviews, Graham and I have, for the first time, brought to life the whole shocking truth concerning Operation Big Ben, a truth that has never been showcased before; at least not as far certainly as the expertise, bravery and common-sense of the pilots who flew during the operation are concerned.* To us, this operation was as important and significant to the liberation of the Allied world during the Second World War as the Battle of Britain and the Dam Busters raid. Because so much secrecy – and dare I say individual modesty – has shrouded the details of the raids, Operation Big Ben has been largely unappreciated until now – its 60th Anniversary.

So for the first time, here are the intricate details of one of the most courageous exploits executed by the Royal Air Force, Royal Canadian Air Force, Royal New Zealand Air Force, Royal Australian Air Force and Polish Spitfire Squadron, during the last days of the Second World War.

Operation Big Ben directly saved British civilian suffering by knocking out V2 rocket sites. The missions were difficult and casualties there inevitably were. To bring home the terror of the V2, let us observe a quote from Lord Alanbrooke's diaries, an entry dated 7 March 1945: 'Herbert Morrison attended the CoS (Chief of Staff) to discuss... (saving) London from rockets and buzz bombs... We listened as sympathetically as we could and then explained to him our difficulties in trying to deal with this threat either by air or by land (while I write I hear the rumble of one landing in the distance!).'

The CoS was very concerned with the cutting-edge technology possessed by the Nazis. The V1s were terrible but at least they gave the warning drone of their engine when they approached; with the V2 there was no warning and, consequently, the fear instilled in the general public was much higher (see 'Memories' for a first-hand account).

Early Crossbow discussions considered the kidnap of top Nazi scientists; but this obviously proved nigh-impossible. Ground troops were deemed necessary but, to begin with, this was too difficult because rocket sites were too far into enemy territory. So bombing raids were the only solution.

For clarity, 'Big Ben' was the codename given to the V2 rockets, hence the codename given to the last all-out assault mission against them: Operation Big Ben. Although certain aspects of the missions under Big Ben have been documented before, no one has truly put together a 'reportage' of events

---

* Operation Crossbow (simplistically, the original counter-attack on V1 rocket sites) has been showcased in other books, such as *Hitler's Rockets* by Norman Longmate (Hutchinson, 1985) and *Hitler's Rocket Sites* by Philip Henshall (Robert Hale, 1985). These books discuss the V1 and V2 from their conception through their development, operational success and then countermeasures against them; this book however, exclusively analyses one set of manoeuvres that came out of the 'lessons learned' from Crossbow and the Crossbow Committee (essentially 1943–45), with specific aircraft – Spitfires – and mission statements: essentially, to dive-bomb rocket sites and supply lines and analyse V2 rocket sites.

distinguishing what Operation Big Ben was, and explaining the subtleties of the mission and how it developed.

It has also been the clear intention of the authors of this book to put the pilot back into his Spitfire and make him fly again. Not only to give the detail of what that pilot did, but who he was, what he looked like and what his personality was like. Perhaps this 'heart-on-sleeve' approach takes the book away from academia; however, it is felt that it offers more depth to the individual squadrons and the decisions made. Just to be confronted by a list of pilots in a squadron history is not enough for a work like this; the camaraderie needs to be appreciated too. It is appropriate to thank again Raymond Baxter for his priceless insight when pulling off this trick successfully.

This book is the most comprehensive study of Operation Big Ben ever published. It is hoped that the men who flew will now receive the praise that has so sadly evaded them over the past sixty years.

Craig Cabell
London, September 2004

Acknowledgements

The authors would like to acknowledge and thank the following people and establishments who assisted and contributed their time and energy to this book, we are forever in their debt: Raymond Baxter, Mavis and Ian, Dennis 'Hurricane' David, John 'Cat's Eyes' Cunningham, John Golly, Jack Brehm, Field Marshal Lord Carver, Frederick Forsyth, Group Captain Jim Spurrell, John Holdcroft, David Downing, Allan House, Jamie Wilson, Beth Macdougall, Andrew Chrysostomou.

Also, thanks are due to Eric B Morgan and Edward Shacklady and their exhaustive work *Spitfire – The History*, for details of aircraft prior and post Big Ben. Your book is a labour of love gentlemen that is an essential reference work for any serious historian or lover of beautiful aircraft.

Many thanks also to The Imperial War Museum, RAF Insworth, the Air Historical Branch, the Douglas Bader Foundation (with special thanks to Lady Bader and Keith Delderfield) and the people who preserve the memory of 453 Squadron down-under.

We would also like to thank the unsung heroes: Anita, Samantha, Nathan and Fern, Shirley and Colin, Berny and Dave and our dear colleague David Barlow.

We would also like to thank the people who made a difference during the Second World War and from whom we learnt much, among them: Field Marshal Montgomery, Field Marshal Lord Alanbrooke, Lord Ismay, Sir Winston Churchill, Dennis Wheatley and also many friends and relations for their memories of the Second World War and perceptions appertaining to it.

Sincerely, many thanks to all.

Craig Cabell and Graham A Thomas
London, September 2004

Foreword

by

Raymond Baxter

The purpose of this book is to draw attention to an aspect of the Second World War which, as its authors acknowledge, has been broadly overlooked. It marked the origins of 'Space Wars' – the operation of unmanned missiles against defenceless civilians.

The German V1 and V2 did just that. They were never aimed at armies on land, ships at sea, nor indeed aircraft or airfields. Their purpose was to destroy, unhindered, the fighting spirit and capability of the British people.

While the lights burned bright in New York City, the long-suffering people of Britain were subjected to an entirely new experience of terrorism. Following their long years of suffering since 1939, they did not flinch.

Since 1940 the Royal Air Force had been familiar with fighting against the odds. But this presented us Fighter pilots, who took up the challenge, with the necessity to develop new tactics and operational skills in double quick time.

The reliance of this book upon day-to-day events as recorded in the official Squadron War Diaries may appear repetitious. Written in the third person they lack the colour of individual comment and, to be frank, do not make light reading. But that in a sense reflects the nature of the campaign. Despite the risks our losses were not heavy but the task was demanding in the extreme. Day after day with no respite. Good weather, bad weather. Good strike, bad strike. Success, frustration, tragedy. Every day was different and to see the next dawn was a blessing for which I, for one, am grateful to this day.

Raymond Baxter, OBE
Henley-on-Thames
September 2004

Introduction

The Glorious Spitfire

It is difficult to write about a legend because people assume you have done so for commercial reasons only. That is not the case with this book. Yes, the Spitfire is a sexy beast, its missions always full of heroism and charm; but when you encounter a mission that has been underplayed *so* much it is almost forgotten, then you disregard your own prejudice and document the heroism. Indeed, dive-bombing Spitfires destroying V2 rocket sites, the great Field Marshal Lord Alanbrooke deeming the mission a great disaster – when it wasn't – and a pilot actually blowing up a ballistic missile as it took off, is obviously worthy of special note.

In the year running up to October 2004, nothing concerning Operation Big Ben was mentioned within the media (even by TV shows covering the threat of V2 rockets during the Second World War), but it did happen and the bravery of those who flew has been largely unappreciated, until now. This is their story.

CC

Memories

by a Child of the Second World War

The V1s and V2s were terrible. I remember that awful deep drone of the V1s. Then suddenly, it would cut out and instantly drop like a stone and explode. There was no escape from a direct hit. Even the after shock. When one landed in the next street, it brought down our ceilings and brought in our windows too.

I lived in Heavitree Road then (Plumstead, south-east London), the V1 took out most of Bramblebury Road, just flattened it. There was rarely any warning from a V1, except that deep drone – I can still hear it now. But when the V2s started, there was less warning, they were silent. So many more people were killed.

I was just a child and regularly had to go to the air raid shelter on Plumstead Common. The one thing I remember about that was the strong smell of Jeyes' fluid. It wasn't an unpleasant smell, just strong. We had our own Anderson shelter, but it was safer going to the main communal shelter.

One day, after an air raid, we returned home and our house had gone. Completely flattened, nothing left. We were taken in by our 'Uncle' Dick who lived nearby, a kind man. On another occasion, a friend of mine asked me to stay in her shelter with her family. I asked my mum but she said no on that occasion. The following day we were told that the whole family had been killed by a direct hit, so I was lucky.

A lot of people died during the blitz by staying at home. Some did survive, having been buried alive and dug out by the ARP.

There was panic one day (1941) as the Battle of Britain raged overhead. A German pilot bailed out of his aircraft and landed on Plumstead Common, there was a lot of screaming and shouting and I'm sure the man was frightened, but the police soon arrested him and took him to a nearby military establishment.

The Spitfires were quite small aircraft. My father used to stand on the roof of our house during the Battle of Britain and watch the dog fights. It was a terrible time really. Going backwards and forwards to the air raid shelter every day for five years, not knowing what was going to happen next, it was very frightening. Then one day I was told I was being taken to Trafalgar Square for the celebrations of Victory in Europe (VE) Day, and that became the start of better times.

MB

CHAPTER I
Fearsome Silhouette

'These new weapons entirely altered all strategic concep-
tions. In November 1940 it was obvious that Britain must do
her utmost to protect herself from future attack by more
powerful air-fleets, but no one then envisaged a war waged
with long-range rockets having thermo-nuclear warheads.'

Stranger than Fiction
Dennis Wheatley

On 15 October 1944 British Intelligence learned that a factory in
Luxembourg was making rockets. Lots of rockets. It appeared that the
Germans had planned to make over 12,000 of what would become the V2
rocket by October 1944, with an eventual rate of production of 1,000 per
month. They were behind schedule, thankfully.

Production may have been slow, but it was almost certain that at least
2,000 rockets had been produced by the end of September and that
something approaching the planned output per month was close to being
achieved.

This was a scary prospect for the British Chiefs of Staff (CoS) to contem-
plate; but what could they do to counter the prospect of a new type of
Blitz? Were they aware of the level of technology harnessed – created – by
Nazi scientists? Well, the answer to the latter question is an emphatic no;
but the former . . .

It was estimated that some 700 rockets were on trial or active operation
by the end of October 1944 and Britain was the obvious target of these
terrible weapons; indeed, the British would soon feel the full force of the
Third Reich's new destructive power.

The CoS had been aware of the production of a new weapon for some
time. The first attack on London of V1 'pilotless planes'occurred on the
night of 12 June 1944 (see Alanbrooke's diaries). As far back as 29 June
1943, Alanbrooke, Eden, Lyttelton, Morrison, Cripps, Sandys, Crow
(rocket expert), Professor Lindemann and others met with the Prime
Minister to discuss the new rocket weapon that the Nazis were 'supposed'

1

to be developing (V2). A conclusion was then drawn that a 'definite threat' existed, and that Peenemünde (the experimental station on the Baltic coast of Germany) should be bombed at the earliest possible date. Interestingly, three days after his promotion to Field Marshal, Alanbrooke had a long CoS meeting (4 January 1944), where they discussed the threat of the rocket and 'pilotless plane' (V2, V1). 'Evidence goes on accumulating', Alanbrooke wrote in his dairies and, indeed, the threat was a constant subject at the weekly CoS meetings. However, Alanbrooke had been aware of the strong 'probability of pilotless aeroplane attacks on London' since 21 December 1943 (as he mentioned in his diaries).

The truth is, nobody really knew how to counter the flying bombs. Peenemünde was difficult to bomb, but obviously something had to be done. Ground troops were not an option, as the launch sites were deep in enemy territory.

Great minds soon went to work on the problem, but in their hearts they knew they couldn't stop the inevitable assault on London and the widespread panic of the British people that would ensue. Could this mean the end of London and a united Britain against the evil of the Nazis?

With hindsight it is easy to shun such thoughts, but at the time the CoS wasn't so sure. Everyone was concerned but some showed it more than others, especially within the government.

CHAPTER II
Anti-V2 Sorties

According to the log book of Raymond Baxter (602 Squadron), Big Ben patrols officially started on 10 October 1944. More precisely, he told me in February 2004: 'the first time "Big Ben" is mentioned in my log book is 10 October 1944, in the form of "Big Ben patrol". Before then it was just "anti-V2 sorties."'

In order to cover every aspect of Big Ben, we first need to start with the reconnaisance that started the operation. For Raymond Baxter and 602 Squadron that started in September 1944. '29 September we went to Coltishall,' Baxter told me. 'We had Spitfire IX Bs. 3 October we were deployed to escort a Liberator. "Escort an anti-V2 Lib at 20,000 feet"' (*Baxter's entry in his log book*). Baxter and his squadron were effectively waiting to be attacked, and they didn't like the thought of that one bit.

For Operation Big Ben, Spitfire squadrons were equipped with clipped-wing Mark XVI Spitfires.

What we learn from Baxter's comments is that there was no layoff period for 602 Squadron, they were quickly deployed from one operation to another (from the 2nd Tactical Air Force front line followers of the Army post D-Day to anti-V2 operations), albeit escort work to begin with. CoS was very concerned about the new Nazi threat and Britain had to get the ball rolling as far as counter-measures were concerned.

All of this activity was probably a direct result of a cabinet meeting, which was held between 18:00hrs and 20:00hrs on 27 July 1944. The meeting exclusively concerned V1s and V2s (see Alanbrooke diaries). The bombing of London by V1s was well underway by then, so dramatic new measures had to be implemented. The answer: reconnaisance and bombing. Anti-V2 measures had to be implemented. This was a separate entity to Operation Crossbow (which had dealt with the V1 threat). So two months later, 602 Squadron was brought in.

Raymond Baxter wrote in his log book, 'On 4 October we undertook anti-V2 raids and that went on through the 6 and 7 October. These raids were two hours fourteen to two hours twenty minutes – a long time in the air in a Spitfire.'

At this stage of the proceedings, there was no dive-bombing because

3

they did not possess the Mark XVIs. However, some form of operation – sweeping in low on the enemy sites – had to be achieved.

On 24 October 1944 a very long CoS meeting took place, primarily concerning V1 missions and proposed counter-measures. The Joint Intelligence Committee was in attendance, also Duncan Sandys. Everybody left the meeting more concerned than when they went in. More intelligence had to be acquired. To counter the rockets was difficult to say the least but something had to be done, the CoS was concerned about widespread panic among the general public and they couldn't afford that; but what should they do?

On 6 November 1944 more was learned about the V2 rocket production. Documents discovered in the Luxembourg factory, along with evidence from prisoners taken, suggested that a very important, if not the only, component assembly plant for the rockets was located at Niedersachswerfen, near Nordhausen in the Harz Mountains. This was the clincher. At last, irrefutable evidence of an assembly factory existed. Fears of heavier attacks from the rockets became prevalent; but the most worrying factor was still counter-measures. The assembly factory was known to British Intelligence. It had been under consideration as a producer of Jumo Jet engines and the difficulties of attacking it were well known and deemed to be great (this was discussed at the weekly CoS Flying Bomb meeting that took place on 8 November).

To reach the plant was not the main problem; the challenge was to damage it effectively. It consisted of two parallel tunnels about one mile long that had been constructed in former gypsum (hydrous calcium sulphate from which plaster of paris is made) quarries and lay for the most part under some 200–300 feet of this mineral. The only bombs available to the Allied air forces that might penetrate to the tunnels were the 12,000 lb 'Tallboy' bombs used by Bomber Command. Production of these during the autumn of 1944 was small and vast quantities were needed for the attacks upon the German pocket battleships, whenever the opportunity arose; and for certain vital communication targets in Germany. The attack on Niedersachswerfen was therefore shelved.

But what of flying operations in September 1944? We know of 602 Squadron's coming into the operation in late September, but were Spitfires operating throughout September? Yes, they were. 229 Squadron got the ball rolling on 10 September 1944; what follows is the detail of anti-V2 sorties conducted by the squadron that month:

10 September 1944

As the morning light crept over Coltishall, two Spitfire IXFs climbed into the air on a Jim Crow[1] over the Den Helder area at 06:50hrs. At 200 feet they crossed over the North Sea and climbed to 10,000 feet over Den Helder sighting two large landing craft patrolling along a line on the south-east coast of Texel. The near vessel stopped and moments later, the two aircraft were buffeted by accurate medium flak from two guns aboard the landing craft. At the same time, flak from (the east coast of) Texel burst near the two Spitfires as they roared along the coastline.

With F/O Walker leading F/Sgt Noneybun, the two aircraft turned south heading back to Den Helder. They sighted more shipping farther south in Ijmuiden harbour and by 08:15hrs they had set course for base, landing back at Coltishall at 08:55hrs.

Later that afternoon (14:02hrs), a squadron of Spitfires took off from Coltishall, climbing into the cold September air heading for the Zeider Zee. They were divided into two sections of four aircraft with F/Lt Patterson leading Green Section and F/O Andrew leading Black Section. Climbing to 10,000 feet the Spitfires crossed into Holland at Egmund at 14:40hrs. Turning south along the Gerredijk Heerenveen patrol line they spotted a solitary locomotive heading towards the town. Seeing the fighters the locomotive stopped. Wheeling around, Patterson led his Section into the attack, the spitfires breaking formation and attacking the locomotive from different angles. Cannon fire raked the steam engine and debris flew everywhere. When Green Section finished its first attack, F/O Andrew led his Section in strafing the now burning locomotive with cannon fire. Green Section attacked again for good measure and, as they climbed away, Patterson could see smoke and flames pouring from the locomotive.

The flight headed towards Swolle where two trains were spotted. A passenger train of eight coaches and a goods train were both travelling north. Seeing the Spitfires, the engineers stopped their trains very close to each other. Immediately, the passengers poured from the coaches as Patterson brought the flight around onto the tempting targets below. Watching the passengers run into the nearby fields and woods he waited until they were clear before leading the attack. Rolling into his dive, Patterson roared down onto the two locomotives below. Splitting up, the Spitfires attacked from different positions, spitting cannon and machine-gun fire onto the vehicles raking the goods locomotive with tracer shells. Suddenly, flames shot up into the air as high as 200 feet (according to the squadron diary). As Patterson pulled out of his dive he could see the goods locomotive had been destroyed and the passenger locomotive severely damaged; but the coaches had remained untouched.

Four more stationary locomotives were spotted a few minutes later by the flight in a wood near Nunspeet. Each aircraft attacked the parked locomotives at least twice, 'but with machine-gun fire only as the cannon had all been used,' wrote the 229 diarist. 'Then F/Lt Patterson who was leading could not resist the temptation of revisiting his favourite haunt of

Amersfoort and not without luck for eight miles east of the town and travelling west towards Appeldoorn was a goods train of four wagons containing timber. It was attacked by three aircraft only as none of the others had any ammunition left!' Patterson saw strikes hit the locomotive and wagons with bits flying off the vehicles.

He turned the flight towards Nijkirk, climbed to 10,000 feet and headed out to sea for home (15:57hrs). The eight Spitfires landed back at Coltishall at 16:40hrs.

11 September 1944

Early morning sorties were Jim Crow missions searching for shipping in Den Helder. But the most interesting flight of the day was later at 17:15hrs when twelve Spitfires, led by W/Cmdr Fitzgerald flew escort for more than 100 Lancaster bombers. Flying at 16,000 feet they turned to starboard north of the target area at Kamen where they spotted a formation of eight unidentified aircraft (probably Me 262 jet fighters) at 35,000 feet. The aircraft left twin vapour trails. Flak was the heaviest they had yet encountered and one bomber was seen to receive a direct hit and explode in mid-air.

Green Section broke away to starboard to investigate the unidentified aircraft but they were too high and too fast so the four Spitfires set a course for Coltishall, covering the straggling bombers. They landed home at 19:55hrs.

With the bombing over, Blue 2, F/Sgt Hayes, developed engine trouble. Escorted by W/Cmdr Fitzgerald the Spitfires headed for a pre-arranged emergency landing field at Brussels. But cloud cover and worsening light made it difficult to find so they continued on. According to 229 Squadron's diarist: 'they turned for base and passed over a town, which F/Sgt Hayes thinks was Antwerp. Over the Albes Canal, they saw the battle now in progress with tanks, flame-throwers and all the implements of war. They crossed out at 19:30hrs and landed at Coltishall at 20:07hrs.'

12 September 1944

The following day the weather was sharp, sunny and clear as it had been the day before (this would not become the norm for the later Big Ben operations). But the CO who had suffered from malaria in the past was fuming because he had to return to hospital for further observation. The diarist wrote: 'He declares himself to be perfectly fit. And regards the Medical authorities as being in league to deprive him of the great activity 229 Squadron is at present experiencing and vows never to put himself into their hands again.'

At 12:55hrs W/Cmdr Fitzgerald was again leading a force of twelve

Spitfires, acting as rear cover to 221 Halifaxes bombing Gelsenkirchen. Flying at 19,000 feet they crossed the Dutch coast. Climbing to 22,000 feet the formation encountered almost continuous flak as they headed for the target. Over the target the flak got worse, becoming very intense. Four of the bombers were hit and exploded in the air. As the bombing took place, the Spitfires made two wide orbits over the area. Below they could see intense black smoke rising from the bombing as high as 10,000 feet and visible for thirty to forty miles. Smoke from generators helped to cover the target area as the bombing continued. One pilot caught sight of six unidentified but very fast aircraft flying east to west at 15,000 feet. The diarist records that these were probably Me 262 jets. However, their vapour trails were seen by all the pilots and some reported that they had twin tails, and F/Lt Lillywhite reported that one aircraft seemed to have a twin boom but it could have been the twin jets.

In the late afternoon F/Lt Patterson led twelve Spitfires on withdrawal cover for returning Halifax bombers that had hit Munster. They took off at 17:30hrs and made contact with the bombers at 18:30hrs. They then orbited the target for four minutes while the Halifaxes dropped their bombs. The diarist recorded: 'The whole town suddenly became alive with flames. Especially in the west and the south where most high explosives were seen to fall first followed by incendiaries, which were seen to fall largely in the west. All pilots reported seeing the dull red flashes of exploding bombs on Munster followed by the bursting incendiaries flashing across the ground.'

The Spitfires, flying at 25,000 feet, escorted the remaining bombers back to England. The spitfires landed at Coltishall at 20:00hrs, the pilots stiff from sitting for more than two and half hours in their cramped cockpits.

13 September 1944

The next day's flying was largely small formations of Jim Crow missions to report shipping activity in Dutch harbours and along its coast. F/Lt Barrett and F/O McKenzie (229 Sqn) took off from Coltishall at 11:15hrs and climbed to 10,000 feet. They crossed in at Egmund and headed along the coast to Terschbelling where they ran into heavy, intense and accurate flak. Undeterred, the two Spitfires carried on reporting shipping. They sighted three naval auxillary vessels in battleship grey of about 500 tons in the area.

The rest of the flights for this day were shipping reconnaissance. However, at 14:45hrs, F/Lt McAndrew and F/Lt Barrett were airborne to escort a Wellington bomber on a mission patrolling over the North Sea. 'Not much was known about the mission,' wrote the Squadron diarist. 'It was either on air-sea rescue work or plotting a Big Ben,' the entry continued (this was the first mention of Big Ben, on which much more enphasis would soon be placed). The bomber had been attacked by enemy aircraft earlier and asked for protection.

The two Spitfires sighted the Wellington at 17:10hrs, flying at 15,000 feet. The patrol was uneventful and the two fighters returned to Coltishall at 19:15hrs.

14 September 1944

Poor weather restricted flying for this day with most of the airfield covered in thick fog. However, after lunch the fog lifted and the airfield was suddenly filled with aircraft as seven squadrons landed to take part in an escort to a bombing operation over Wilhelmshaven (17:30hrs). However, one Spitfire from 611 Squadron, after landing, taxied straight into the CO's Spitfire 'Judy' that was sitting in its pen. In the word of the diarist: 'P/O Andrews who was in the cockpit of the CO's Spitfire cleaning the Perspex escaped with severe injuries and shock, with the blue Perspex cleaner streaming down his face he staggered from the wreckage giving one the first impression that his injuries would be little less than fatal. Within three minutes of this happening a second Spitfire of 126 Squadron overshot and hit a raised bank on the other side of 229 dispersal, breaking the aircraft . . . in a flash flames leapt into the sky.'

Sadly, the pilot (F/O Fortes) died within a few months and it was later discovered that he had been married only three days before the incident.

15 September 1944

More sadness occurred the following day, during the first sortie at 09:10hrs. On a Jim Crow mission to patrol the Ijmuiden to Terschelling area, F/Sgt Manley and F/Sgt O'Reilly climbed into the early morning air. The weather was not good, but as they crossed over the North Sea to the Dutch coast it got worse. Below them was a heavy sea fog.

Both aircraft flew very low. Through a break in the mist they saw land and F/Sgt O'Reilly reported they were about six miles south of Den Helder. Turning north, flying at 200 feet, they crossed out towards England and were met by sudden, intense flak. F/Sgt Manley (Black 1) suddenly reported he'd been hit. Climbing to 3,000 feet, the fighters changed course and headed back to base.

'I'll probably have to bale out,' reported Manley over the R/T. O'Reilly formated on the stricken Spitfire and saw the rudder ailerons had been shot away. About thirty miles west of Den Helder, according to O'Reilly's report, Manley prepared to bale out. But before he could, flames and white smoke leapt from the Spitfire's exhaust and the aircraft went into a spiral.

O'Reilly watched his friend go down, praying for a parachute to open. At 500 feet he saw Manley's chute open. It remained on the water for five minutes only, a few hundred yards from where the Spitfire had crashed. However, O'Reilly didn't see Manley, and he climbed to 5,000 feet reporting the crash and the shipping they'd seen during their patrol. 'The shipping seen through the gap in the clouds was five barge type vessels,' recorded the Squadron diarist.

At 10:45hrs O'Reilly who had been orbiting an oil patch where Manley's Spitfire had crashed, was relieved from duty and headed back to base. Throughout the day, Spitfires from 229 Squadron were scrambled on air-sea rescue search missions to search for Manley but no sign of the pilot was found.[2]

16 September 1944

F/Lt Patterson led a formation of eight Spitfires looking for targets over the north of Holland. They were airborne from Coltishall at 10:55hrs and headed for the Dutch coast. Over Texel, Patterson climbed the formation to 10,000 feet and turned inland. Within minutes he saw a small goods train of eight trucks south of Crondngien. The train stopped, its crew diving for cover as the Spitfires attacked. From all directions the fighters shot across the area pouring cannon shells into the locomotive. Debris, including the funnel, flew from the stricken locomotive as the shells hammered into it. Thick smoke poured out as the locomotive was destroyed. The trucks were heavily damaged as the Spitfires raked them with shells.

On the same flight, a six-wheeled vehicle was attacked by four aircraft and destroyed on the Meppel road. Three army vehicles were also attacked and another heavily camouflaged vehicle on a common east of Aburg was destroyed, and several grey clad figures were seen scurrying for cover. The flight landed back at base at 13:50hrs.

17 September 1944

The squadron was involved in a major airborne operation in the south of Holland to Eindhoven and Nijmegan. 'Troops were carried in 623 aircraft and 408 Horsa gliders towed by tugs,' wrote 229 Squadron's diarist. 'A considerable stream of aircraft escorted by fighters swept over the North Sea for three to four hours.'

The role of 229 was to patrol a stretch of the Dutch Coast. Led by W/Cmdr Fitzgerald, twelve Spitfires took off from Coltishall at 12:20hrs. Over their patrol lines, the Spitfires climbed to 5,000 feet but they saw no sign of enemy activity either in the air or on the ground. However, Green Section (led by F/Lt Patterson) patrolling at 12,000 feet, caught sight of the

Squadron's first V2. 'It was a vapour trail beginning at 20,000 feet and ending at 35,000 feet going up vertically at terrific speed originating somewhere to the south of the Zeider Zee. It fell to earth we know not where but this was a phenomenon we had been trained to watch for.' (Again, the Big Ben mentality was there and target areas would be sourced from this intelligence.)

Minutes later, Patterson reported over the R/T that two Horsa gliders were floating in the water but there was no sign of life.

18 September 1944

Flying activity was limited to one sortie. During the morning the Squadron practised dive-bombing with their Spitfires (the real start of Operation Big Ben). But at 16:15hrs, Major Harrison led a formation of eight Spitfires to the north of Holland. At 10,000 feet they reached landfall over Texel, then turned towards Vinshoven and then south to Meppel. On the Meppel/Belkbrug road the Spitfires attacked two vehicles leaving them both blazing.

Turning to the Meppel railway yards there were no targets of interest for the attacking Spitfires but they were met by such heavy and intense flak that all the pilots suffered anxious moments. 'Especially the CO whose engine cut at the psychological moment and was some seconds picking up after he had switched over to the main tanks,' wrote the Squadron diarist.

They landed back at Coltishall at 18:40hrs.

20 September 1944

20 September was a turning point for 229 Squadron. The squadron history records that 12 Group Operation Instruction No.19/44 considerably altered the shape of things to come for the Squadron. 'It is now committed to work in conjunction with Nos 80, 274, 3, 56 and 486 Tempest squadrons in the location and destruction of Big Ben locations in Holland.'

Throughout the day, despite the new orders, there was little flying done in search of Big Ben sites. One flight of two Spitfires escorted a Mitchell flying over the north of Holland while another flight of two Spitfires were on air-sea rescue in search of a downed Mustang pilot. Fortunately, the pilot, who was in a dinghy one mile off shore between Yarmouth and Lowestoft, was picked up and brought to safety.

That evening things did change as a new Tempest Squadron arrived at Coltishall. The Squadron diarist recorded: 'There was much briefing and organising in the Station Intelligence Office supporting new duties of Coltishall regarding Big Ben.' As 229 Squadron was the most familiar with the area it was assigned the first patrols escorting the 100 Group on patrol.

Over the next few days the Squadron conducted escort work, mostly of single bombers such as a Mitchell, Halifax or Wellington over Holland. No attacks on land targets took place at this time.

25 September 1944

229 Squadron moved to Manston and the following day the first patrol took place in conjunction with 504 Squadron, escorting Dakotas to Hetchell and north of Ostend before returning to Manston.

27 September 1944

In the morning, at 09:00hrs, twelve Spitfires from 229 Squadron took off from Manston on an escort mission. Together with 504, 124, 119 and 134 Squadrons, the fighters escorted 130 Halifax heavy bombers, which were tasked to bomb Sterkrade in the Ruhr. Three Spitfires, including the CO and Major Harrison, turned back due to mechanical problems. The fighters climbed to 24,000 feet and rendezvoused with the bombers at 09:55hrs. About ten miles north of the target, a Big Ben trail was sighted rising vertically from 20,000 feet to 35,000 feet, going 'at terrific speed' recorded 229 Squadron's diarist. The Squadron landed back at Manston at 11:30hrs.

28 September 1944

The weather proved to be sunny, cold and clear, as it had been the day before. The Manston wing was airborne again to provide escort for two groups of Mitchell bombers attacking Enmerick. At 15:50hrs eleven Spitfires led by W/Cmdr Balmforth, in conjunction with 504 Squadron and the two other squadrons, took off from Manston. At 16:30hrs they rendezvoused over Diest flying at 15,000 feet with the bombers 12,000 feet below them. Over the target the Spitfires orbited for five minutes while the Mitchells dropped their bombs on the marshalling yards in the town.

A vapour trail from a Big Ben was seen at 20,000 feet to 35,000 feet rising vertically at terrific speed. The bombers were escorted out as far as Ghent and the fighters then set course and landed back at Coltishall at 18:00hrs.

In the next couple of days the squadron's Spitfires were again escorting heavy and medium bombers attacking targets in the Ruhr and in Holland.

Pilots of 229 Squadron returned to armed recce patrols, and patrolling over Holland in late October. But it wasn't until December that they began dive-bombing sites in Holland using the new Spitfire XVI (the detail of this can be found in Appendix C, which showcases the rest of 229 Squadron's Big Ben duties and again Appendix D, which looks at the squadron's continued duties renamed as 603 City of Edinburgh Squadron).

So how did the operation now evolve after the foundations laid by 229 in September 1944?

NOTES

1   The definition of a Jim Crow is a sortie that patrols the home coastline in order to intercept hostile aircraft; its additional role is to spot invasion forces (Air Historical Branch).

2   When the squadron was re-named 603 City of Edinburgh Squadron – see Appendix D – a body was discovered washed up on the Dutch coast, which was identified as Manley – see entry for 31 January 1945.

CHAPTER III

Early Days

The vast majority of targets in Holland from which rockets were being fired at the UK were difficult for heavy bombing (as was found throughout September). Essentially, these areas lay between The Hague and Leiden and The Hague and Hook of Holland. Much of this country was heavily wooded and the precise location of firing points and storage depots was not always known (although a lot of important intelligence had been gathered by 229 Squadron during September). And where the hand of nature was not an obstacle that of man was: certain possible targets lay in, or close to, built-up areas and could only have been attacked by heavy bombers at the cost of civilian life. The less devastating attacks of fighter-bombers against targets of this type were also prohibited, because of concern for the Dutch population.

So the offensive took the form of sweeps and reconnaissance in which fighter-bombers attacked targets of opportunity rather than specific, pre-selected objectives. This was work better suited to 2nd Tactical Air Force rather than Fighter Command: because, to be effective, a large number of sorties was needed and 2nd Tactical Air Force was a much stronger force than Fighter Command; second, because 2nd Tactical Air Force was continentally based within easy reach of the areas to be attacked, whereas Fighter Command squadrons had to fly approximately a hundred miles across the sea before they reached western Holland. The sorties flown over Holland and north-west Germany by the two forces reflect the differences. For example, during the period 15 October–25 November 1944, there were only six hundred sorties by Fighter Command and nearly ten thousand by 2nd Tactical Air Force. Much German transport was destroyed in this offensive: forty barges, forty locomotives, over two hundred railway vehicles and nearly two hundred motor vehicles were claimed as destroyed, by the two forces. It is unlikely that the German rocket batteries were unaffected by these attacks, but those by 2nd Tactical Air Force were not carried out specifically for that purpose. Insofar as they were affected, it was as a by-product of the larger purpose of preparing for the final offensive against Germany. Their real strength, in and near The Hague, was not directly attacked.

This was far from being a satisfactory situation for Fighter Command. It was appreciated that the scale of rocket attack was low and did not warrant any important diversion of bomber forces; it was appreciated also that the heavy bombers and tactical air forces had more important tasks than the bombing of 'crossbow' targets (well, apparently). But there was intelligence during October that the Nazis were accumulating supplies of rockets near The Hague, which might be the prelude to a heavier attack. Air Marshal Hill argued, therefore, in a letter to the Deputy Chief of Air Staff on 24 October, that an immediate, small offensive effort might avoid the need for a heavier effort later (at a time when it might be embarrassing to the conduct of the offensive against Germany).

There were, in particular, two areas near The Hague which were believed to be actively employed both for firing and storing rockets. They were at Bloemendaal and Ockenburg Klinier, which adjoined and together covered a large area, well away from any important built-up area. They were recommended as targets to Bomber Command on 17 October. By 10 November their importance was judged to have diminished and they were withdrawn from the list of targets. They were not attacked during those three weeks.

Fighter Command had no better response from 2nd Tactical Air Force to requests made on 16 and 18 October for the attack on two stations at Leiden, through which rocket supplies were thought to be passing, and the Hotel Promenade at The Hague, which was used as a vehicle park.

However, a better argument (than the wisdom of insuring against heavier attack for direct action against targets near The Hague) came to hand at this time in the form of an increase from 26 October in the Nazi fire against London; though the fact that this occurred is proof of the validity of the Big Ben operations.

In the twelve days from 15 to 26 October only nineteen rocket incidents had been reported in the United Kingdom. All were aimed at London but only two fell in the London Civil Defence Region. But on 26 October alone, eight incidents were reported and nine on the following day; and by 4 November a further twenty-seven incidents had occurred. The attack was not only heavier than any hitherto made in a similar period, it was also more accurate. Thirty-three of the incidents were in the London Civil Defence Region and a further seven within twenty-five miles of Charing Cross. The central point of impact of these forty rockets fell in Poplar.

The attacks did not slacken. In the fortnight following 4 November they increased a little, sixty-two incidents being reported in the UK in total. Accuracy, however, fell away, only twenty-six of the incidents occurring in the London Civil Defence Region. During the week ending 25 November the accuracy of fire again improved as did its weight: forty-five incidents were reported in the UK, thirty-three of them in the London area.

Casualties in the weeks following 25 October rose sharply. In the seven weeks up to that date, rockets had killed only eighty-two people and injured 164 in the UK; whereas in the following month, 406 people were killed and 1,002 injured. The first incidents causing heavy loss of life were recorded during these weeks. Seven incidents each caused the deaths of more than twenty people; while on 25 November there was a terrible incident in New Cross Road, Deptford, where at 12:25hrs a rocket hit a crowded Woolworth's store, and 160 people were killed and 108 injured.[1]

It is useful to looks at these statistics because Big Ben operations have been deemed to be of little significance, and too much enthasis has been placed on ground troop activities to 'arrest' rocket sites in mid-1945. Field Marshal Alanbrooke was one to compliment the army for their work, to which F/Lt Raymond Baxter has stated in response, 'typical bloody soldier'. Indeed, it appears that Alanbrooke was not aware of the complexity and intensity of the air force's contribution (unlikely, when we take in how many CoS meetings he attended during 1944 at least connected with the threat of V1s and V2s, it is more likely that he simply concerned himself with other matters).

So what activity was going on during October and November 1944 to counter the rapidly growing threat of V2 rockets?

This can be clearly showcased through the detail of 303 Polish Squadron, who built upon 229's work and cut down the Nazis' V2 success rate on London.

1 October 1944

Big Ben patrols took place at 08:20hrs when a section of Six Spitfire IXFs took off from their base at Coltishall. They landed according to Squadron Histories at 17:50hrs but this is assumed to be the final section of aircraft to fly that day. Patrols of one hour's duration were carried out by each section as detailed and were accompanied by a Liberator bomber on Special Mission. Big Ben patrols were deemed uneventful.

In the afternoon a small section of two Spitfire IXFs climbed rapidly into the sky at 14:45hrs led by P/O Krezeptowski to practise airborne interception; but they were quickly diverted to search for eleven damaged MTBs. The two pilots spotted the vessels sixty miles from Coltishall and reported their position to the Controller. The weather was fairly cloudy at 6,000–7,000 feet. The section landed back at base at 16:21hrs.

2 October 1944

303 Squadron HQ received the posting notice of the new Squadron Commander, Acting S/Ldr B H Drobinski, DFC who took over command from S/Ldr T Koc, DFC on 28 September.

By dawn's early light, Big Ben patrols began with the first section of two Spitfires airborne at 07:20hrs. In total, six sections of two Spitfire IXFs carried out the patrols and the last one arrived back at Coltishall at 14:50hrs. Again these were patrols of one hour's duration, carried out by each section with the Liberator acting on Special Mission.

One section caught sight of five small ships and their position was radioed back to the Controller by F/Lt Socha.

3 October 1944

Two sections of two Spitfire IXFs were up from Coltishall at 13:05hrs on Big Ben patrols. These were uneventful and they were again accompanied by the Liberator. The last section landed back at base at 16:20hrs.

Five minutes earlier (16:15hrs), ten Spitfires took off on a Ranger patrol flying a route over Bergen, Leeuwarden, Gronigen, Eedle, Hoogeveen, and Egmond led by F/Lt Ochs. Landfall was made at Den Helder at which point a Big Ben contrail was reported by the leader. It was at 20,000–30,000 feet and still climbing. A white corkscrew contrail seemed to come from the Leeuwarden area. The cloud base wasn't particularly heavy (at 4,000 feet), so visibility was good.

Practice interceptions of Big Bens were carried out by a flight of Spitfires IXF led by F/Lt. Kedzeirski on twenty-four Halifax bombers. The flight was airborne at 13:00hrs and was vectored onto their targets over Norwich above cloud. Attacks were made by the Spitfires from all angles using camera guns instead of live ammunition. As the fighters attacked, the bombers took evasive action, splitting their formation and weaving to avoid being 'shot down'. On landing the flight leader discussed the attacks with the pilots and then flew over to the bomber base, Spolding Moor, where the tactics were discussed with bomber crews. The main criticism was that the bombers were too dispersed, which left them open to attacks from fighters (there being no protection from the other bombers owing to their distance from each other).

4 October 1944

F/Lt S Szpakowice was posted from 316 Polish squadron for flying duties. In the afternoon, three sections of two Spitfire IXFs climbed slowly into the October sky (15:25hrs) on Big Ben patrols, flying a patrol of one hour for each section. These were uneventful and they landed back at base at 18:45hrs.

Later, at approximately 17:25hrs, one section of two Spitfires were scrambled to intercept an unidentified aircraft that turned out to be a B17 heavy bomber.

5 October 1944

A Jim Crow mission started the day, with two Spitfire IXFs led by W/O Rutecki taking off from Coltishall at 06:37hrs. The aircraft climbed to 4,500 feet and followed shipping in the Den Helder area. The pilots reported spotting two Fanker vessels of 3,000 tons, facing west about three miles east with one destroyer to the south-west. A further eleven escort type vessels were spotted to the south-west, off the east coast of Den Helder. As the Spitfires approached Den Helder they spotted a Big Ben contrail rising from between Toure and Ankrum vertically and disappearing at 30,000 feet (visibility was good from 2,000 feet upwards).

At 07:40hrs Big Ben patrols took place with five sections of two Spitfires taking off from Coltishall on patrols of one hour's duration. Yellow Leader P/O Krezeptowski reported seeing a white cone shape at 40,000 feet approximately twelve miles south-east of Rotterdam. Flying at 23,000 feet fifteen miles north-west of The Hague, Krezeptowski had a visual sighting for twenty seconds. An unidentified aircraft was later seen heading at speed south-west at 25,000 feet and another was seen circling over Waecheren. The visibility for these patrols was excellent.

6 October 1944

The Squadron diary states that a Day Ranger patrol of three sections of Spitfires took off from Coltishall at 09:00hrs, heading towards Egmond via Lingen, but the patrols were uneventful. However, one Spitfire was damaged when F/Lt L Kraszewski forgot to lower his undercarriage lever on his approach. The ADC signalled to the pilot with a red lamp but it didn't register and Kraszewski landed without his undercarriage open.

7 October 1944

Nine Spitfires took off at 06:20hrs on a Day Ranger sweep led by F/Lt Kedzierski. Blue section, led by F/Lt Zmierodzki, sighted two goods trains immediately south of Leiwarden, both stationary, one in the marshalling yards and the other on the main line. A passenger train south-east of Leiwarden was also spotted heading west. Leaving the other sections to attack the two goods trains, two Spitfires from Blue Section peeled off and attacked the passenger train making two passes each. Light but inaccurate flak from the tender of the train reached up towards the marauding Spitfires but missed the aircraft completely. After the first strikes, the train stopped, and hits were observed by the pilots on the locomotive and front coaches. Huge columns of white smoke were seen pouring from the locomotive. Blue Section then formed up over the target area and headed back towards base landing at 09:05hrs. The remaining six aircraft continued on course but no other targets were encountered for them to attack.

At 12:50hrs ten Spitfires, led by F/Lt E Szaposznikow, DFM were airborne from Coltishall and formed up with Lancasters and Halifax bombers for escort duties over Cleeve. Ground mist made the bombing results difficult to see but thick, black smoke rose 4,000 feet into the air from the intense bombing. However, from the target area the bombers ran into heavy, intense and accurate flak. No enemy aircraft were encountered but one Halifax received a direct hit from anti-aircraft fire and disintegrated. The Spitfire escorts saw ten parachutes come tumbling out of the wreckage. Two Big Ben patrols were carried out but were un-eventful.

8 October 1944

At 09:35hrs two Spitfires took off from Coltishall on an air-sea rescue mission led by F/O Maksymowicz to search for survivors of a Mosquito from 215 Squadron that had crashed in the North Sea during the night. A large patch of oil was sighted sixty miles from Coltishall. Two Mosquitoes also searching the area joined the Spitfires. The only thing found during the square search was a piece of yellow wood and a tyre floating on the water five miles from the oil patch. There were no other signs of the downed aircraft. The height of the patrol varied from 100 to 1,000 feet. Dejected, the pilots landed back at base at 11:35hrs.

9 October 1944

Three sections of two Spitfires were airborne from base on Big Ben patrols. Owing to the bad weather the second section led by F/Lt Malarowski was recalled before reaching the patrol line. The remaining sections continued with the first section led by F/Lt M Szalestowski climbing to 20,000 feet. The remaining section dropped down to 8,000 feet. Suddenly there was a shout over the R/T as a vapour trail was sighted stretching from approximately 25,000 feet up to 40,000 feet. The first section reported the sighting to Control before they headed back to base.

10 October 1944

Big Ben patrols were uneventful. One section of two Spitfires, led by F/Lt Malarowski, took off from Coltishall at 11:15hrs. The visibility was excellent. The squadron also carried out some flying training, taking advantage of the fine weather. The cloud cover was heavy at 6,000 feet with patches from 20,000–24,000 feet.

11 October 1944

Mist and a cloud base at 5,000–6,000 feet hampered flying as F/Lt Kedzierski led a section of eight Spitfires on a sweep over Texel, Leeuwarden, Leer, Lathen and Egmond. The sweep was uneventful and the squadron carried out more training later in the day.

12 October 1944

Following the route flown the day before, eight Spitfires led by F/Lt Szaposznikow roared off the airfield at 09:25hrs on a Day Ranger sweep. The patrol sighted no targets of opportunity and returned at 11:35hrs. However, 303 Squadron pilots sighted shipping as well. In the gap between Den Helder and Texel 4 M/Vs were sighted of 2,000–3,000 tons and four escort vessels. In Den Helder harbour itself two M/Vs were seen tied up at the quay with another steaming out of the harbour, heading north-east.

At 10:40hrs Szaposnikow's section sighted a vertical Big Ben contrail forty to sixty miles from their position. The contrail appeared to come from somewhere between Rotterdam and Utrecht but the pilots were unable to fix the position owing to the cloud cover over the Rotterdam area. The Spitfires themselves were between Aoorn and Egmond flying at 9,000 feet when the contrail was spotted. The visibility on this patrol was fine at 5,000–6,000 feet over the Ranger area.

At 13:30hrs four sections of two Spitfires took off from Coltishall on a Big Ben patrol over Holland but the patrol was uneventful and no sign was seen of the elusive V2s. The day ended for 303 Squadron with two Spitfires being vectored seventy miles from their base on an air-sea rescue mission. Dropping down to 100 feet, the two pilots criss-crossed the search area looking for debris but found nothing.

13 October 1944

F/Lt Franckiewicz led another Spitfire sortie on a routine Big Ben patrol. They took off at 11:15hrs but the flight was uneventful and they returned to base at 13:25hrs.

However, the day was not without drama. On a routine Ranger patrol over the Texel to Egmond area that they had patrolled so often before, eight Spitfires from 303 squadron, led by S/Ldr D H Drobinski, DFC, climbed into the early afternoon sky over Coltishall (13:55hrs). Roaring over the North Sea the aircraft headed for Holland. Almost two hours later, Sgt Stankienwicz called over the radio that he was in trouble and would have to ditch. Glycol poured from his engine. With smoke billowing from the aircraft, Stankienwicz managed to land the aircraft in Holland and reported back to Drobinski that he was unhurt. The S/Ldr told him to get out fast and head south towards the advancing allied troops.

Cloud base was at 4,000–12,000 feet and thickening as the patrol wheeled away and headed home. They sighted shipping in Den Helder. Stankiewicz was officially reported as missing that day along with his aircraft (Spitfire BS543).

14 October 1944

The day started with heavy action for the pilots and ground crew of 303 Squadron. This was a Ramrod patrol with twenty-one aircraft taking part. At 07:45hrs F/Lt Socha's wheels left the ground as he led the formation of fighters into the sky. They formed up with 100 Lancasters and 100 Halifaxes that were on a bombing mission to Duisburg. According to 303 Squadron's diarist, the formation of escorts was made up of twenty Spitfire squadrons and several Mustang squadrons. As the huge formation pushed on, heading over land towards the target, heavy flak began peppering the air over Texel. Visibility for the raid was excellent with the cloud cover at 10,000 feet and some haze at 25,000 feet. Fortunately, the intense flak was inaccurate.

Later in the afternoon, on another Ramrod mission, S/Ldr Drobinski led his ten Spitfires to the rendezvous point with twelve Mitchells and twenty-four Boston medium bombers. Heading for Zutphen, the object was to hit the railway station by the river and a bridge over the river in the centre of the town. As the bombers ran in on the targets, the Spitfire pilots could see the hits. Several buildings near the station and on one side of the river erupted into flames, fire spreading through the structures. Bombs rained down on the area near the bridge.

Turning away from the target the formation headed home. At 16:25hrs a Big Ben contrail was seen apparently coming from somewhere north of Apeldoorn and tilted towards the west. No flak of any kind was encountered on the raid. Over the target the weather was clear, making the bomb burst identification easy to see, but as the aircraft headed back to England cloud was beginning to form.

15 October 1944

A busy day for the Squadron. At 10:20hrs eight Spitfires led by S/Ldr Drobinski took off on a Day Ranger to sweep the Texel to Egmond area but found no targets. Forty minutes after take off the patrol sighted a ship of 3,000–4,000 tons with three escorts steaming very slowly north-east. The fighters were at 12,000 feet. Thirty minutes later they sighted some barges tied up in a canal and after a further few minutes saw more M/Vs tied up near Marken Island.

One of the pilots saw a Big Ben contrail towards the west coming out of the area near Heerenveen. As they headed towards the area, flak burst all around them just as they crossed over Leer. The flak was intense and accurate. At 5,000 feet the fighters were in danger, so Drobinski quickly turned the Squadron, climbing hard out of the range of the gunners below. The weather for this patrol was clear over Holland but deteriorated badly at 2,000 feet over Germany. The entry in the Squadron history reads: 'Pilots report that water in the canals in north-east Polder has been of a reddish colour the last few days.'

On 16 and 17 October low cloud and heavy rain stopped any operational flying for 303 Squadron. However, on 18 October the weather cleared enough for four sections of two Spitfires to get airborne for a Big Ben patrol. It was uneventful and the aircraft landed back at Coltishall without sighting anything.

Again, the weather closed in over the next few days until 22 October, when it cleared enough for 303 Squadron to launch an armed recce. The route was to make landfall at Egmond and head out back across the sea to England at Westhood. Four Spitfires, led by F/Lt Szpakowicz, took off at 12:59hrs but when they reached Egmond the cloud cover had dropped to 1,000 feet and they were forced to turn back.

24 October 1944

Big Ben patrols took place as three sections of two Spitfires roared away from Coltishall, climbing rapidly into the October sky. Visibility was poor on this flight with the cloud base at 3,000–4,000 feet and top cover at 9,000 feet. They saw nothing and landed back at base at 15:30hrs.

Another section of two Spitfires took off at 12:40hrs, but the section soon returned as one of the fighters had mechanical trouble. Another section of two Spitfires left Coltishall at 13:05hrs but came back again only twenty minutes later with mechanical trouble.

The day was not entirely a washout. At 14:20hrs F/Lt Szaposznikow led four Spitfires on an armed recce. They crossed land at Westhoofd and came out of the cloud base at 4,000 feet over The Hague where twenty stationary barges were observed on one of the canals. Just as they emerged from the cloud cover, intense, heavy and accurate flak burst all around them. The fighters saw the barges, reported them back to Control then quickly left the area.

25 October 1944

S/Ldr Drobinski led a section of four Spitfires on an armed recce towards the Egmond area. Taking off at 14:20hrs the aircraft roared across the sea heading towards Holland. Drobinski kept the flight low as the cloud base was at 1,500 to 5,000 feet and visibility was poor. Braving heavy flak the Spitfires headed towards The Hague then turned for home.

Dropping down to 400 feet under the low cloud the aircraft raced across the water towards base when they spotted an unidentified object slip beneath the surface of the sea (16:00hrs). Looking ahead, Drobinski saw six MTBs converging on the spot where the object had submerged.

28 October 1944

Pilots of 303 Squadron took to the air at 14:20hrs. F/Lt Socha led four Spitfires on an armed recce towards Katwijk. Spotting a locomotive and trucks Socha rolled into a dive and sprayed the targets with cannon fire. His shells ripped into the locomotive which began gushing steam and smoke as the aircraft roared overhead. Climbing, Socha could see F/Sgt Michalak's aircraft strafing the train. Flames shot from the damaged trucks and locomotive.

Continuing the patrol F/Lt Franckiewicz spotted a large lorry and attacked, diving on it raking it with cannon fire. The lorry burst into flames as the high explosive shells struck the vehicle. Satisfied, the pilots continued their patrol landing back at base at 16:35hrs.

29 October 1944

An eventful day for the Squadron. Again, F/Lt Socha led four Spitfires on an armed recce over Holland. Lifting off at 08:20hrs they crossed at West Schouwen flying at 10,000 feet. Over Alkmaar the other pilots suddenly heard their leader reporting a V2 sighting coming from the Meppel area. Socha saw the contrail at 6,000 feet and watched it climb to 20,000 feet before losing sight of it.

Continuing on the patrol, Socha spotted five barges on a canal moving south. Rolling into a dive he screamed down on the vessels, pumping cannon shells into them. Right behind him came F/O Maksymowicz, his wingman, his cannon blasting away at the vessels. The pilots watched shells strike the barges and one was left in flames.

Later that day another Armed recce patrol, led by F/Lt Kedzierski, climbed to 10,000 feet and flew as far as Egmond before turning south where they encountered heavy, accurate flak over the Rotterdam/Hague area. Two hours later the section touched down at Coltishall unscathed. The visibility for that flight had been good with no cloud over the target areas.

The following day two armed recces were flown by the Squadron but no targets were spotted to attack and the weather locked in, forcing the afternoon's recce to be aborted early.

1 November 1944

At 14:00hrs four Spitfires, led by S/Ldr Drobinski, took to the sky. Climbing to 9,000 feet, the fighters formed up and turned towards Holland. They crossed the coast at Bergen then turned south, flying to Westhoofd then back to The Hague and onwards (north-east) to Amsterdam. Drobinski pushed his stick forward as he descended to 6,000 feet, the three other Spitfires following him. Below, he could see several barges on the canal, and calling to the rest of the section, he tipped his wing over into a steep dive. The Spitfire tore down on the vessels, but as his altimeter reached 500 feet, Drobinski saw red crosses painted on the ships so he pulled back sharply climbing rapidly away into the cloud base. Above the cloud, the other Spitfires formed up on Drobinski's wing but one was missing. Sgt Wierchowicz's aircraft was nowhere to be seen. Drobinski and the remaining pilots scanned the area below the cloud for some sign of Spitfire MH910. But they saw nothing. Saddened the fighters crossed the coast over Ijkmiden heading for home.

Sgt Wierchowicz never returned.

2 November 1944

As dawn broke on the cold winter morning visibility for flying was good at twenty miles. Over Coltishall the cloud base was approximately 3,000 feet. Engines burst into life as two Spitfires, led by F/Lt Bartys, headed the small section on a Jim Crow mission. The two fighters roared down the field and leapt into the grey sky heading towards Den Helder. Climbing to 9,000 feet they observed eleven ships with approximately five destroyers surrounding one large merchant ship of about 6,000–8,000 tons. The merchant ship had one funnel painted red and grey. Flak from the destroyers arced up towards the Spitfires but it was out of range and inaccurate. The rest of the patrol was uneventful and the aircraft landed at base at 09:30hrs.

While Bartys and his wingman were flying over Den Helder, another four Spitfire IXFs from 303 Squadron took off from Coltishall led by F/Lt Malarowski. Climbing to 10,000 feet they crossed the coast over Velkenburg. Turning north towards Amsterdam Malarowski spotted four stationary barges and seven small M/Vs nearby. He wheeled the section around, dropped into a dive and raked the vessels with cannon fire. The remaining three Spitfires followed suit. Shell strikes ripped up and down the length of the barges as the Spitfires let rip. Suddenly, 20mm flak opened up on the fighters but they had climbed rapidly away after only one pass. Moments later, they spotted one tug towing four barges heading south and pounced on this target raking the tug with their gunfire. Each pilot reported seeing hits on the barges and the tug before they climbed away.

On this same patrol, a camouflaged lorry was attacked and set on fire. They landed back at base at 09:30hrs.

Later that same morning, S/Ldr Drobinski led a section of four Spitfires on an armed recce. They climbed quickly into the sky at 10:40hrs, their engines purring as the Spitfires reached 10,000 feet. Crossing the Dutch coast at Westhoofd they turned north towards The Hague then north again to Leiden and then to Haarlem and up to Ijmuiden and back over the sea at Egmond. The flight spotted a barge moving south on a canal. Drobinski and his wingman peeled away to attack, ready to jettison their underwing fuel tanks for the steep dives, but the tanks remained firmly fixed to their wings. Aborting the attack, the two Spitfires formed up with the rest of the section and continued on. The rest of the flight was uneventful and they returned to base, their wheels touching down at Coltishall at 12:40hrs.

By the early afternoon the visibility was excellent and at 13:45hrs F/Lt Rzyski led a section of four Spitfires across the North Sea to Holland. Hitting landfall over Westhoofd they then turned towards Leiden and again towards Amsterdam when a military car was spotted by one of the pilots. Two Spitfires peeled away from the section, dropping into steep dives, they roared down on their hapless target. They raked the vehicle with cannon shells, and the car exploded into flames as the aircraft roared overhead and quickly climbed away. They landed back at base at 15:25hrs.

4 November 1944

Bad weather (heavy rain and mist) had forced operational flying to stop at Coltishall on 3 November. But 4 November proved to be better and flying recommenced. At 08:40hrs a section of four Spitfire IXFs climbed quickly into the morning sky heading towards the continent on an armed recce. They crossed the coast and then headed south to Rotterdam. The patrol was uneventful and they crossed the coast, heading back to England from Egmond.

Once again the weather played havoc with flying and no operational or practice flying took place on 5 November, the visibility being very poor.

6 November 1944

The weather had cleared and visibility was good. At 07:50hrs a section of four Spitfires, led by F/Lt Socha, took off from Coltishall on an armed recce. Crossing land at Westhoofd then turned north to Egmond then south-east of Haarlem when they spotted a camouflaged car with a trailer. Wheeling around the Spitfires dived on the vehicle peppering it with cannon fire. As the pilots attacked they could see strikes on and around the vehicle. A German soldier was seen approaching the car as the British fighters attacked and was believed to have been killed in the hail of bullets from the Spitfires. They landed back at Coltishall two hours and twenty minutes after take off.

While Socha and the rest of his section were shooting up the camouflaged car, F/Lt Malarowski and his wingman climbed away from base at 08:05hrs, heading towards Den Helder on a Jim Crow mission. Over Terschealing they dropped down to 3,000 feet and spotted two stationary ships of approximately 200 tons each and reported their findings to Control. Turning, they headed back to base and landed at 09:15hrs.

While visibility remained, the squadron took full advantage and another armed recce was launched at 10:45hrs with F/Lt Kedzierski leading a section of Spitfires. The four fighters climbed to 10,000 feet and crossed over land at Ijmuden heading north towards The Hague. Dropping to 7,000 feet they headed on to Rotterdam. Although they saw no targets to attack on this patrol, the fighters ran into intense and accurate flak from the Hook of Holland. The Spitfires landed back at Coltishall at 12:40hrs, the pilots glad to be on solid ground once more.

F/Lt Socha was up again that afternoon and his section spotted a Big Ben contrail. Engines roared as the four Spitfires rolled away from dispersal. Moments later, the pilots pushed their throttles forward and the four aircraft climbed gracefully into the sky heading towards the North Sea. At 10,000 feet they crossed land at Nadvlyk and headed for their patrol area between The Hague and Haarlem. Suddenly, Socha's engine began running rough and he quickly called up Control, reporting engine trouble. Spluttering and coughing the engine started to get worse. The rest of the section split up, as he turned away, escorted by his wingman. Searching for a place to land Socha headed for Belgium and managed to get his Spitfire onto hard ground at a tactical airfield behind the Allied lines. The airfield was designated as B 61 Belgium. He was back at Coltishall two days later. But as the rest of the section flew on, they spotted a squadron of Tempests patrolling north-west of The Hague. Suddenly, the remaining Spitfires ran into intense, accurate flak coming from far below them. Climbing to avoid the danger they saw the contrail come from somewhere between The Hague and Rotterdam. Flying at 10,000 feet the Spitfires saw the contrail at 16,000 feet before it disappeared on its way to England. At 16:45hrs their wheels touched the ground at Coltishall and they taxied into dispersal.

7 November 1944

The Squadron flew three armed recces. The first was at 10:00hrs when F/Lt Malarowski led a section of Spitfires on a patrol over the Rotterdam/Utrecht area. They spotted no targets but did run into light flak coming from Rotterdam. They were back on solid ground at 12:15hrs.

The second armed recce began at 12:50hrs when four Spitfires led by F/Lt Szklestowski took off from Coltishall. Climbing to 9,000 feet he crossed land at Schouen then turned north to Rotterdam and then to The Hague. Dropping to 3,000 feet they attacked four trucks (two with cranes) and a car. One by one, in line astern, the Spitfires dived on the vehicles strafing them with High Explosive cannon shells. The pilots reported strikes on all the vehicles. Turning back towards the North Sea they opened their throttles, speeding through light flak as they headed out over the water back to the safety of England. They landed at 15:00hrs.

Two hours later visibility was getting bad as mist began to cover the base. Below the cloud level pilots could see for roughly five miles. The cloud base was at 5,000 feet and the cloud top was at 9,000 feet. Despite the weather conditions, another section of Spitfires took off from Coltishall at 15:30hrs. Led by F/Lt Malarowski, they crossed to Ijmuden and continued their sweep as far as Rotterdam but found no targets, so turned for home, heading out to sea over Westhoofd.

8 November 1944

One patrol of four Spitfires took to the air from Coltishall at 08:55hrs, heading towards Amsterdam. They climbed to 10,000 feet and turned out to sea towards the Hook. However, the patrol was uneventful and they found no targets to attack. Later that morning another armed recce took to the sky but again no targets were found to attack.

Between 9 and 11 November, pilots of 303 Squadron remained on the ground as the weather worsened and visibility was cut to less than a mile. No practice or operational flying took place over these three days.

12 November 1944

The weather cleared and visibility was good. The cloud base was at 4,000 feet making flying possible. Four Spitfires, led by F/Lt Socha, roared off the airfield at 08:45hrs, their undercarriages closing as they climbed quickly into the sky. Turning out to sea they headed once more for Holland but on this armed recce they found no targets to attack and returned to base at 11:00hrs.

For the next two days rain lashed the airfield keeping the Spitfires on the ground with visibility down to less than half a mile.

15 November 1944

F/Lt Bartys and his wingman took off at 09:45hrs on a weather reconnaissance flight. Rain streamed down their windshields as they climbed, buffeted by wind. The freezing point was at 3,000–4,000 feet and within twenty-six minutes of take off both Spitfires were in trouble. Realising the dangers of ditching in the sea, Bartys turned his Spitfire for home, ice and rain causing havoc. Behind him, his wingman did the same. Bartys flew up alongside the other aircraft touching his headphones. There was nothing but static in his ears as his R/T had failed. The engine temperature gauge was climbing. He tried desperately to raise Control but only succeeded in relaying a short message before the R/T cut out again.

Back at Coltishall, at 10:15hrs F/Lt Socha ran to his aircraft, the engine ticking over. The order to scramble two aircraft had just come through. Within minutes he was strapped in, throttle open and tearing towards take off, the second Spitfire behind him. They climbed into the cold November morning sky pummelled by wind and rain. Calling up Bartys several times Socha finally managed to contact the stricken fighters and he formed up with them escorting them back to base. The four aircraft all landed safely at 10:40hrs.

Five minutes later another section of two Spitfires, led by F/Lt Rzyski, took off heading for Holland. The cloud base was 5,000 feet and the top at 7,000 feet. Climbing through the rain, they flew through the cloud and found good visibility above the cumulus layer. But after sixty miles both aircraft had to turn back due to engine trouble. It had been a frustrating day.

21 November 1944

Bad weather kept the Squadron grounded until 21 November when visibility was good enough for them to fly. The cloud base was at 3,000 feet with the top between 5,000 and 6,000 feet. Below the cloud base visibility was hazy but it was good enough to fly and above the cloud the sun shone brightly.

In the afternoon (14:30hrs) S/Ldr Drobinski led three other Spitfires on an armed recce over Holland. The four fighters crossed at the Hook and turned north towards Wassenaur/Rust-en-Vreugt. As they flew north-east of The Hague, Drobinski spotted a Big Ben contrail shooting vertically into the sky. Checking his altimeter he reported the sighting to Control at 10,000 feet and watched the contrail rise high above them, disappearing at 30,000 feet. Control asked where the contrail had come from and Drobinski replied in the Huis-Te-Werve area. The rest of the patrol was uneventful and the Spitfires landed back at base at 16:15hrs, having gained some vital intelligence.

Bad weather again kept the Squadron grounded the next day but on 23 November F/Lt Socha led a section of four Spitfires on an armed recce over Holland. The four aircraft took off from Coltishall at 12:40hrs climbing to 12,000 feet. Socha scanned the area below his aircraft for a sign of land but saw nothing through the thick layer of cloud. He knew they had reached Holland, but as far as he could see there was nothing but cloud obscuring any targets they might have attacked. Suddenly from the layer of cloud below Socha caught sight of a white Big Ben contrail shooting vertically into the sky. It was gone in a few seconds. But because of the cloud cover there was no indication of the firing point. Disgusted, Socha turned the section back towards base. They landed at 14:30hrs.

26 November 1944

303 Squadron was back in action again after two days of bad weather. This time it was F/O Maksymowicz who led the section of Spitfires on an armed recce over Holland searching for targets of opportunity. The four Spitfires climbed into the morning sky at 08:35hrs and levelled out at 10,000 feet. Crossing at Egmond, they turned south and headed to the west of Amsterdam. The cloud base was at 3,000 feet with the cloud top at 4,000–5,000 feet. Maksymowicz dropped down to 2,500 feet, just below the cloud base, the other three Spitfires following. But at this level the visibility was poor owing to mist, so he climbed through the cloud into clear sky. High above them at 20,000 feet he caught sight of a Big Ben contrail shooting vertically into the sky. It appeared to come from Nunspeet so Maksymowicz reported the sighting to Control and turned the section for home. They crossed the North Sea at Egmond and touched down at Coltishall at 11:00hrs.

During the month of November the squadron had flown 195.15 operational hours by day. An additional 67.55 hours had been flown on training sorties all on Spitfire IXFs (also during the day). Another 14:35 hours had been taken up on practice flying with Spitfire Vbs. They flew no night sorties at all.

Although they did attack the enemy, the work carried out was more useful as intelligence – actually pin-pointing major V2 rocket sites and getting into the mind-set of the enemy. This was still early days for Big Ben, clipped winged Mark XVIs had not been introduced yet, and that was when the fun really started.

NOTE

1   See Vol. 6 (formerly Vol. 17) of *Air Defence of Great Britain*, which contradicts Douglas Bader's figure of 135 injured in *Fight For The Sky – The Story of the Spitfire and Hurricane*.

CHAPTER IV

Operation Big Ben

'As winter approached, the bad weather was upon them, bringing long nights and low temperatures. Diving ... resulted in frozen windscreens, and engines which had been repeatedly flogged were getting tired.'

John 'Cat's-Eyes' Cunningham – The Aviation Legend
John Golly

For the detail of Operation Big Ben – the dive-bombing Spitfire missions themselves, we have exclusively turned to 602 City of Glasgow Squadron. We have done this largely because it appeared to be the most dramatically built and comprehensive history of events; especially when we could include extracts from the log book of Raymond Baxter and interview him concerning the Squadron history accuracy.[1]

We begin Operation Big Ben on 4 December 1944, Baxter saying of it: '4 December. Dive-bombing V2 site. Bombed through gap (in clouds) and got train. A rare occasion when we got a train.'

For clarity's sake, when did 602 Squadron convert to Mark XVI Spitfires from Mark IXs? Baxter explained: 'I first flew in Spitfires XVIs on 27 November 1944. I loved that aircraft from the word go. I did a familiarisation and air test, and then straight into the dive-bombing ... We dive-bombed once or twice a day. I used to chew gum when I started, but I had to give it up, because as soon as we started to cross enemy territory, the gum used to turn to chalk. It was terrible to try and get it out of an oxygen mask.'

Raymond Baxter concluding with an anecdote about his personal discomfort; but what of the difficulties in carrying out sorties, especially locating prime targets; Baxter explained: 'We were very reliant on aerial photography ... We had a fair amount, although I wouldn't call it a flood or, an integral part. If we couldn't see a target we wouldn't bomb; however there was no excuse for not finding the target.'

Throughout the operation the weather conditions were very poor, but before we look in some detail at the missions flown by 602 Squadron

29

between 4 December 1944 and 31 March 1945, we must ask how did the Spitfire pilots dive-bomb their Mark XVIs? Baxter again: 'It was a close formation exercise and we bombed in sections of four or more. And if you were leading, you flew over the target, and you would round your wing and count two and roll on your back and come down like that. And every aeroplane would do the same thing. So, ideally, it was a stream of four aeroplanes very close together. And you bombed individually, but obviously you didn't drop your bombs[2] until your leader pulled away. And that was the trick to make it successful. It all depended to a considerable extent on how good the leader was. Because if he was too far away and his dive wasn't steep enough, then the other dives would tend to be flatter and flatter, which was dangerous.

'On one occasion, I looked in my mirror, and one chap was pulling out – this was my No. 3 – he was pulling out before I dropped my load. So I posted him. He never flew with us again.

'The dive itself was always seventy to seventy five degrees. Ideally, you would start at 8,000 feet, drop the bombs at 3,000 feet and pull out.

'We did a couple of practices and then we were into the thick of it.'

And now the detail of Operation Big Ben as seen through the eyes of 602 City of Glasgow Squadron:[3]

4 December 1944

From first light to 13:00hrs, the squadron kept two aircraft at readiness and two at fifteen minutes readiness state.

Four aircraft took off on an armed recce and dive-bombing show at 14:30hrs. Low cloud obscured the priority target, so S/Ldr Sutherland led the section up to the Wassenaar/Rust-en-Vreugd target, which they bombed successfully from 5,000–1,000 feet, north to south, all the bombs falling on the target area. The recce of the Helden/Amsterdam/Laandam area, which followed, proved equally successful. A goods train was attacked with cannon and machine-guns by three aircraft, five attacks in all being made from 2,000 feet to heights varying from fifty to 200 feet. Many strikes were seen all along the train, which came to a standstill and an excessive amount of steam was seen coming from the locomotive. A number of motor vehicles were seen on the road parallel to the railway but lack of fuel and ammunition prevented an attack. However, no flak was encountered during the mission.

5 December 1944

Due to the absence of suitable weather conditions over the Dutch coast and capital, it was decided to cancel the combined 453/602 Squadrons' dive-bombing show and send only four aircraft of 602 on an armed recce fitted with bombs, in the hope that they might find the weather improved a little and be able to bomb one of the three given targets. Heavy cloud made dive-bombing (or a recce of V2 launch sites) impossible. Flying north up to Egmond F/Lt Lloyd, who led the section, found the weather conditions very similar to those at The Hague, and therefore set course for base. Two aircraft jettisoned their bombs in the sea, the others bringing theirs back to base.

S/Ldr Sutherland led the next section which took off at 13:35hrs to bomb the Wassenaar/Langenhorst target. Cloud from 2,000–5,000 feet obscured the target, and three attempts were made to pin-point it without success. The CO then took the section up to the Wassenaar/Rust-en-Vreugd target and diving from 9,000–4,000 feet, dropped eight 250 lb bombs on the target area. A large covered truck moving towards Leiden was seen about ten miles due east at 14:20hrs and was attacked. Many strikes were seen and the vehicle was left smoking.

6 December 1944

602 and 453 Squadrons again combined forces and took off in the morning to dive-bomb The Hague/Hargsches Bosch target.

Carrying 250 lb bombs – two aircraft of 453 returned early, one with engine trouble, the other as an escort. The remainder continued to the target and with the exception of F/O Thomerson (602), who had difficulty in jettisoning his tank, which rather upset his attack, dropped their bombs from 12,000–2,000 feet, in a north-east/south-west direction. Four bombs fell on the target with the remainder a short distance to the south and south-west of it.

Sutherland, who led the attack, was unable to jettison his tank, and in the dive towards the target had it shot off with flak, his number two seeing it hurtling through the air in flames, otherwise no damage was sustained. Very intense and accurate flak was encountered in the target area, but all the aircraft returned safely to base.

At 11:05hrs, as they were crossing out north of The Hague, the pilots saw two twin V2 contrails rising from 4,000–20,000 feet, from the Den Helder area.

The next show took off at 15:05hrs but was aborted, due to the bad weather, the section flying only a few miles from the English coast before receiving a report from 453 Squadron of unfavourable weather conditions over Holland.

7 December 1944

Once again a combined 602/453 Squadron dive-bombing show was cancelled, due to adverse weather conditions over The Hague.

At 13:00hrs the squadron took over the defensive state of readiness, and the pilots not employed on this duty carried out practice flying.

W/O Daggett and W/O Jenkins were Tour Expired and were posted with effect from (w.e.f) 8 December for flying instructor duties. P/O F J Fox was also posted with effect the same day, also to 57 OUT. W/O Crosland was a new arrival to make up the strength.

8 December 1944

The Squadron was kept grounded, the weather both in England and Holland being the worst experienced since the operation in Swannington.

During the morning, the commanding officer talked to the pilots about dive-bombing tactics. At 12:30hrs the Squadron was released.

9 December 1944

At 08:30hrs four aircraft fitted with 250 lb bombs took off to dive-bomb one of the V2 storage sites, north-east of The Hague. At the same time two aircraft took off on a Jim Crow, over the Den Helder area. The section of four aircraft flew within a few miles of the Dutch coast; but the weather was poor, with thick cloud layers from 1,000–25,000 feet, so they had to abandon their mission. They set a course for base, taking their bombs with them.

The Jim Crow section operating farther north had better luck, and on their return reported sighting three merchant vessels in the harbour of Ijmuiden. Flying north they recced Den Helder harbour, but saw no shipping there, except a small tramp steamer ploughing its way south from Texel, towards Den Helder. They then carried out a recce over the northern part of the Zeider Zee, but apart from the usual small sailing craft no shipping was seen. Crossing in at Edam they observed a stationary ferry boat about ten miles from the coast. Flying over the area north of Edam to the northern part of the Zeider Zee, they again recced Den Helder harbour. Apart from the small tramp steamer, which had been seen earlier and was now entering the harbour, no shipping was seen. Climbing to 9,000 feet and diving across the Den Helder Gap in a shallow dive, the section, which was led by F/O Thomerson, encountered intense, accurate flak from the harbour area; also from a cluster of large blue vessels in the centre of the strait.

As there was no improvement in the weather, the Squadron was released from operations. The afternoon was spent undertaking practice dive-bombing.

10 December 1944

F/Lt Waterhouse led the first dive-bombing section, which took off at 10:00hrs. They dive-bombed the target at the Hotel Promenade in The Hague. Crossing in over The Hague they pin-pointed their target and bombed it south-east to north-west from 11,000–3,000 feet. Two bombs were seen just north of the hotel whilst two others exploded east of the building – the other results were not observed due to cloud obscuring the target (as the aircraft pulled out of their dive). No flak was encountered from the target area or during the recce of the Leiden area, which followed.

At 12:35hrs the next section took off, this time the target being Wassenaar/Rust-en-Vreugd. After making a recce of the railway and roads from Noordwijk to Alkmaar and south again to The Hague, the section saw three M/Vs in Ijmuiden harbour, and meagre, though accurate, light flak was experienced from north of The Hague. F/Lt Pertwee led the section to the target, which was dive-bombed south-east to north-west from 8,000–2,000 feet; two bombs fell only a short distance from the target pin-point but unfortunately the position of the other was not observed.

Bad weather caused the third recce to be cancelled and, at 15:00hrs the squadron was released.

11 December 1944

At 09:00hrs S/Ldr Sutherland took off with five other pilots to dive-bomb (with 250 lb bombs) Staatsspoor station in the Dutch capital, where it was reported that there was a filling point for liquid oxygen lorries. On his return, he was delighted with the result of the mission. Crossing in at 15,000 feet north of The Hague over a large patch of cloud, the commanding officer orbited the target three times until he found a convenient hole through which he could dive-bomb.[4] When the opportunity arose, the aircraft dived from 10,000–4,000 feet, north to south, turning at 4,000–2,000 feet and dropping their bombs in a north-west to south-east direction.

Four of the bombs were dropped on the east end of the station awning from which a dense cloud of white smoke and debris arose. Four fell in the centre of the target area amongst trucks and railway buildings, approximately 100 yards from the station and two more fell on the railway line less than fifty yards farther east. These observations were made by the commanding officer, who after his dive did a climbing turn up to 2,000 feet, watching closely the results of the bombing. Although the target was in the centre of The Hague, no flak was encountered. S/Ldr Sutherland stated that this was the finest piece of dive-bombing he had ever seen.

The next show was for four aircraft and at 11:25hrs they took off to dive-bomb the Hotel Promenade target. After pin-pointing the target F/Lt Lloyd led the section in a dive-bombing attack from 7,000–3,000 feet, and four bombs were seen to fall east of the hotel. The results of the other bombs were not observed. On the recce which followed, a light truck was moving towards Amsterdam from Wesp and was attacked and left smoking.

12 December 1944

A new Commitment Programme having come into effect, 602 Squadron continued at a sixty minute readiness state in the Fighter Defence system of the UK. The weather, however, made flying impossible, and during the morning combat films were shown.

13 December 1944

Thick mist kept the Squadron grounded all day.

14 December 1944

Bad weather prevented the Squadron from carrying out any show.

15 December 1944

The spell of bad weather continued and again no flying was done.

16 December 1944

Another day of mist and rain, which kept the Squadron grounded.

17 December 1944

Although the weather was not perfect, by 12:00hrs it was good enough to send four aircraft on a combined armed weather recce. Some miles from base, cloud cover made conditions difficult, frequent rainstorms were also experienced, so the section (carrying 250 lb bombs) realised it was hopeless to continue, and set a course back for base.

Throughout the day, a state of readiness was observed (for four aircraft), and although they were scrambled once, this proved a false alarm and they were stopped before take off.

18 December 1944

At 08:35hrs four aircraft took off on an armed recce/dive-bombing show, and two others on a Jim Crow. The target to be bombed was The Hague/Haagsche Bosch but as the weather was quite unsuitable for dive-bombing, all the section brought their bombs home.

On the return of the Jim Crow section at 10:15hrs, S/Ldr Sutherland reported that when flying at 09:20hrs he saw a funnel-less merchant ship of about 2,000–3,000 tons stationary in the centre of the Van Helden Gap, surrounded by seven smaller ships of approximately 100 feet in length and of the motor minesweeper type, as well as two motor launchers. Apart from this no other shipping was seen, and the mild flak which the Spitfires usually encountered in this area never occurred.

19 December 1944

Thick mist with visibility varying from fifty to 300 yards persisted throughout the day and made it impossible for flying to be done.[5]

20 December 1944

The Squadron was fog-bound and no flying was done.

21 December 1944

Thick fog. No flying.

22 December 1944

Still fog-bound. No flying.

23 December 1944

Although the weather improved, the conditions were not good enough for flying.

24 December 1944

A cloudless sky and unlimited visibility made it a perfect day for dive-bombing and at 10:05hrs ten aircraft of the squadron took off. This was one of three squadrons whose task it was to bomb a new target in The Hague with 250 lb and 500 lb bombs: a block of flats, which were reputably being used as a headquarters and billets.

229 Squadron led by W/Cdr Fitzgerald were first over the target, and when they had completed their attack F/Lt Waterhouse led the pilots in a dive from 9,000–2,000 feet, bombing in a south-east to north-west direction. Apart from two overshots and one undershot, all the bombs fell

on the west corner of the building and on the ground nearby. From the amount of smoke and debris witnessed, it was considered that the bombs caused considerable damage.

All the aircraft then flew to Ursel where, after re-fuelling, eight aircraft of 602 Squadron carried out a strafing attack on two targets south of The Hague, the other aircraft, which had developed engine trouble, returning to base. No results were seen from the strafing attack but the photographs, which were taken by PRU aircraft of the bombing attack on the target in The Hague, showed that a fair amount of damage had been caused.

25 December 1944

Although pilots journeyed to Swannington to carry out an armed recce at 08:30hrs, a very thick mist descended from about this time and made it impossible to take off. The show was cancelled and the Squadron put to sixty minutes readiness (a state which allowed them to return to Matlaske). The weather did not improve sufficiently to allow them to take off and the Squadron was eventually released in the early afternoon.

26 December 1944

As the weather was still unsuitable for flying, the Squadron were put to sixty minutes readiness and did not travel to Swannington. A heavy pall of mist hung over the aerodrome all day and all aircraft were kept grounded.

27 December 1944

The weather was still unsuitable for flying; the Squadron was released quite early in the morning.

28 December 1944

The weather improved considerably, the Squadron was at a sixty minutes state for training, and an extensive programme was carried out throughout the day.

29 December 1944

Weather still improving, but as the day developed, not much could be done.

Seven of the Auxiliary members were posted to 56 OTU. Two new members including Australian F/Sgt Zuber and F/O Rudkin were among the new members of the squadron.

Link Trainer[6] from Coltishall claimed some of the pilots and numbers were placed on the list for training.

30 December 1944

Armed recce by four aircraft led by F/Lt Waterhouse took off at 10:45hrs to bomb V2 sites near The Hague, but the weather clamped down on both sides of the North Sea and the pilots had to be diverted to Wittering. They were able to return to Swannington later in the afternoon.

31 December 1944

Once again, the weather had the last say. Four aircraft led by F/O Thomerson were airborne at 14:30hrs to visit The Hague, but were recalled and made their way back to base on the outskirts of various storms.

The year 1944 finished without too much incident other than an appropriate New Year party that night.

1 January 1945

The Squadron commenced the New Year with no operational commitments, and the day's programme consisted of practice dive-bombing and cine gun exercises (some air to air firing was also carried out).

2 January 1945

In the early morning, the Squadron was released for the day.

3 and 4 January 1945

Although no operational flying was carried out by the Squadron, due to unsuitable weather conditions over Holland, a number of practice flying exercises were carried out on both days.

5 January 1945

Only one mission was carried out by the Squadron, when four aircraft took off on armed recce and dive-bombing show over The Hague/Voorde target. Crossing in at Westhoofd at 14,000 feet, the section flew to Leiden, turned towards the target and having pin-pointed it, bombed it from north-east to south-west, from 8,000–2,000 feet. Two bombs were seen to fall on the south of the target. The results of the others were not observed. The section broke south towards Rotterdam where moderate heavy flak was encountered, and recced the area as far as Leiden, crossing out south of Katwijk, but no movement was seen. At 15:20hrs when at 8,000 feet, a V2 was seen fired north-east of The Hague, the trail being seen to rise to a height of 40,000 feet. On their return, the pilots were able to pin-point exactly where the V2 originated.

6 January 1945

At 14:00hrs the weather was deemed unsuitable for dive-bombing. The section of four aircraft (which took off at that time) was recalled by the Controller. No other operational flying was carried out.

7 January 1945

A combined Jim Crow and armed recce was flown by four aircraft, which took off at 13:55hrs. The section made landfall south of Den Helder through a very heavy snowstorm, which made visibility nil. Flying south to Ijmuiden and then climbing to 5,000 feet, the section arrived at Zanouvoort carrying out a recce of the Haarlem/Alkmaar area, but no movement was seen. Yellow 1 flew just south of Ijmuiden to investigate a vessel of approximately 3,000 tons, which was moored in the northern basin of the harbour and recognised it as the same ship that had been seen some weeks before. The section then set course for base, flying back through very heavy snowstorms. No other operational flying was carried out.

8, 9 and 10 January 1945

Another spell of bad weather kept the Squadron grounded. Heavy snowstorms fell over the three-day period. Although the pilots journeyed to Swannington each morning, the Squadron was released before noon each day. The available airfields were effectively snowbound with deep drifts.

11 January 1945

An adverse weather report from the pilots of 453 Squadron on their return from a weather recce over the Dutch coast cancelled the twelve-aircraft dive-bombing mission, which was due to have been carried out by 602 Squadron.

At 13:05hrs four aircraft took off on a weather recce, but after encountering heavy snowstorms off the English coast, they found the cloud increased over the Dutch coast. In addition, visibility decreased to almost nil. Having flown south to Westhoofd, they found no improvement and set course for base.

12 January 1945

There was no flying as the weather was unsuitable.

13 January 1945

Some practice flying was carried out but no operational flying was done.

14 January 1945

At 09:35hrs the Squadron (the usual section of four aircraft) took off for an armed recce. They crossed in at 12,000 feet; unfortunately, cloud obscured the whole of the target area (from Hook of Holland to Staalduine Bosch), and consequently prevented any bombing or strafing to be carried out. They set course for base.

At 15:40hrs, twelve aircraft, having flown to within fifty yards of the Dutch coast, were advised that the weather was unsuitable and the mission proved abortive. Cloud cover was heavy, which made strafing and bombing useless.

15 January 1945

Once again, poor weather conditions over Holland upset the programme. A twelve-aircraft show with the aircraft carrying 1,000 lbs[7] bombs was cancelled, and instead four aircraft took off at 12:30hrs with two 250 lb bombs on each to bomb the Staalduineche Bosch target. However, cloud cover over the coast of Holland was heavy, and the section found it impossible to make their attack and set a course for base (bringing their bombs back with them).

16 January 1945

Due to adverse weather conditions over Holland, none of the aircraft took part in any operational missions throughout the day.

17 January 1945

At 08:30hrs two aircraft of the readiness section took off on a Jim Crow, led by F/Lt Thomerson. During the recce, which lasted from 09:05hrs to 09:15hrs, the section saw five minesweeper type vessels moving west, grouped round a hulk that had neither funnels nor masts, lying stationary in the centre of the Gap. About a quarter of a mile farther west, three smaller ships were moving slowly westward. A merchant vessel of approximately 5,000–6,000 tons was seen moving out of Den Helder harbour and another vessel of the same type and tonnage was seen in the harbour with smoke up.

At 13:15hrs the Squadron, led by S/Ldr Sutherland, took off to rendezvous with 603 Squadron and a number of Beaufighters whose mission it was to attack the shipping, which 602 Jim Crow section had reported earlier in the day. The two Spitfire Squadrons were led by W/Cdr Burke and their task was to escort the Beaufighters, and before the shipping attack, dive-bomb 'flak' positions north of Den Helder, and on the southern tip of Texel. After escorting the Beaufighters to five miles south-west of the target, the two Squadrons, separated at 14:05hrs with 602 attacking the 'flak' positions with 250 lb bombs; all with good results. Synchronisation of the attacks was perfect and the Squadron broke port across the harbour, and started to climb to 10,000 feet, the Beaufighters were flying through the Straits, to make their attack. S/Ldr Sutherland then led the Squadron in a dive down to 3,500 feet, strafing the flak positions, which were then concentrating their fire on the Beaufighters. A minesweeper type of vessel was seen to be on fire and one of the Beaufighters was observed to crash into the sea in flames. The Squadron then rendezvoused with the wing commander about ten miles west of Egmond and set course for base. Two pilots returned early from the operation, their aircraft having developed engine trouble.

18 January 1945

Four aircraft of 602 Squadron took off on a weather recce over The Hague. They found that cloud cover was heavy. F/O Farfan, who led the section, flew inland for five minutes, turned 180 degrees, and then flew north climbing to 4,000 feet above cloud tops. He and his No. 2 dived through cloud to 900 feet, which was the height of cloud base and where visibility was one mile. Rejoining the other aircraft, the section then set course for base, where they reported that the weather was unsuitable for either dive-bombing or recces. The Squadron was released at 11:30hrs. 'That meant a day off, and the possibility to go into Norwich to visit, as well as pubs and dance halls.'

A large part of the Big Ben operations was to deny the Germans their ability to supply the launching sites and factories with the supplies they needed. That meant all sorts of targets from shipping to railyards, factories, anything that could possibly help to stop the onslaught of the terrible weapons falling on London, had to be attacked. The Squadron was convinced that they were doing a good job, as Raymond Baxter enthuses: 'We were a crack squadron.'

19 January 1945

A twelve-aircraft dive-bombing mission, took off at 12:30hrs against The

Hague/Haagsche Bosch target.[8] Unfortunately due to mechanical trouble one of the aircraft did not take off and a second returned early, but the remainder, crossing in south of The Hague, found the target obscured with heavy cloud and attacked The Hook of Holland/Staalduine Bosch targets over which cloud was less dense. Attacking south to north from 9,000–3,000 feet, with eighteen 250 lb bombs through intense but inaccurate flak, they saw six bombs fall in the target area, between two given pin-pointing aiming positions. Four others undershot that pin-point and the remainder were not seen due to cloud. Blue 4 (F/Sgt Francis) was hit by flak and did not bomb, jettisoning his load into the sea. On his return it was found that a fragment of flak had hit his tail unit, but the pilot was unhurt. This was the only mission to be carried out by the Squadron throughout the day.

20 January 1945

The Squadron was at sixty minutes readiness, and although the weather was somewhat adverse, a moderate amount of practice flying was carried out.

21 January 1945

A section of two aircraft took off this morning on a weather recce at 4,000–5,000 feet. Ten miles from the Dutch coast the cloud began to thicken. The section made landfall at Westhoofd where the cloud base was 4,000 feet, with tops at 10,000 feet, while above this was a layer of cloud at 13,000–15,000 feet. The section reported the weather as being unsuitable for bombing or recces and then set course for base. No other shows were flown.

22 January 1945

The first flight on the day was a four-aircraft dive-bombing armed recce mission, and at 14:30hrs three aircraft were over the Hook of Holland/ Staalduine Bosch target, which they attacked with six 250 lb bombs. Two bombs fell approximately thirty yards from one of the aiming points, whilst two slightly overshot. The position of the remaining two was not observed. The fourth aircraft had to return early due to engine trouble. During the recce that followed the bombing, a small van and a three-ton truck were attacked south-east of Katwijk and the latter was left smoking. Some inaccurate light flak was encountered as the section flew out over Katwijk.

At 13:50hrs two of the 602 aircraft that were at readiness were scrambled to escort W/O Sollitt back to base. His aircraft had developed engine trouble whilst he was flying with the armed recce section, and the escort, after having recced out to the coast, saw the pilot's aircraft fifteen miles from base.

At 14:35hrs the next armed recce made landfall south of Egmond, and having pin-pointed the target at Hague/Haagsche Bosch where some flak was encountered, attacked it with six 250 lb bombs from 8,000–3,000 feet from south-west to north-east. Four bombs fell in the target area in line twenty to 100 yards south-west of one aiming point, and two others approximately 100 yards north-west of another aiming point. Again, one of the aircraft had to return early due to engine trouble. F/Lt Sutherland led the section on a recce of the roads and railways at Gouda and he made three attacks on two stationary railway box wagons observing many strikes on both, and smoke coming from one.

The last mission was another attack on the target at The Hook of Holland/Staalduine Bosch, this time with eight 250 lb bombs. These were dropped in a dive from 9,000–2,000 feet, and all bombs fell on the target area. In most cases the squadron histories and pilots' log books do not specify the targets they were bombing. But as these were Big Ben missions on V2 sites it can be assumed they were attacking the largely wooded areas, which would have had several launch vehicles, fuel trucks, tents, huts and flak positions. Much flak opposition was experienced whilst over the target, but there were no casualties.

23 January 1945

Because of poor weather conditions over The Hague, it was decided that bombs could not be carried and that armed recces would be necessary. Engine trouble developed in two of the four aircraft that took off on an armed recce, one prior to crossing the English coast and the other when about five miles off the Dutch coast. The operation was aborted.

Four aircraft took off at 14:30hrs and, when half way across the North Sea, one of them had to turn back (due to engine trouble) and was escorted by another aircraft of the section. The remaining two aircraft crossed in north of The Hague and carried out a recce over the Leiden/Ijmuiden Opmeer area but no movement was seen. At Uitgeest, two rows of railway box cars on a siding were attacked from 3,000 feet to deck level and although many strikes were seen, no results were observed. Flying north up to the Alkmeer, a three-ton motor truck was seen and attacked three times, many strikes being observed.

24 to 31 January 1945

Widespread snowstorms prevented any operational flying from being carried out. But on the days when weather permitted (not detailed in the Squadron history), extensive practice flying programmes were completed.

A total of 117 hours (non operational) was flown by the Squadron during the month. The non-flying days were occupied (according to Squadron history, not Raymond Baxter) in Link Trainer instruction, aircraft recognition, discussions on dive-bombing tactics and other subjects.

Despite the adverse weather the Squadron carried out practice flying and fifteen hours were flown.

A very interesting lecture was given at Station Intelligence on escape and evasion.

1 February 1945

Four aircraft took off to rendezvous over Antwerp with a Halifax, which was patrolling the area from Antwerp to Nijmegen, and having made contact, they escorted the aircraft on its patrol, which was carried out at a height of 22,000 feet. Although the Spitfires were carrying ninety gallon tanks, the first section found it necessary to land at Uraal airfield to re-fuel, as did the section which relieved them.

The third section however, after completing their patrol, returned direct to Swannington. Apart from seeing and reporting a number of V2 contrails, all the patrols were uneventful.

2 February 1945

Owing to unfavourable weather conditions, a combined 602 and 453 Squadron dive-bombing mission was cancelled, and no operations were carried out.

3 February 1945

At 08:00hrs two aircraft were airborne on a weather recce over The Hague area and reported that the weather was ideal for the combined 453 and 602 Squadrons' dive-bombing operation.

Twelve Spitfires took off at 09:55hrs and formed with 453 Squadron to dive-bomb a liquid oxygen factory at Coosduinen. Unfortunately, one of the aircraft had to return early, due to a mechanical failure, but the remainder, after crossing in north of The Hook of Holland at 12,000 feet, decreased their height to 8,000 feet, over the target area. Here they dive-bombed it with ten 500 lb and nineteen 250 lb bombs, from 9,000–2,500 feet. Of the bombs, several landed in and around the sheds in the canal basin east of the target, but the majority undershot. Very intense, accurate flak was encountered in the dive and a moderate amount of heavy flak as the Squadron crossed out just south of The Hague.

Having been given permission by No. 12 Group to attack the same target with 250 lb bombs, both squadrons, this time led by S/Ldr Sutherland, took off exactly two hours after landing back from the first show. This time two aircraft returned early, one due to mechanical trouble, the second as escort. The other aircraft proceeded to the target, which they bombed with nineteen 250 lb bombs, from east to west, with good results. Two bombs fell on the buildings in the southern end of the target area, and four to six bombs on the western end by the canal basin. Two others landed squarely in the middle of a building due west, a column of smoke rising to about 1,000 feet was seen to come from it. There were many near misses round the buildings given as aiming points and it is felt that a fair amount of damage must have been done. A number of bomb craters (presumably from the first attack) were seen in the target area, and it was the opinion of all the pilots that the result of this mission was infinitely better than had been considered.

4 February 1945

At 11:15hrs four aircraft were despatched on a combined weather and armed recce, but weather conditions over the continent prevented an attack being made, and the aircraft returned to base with their bombs. Raymond Baxter explains why: 'Landing a Spitfire with a full bomb load had to be approached with total concentration and skill. It would have been far easier to jettison over the sea, but we did not do that.'

At 13:10hrs a further four aircraft took off to dive-bomb the Hotel Promenade target at The Hague. Although the weather conditions were still poor, they were fortunate in finding a break in the cloud and they attacked the target from 8,000–3,000 feet, south-east to north-west. Unfortunately, the bombs on two of the aircraft hung up but the others fell very close to the hotel (two bombs only a few feet from the south-west end and two on the junction of the roadways near by). During the attack some heavy flak was encountered. A recce of the Leiden / Amsterdam, Haarlem / Leiden area was then carried out. Apart from an unusual amount of barge activity on the canal north of Leiden, no movement was seen.

At 15:25hrs the last operation of the day, an attack on the railway junction between Utretch and Woerden, was aborted. Heavy cloud covered the whole area and the aircraft returned to Swannington bringing all bombs back with them.

5 February 1945

At 12:45hrs the first section of four aircraft was airborne as escort to a Halifax aircraft from Antwerp to Nijmegen. Four sections were despatched throughout the day, all patrols being uneventful.

6 February 1945

At 08:15hrs a combined armed and weather recce was carried out this morning. Three aircraft took off each with 250 lb bombs, and finding that the weather was suitable, dive-bombed the Haagsche Bosch target. Two bombs fell on the south-west edge of the woods and four farther south; a recce followed but no movement was seen.

At 12:25hrs five aircraft led by F/Lt Thomerson were despatched to attack with 250 lb bombs the railway junction between Utrecht and Worden. Diving from 7,000 feet along the railway line, they dropped their bombs at 1,000 feet, with very good results. The railway line was hit in two places and a mixed passenger and goods train, which was stationary on the track next to where the bombs burst, severely damaged. Two bombs fell on some railway buildings and two more were near misses to the track. After their initial attack the aircraft made two more cannon and machine-gun attacks on the train, giving the locomotive and all the rolling stock an equal share of their ammunition. No flak was experienced throughout the operation.

At 13:15hrs another five aircraft attacked a railway junction at Gouda and again cut the railway line. Two bombs fell on the centre of the track west of the station. There were four near misses, two to the left and two to the right (at approximately the same position). The sites of the other bombs were not observed. This time the section encountered some meagre heavy flak from Rotterdam, but no casualties were suffered.

New arrival Sgt Love was posted to the unit for flying duties with effect from 5 February 1945. He became a devoted No. 2 to F/Lt Baxter and is credited as the only pilot to have engaged a ballistic missile in flight.

7 February 1945

At 10:20hrs four aircraft took off for a Jim Crow and weather recce, but after flying for twenty-five minutes at various heights through two layers of thick cloud, they were faced with a solid wall of cloud from 1,500 feet down to 150 feet and were forced to return to base.

At 13:15hrs the Halifax escort patrol, which was due to take off at 12:45hrs, was finally postponed until 13:30hrs, then cancelled. However, S/Ldr Sutherland, who was to have led the first section, got permission to carry out a Jim Crow and armed recce. Flying between layers of cloud, they found Den Helder and the whole area to the south obscured by cloud. The section set course for base.

8 February 1945

A three-squadron ramrod on the liquid oxygen works in the Dutch capital was the only operation flown. 602/453 Squadrons again combined forces and, led by S/Ldr Sutherland, took off at 09:25hrs; the third Squadron was 603, which took off forty-five minutes later. Flying out at 9,000 feet in heavy cloud, the Squadrons found the target area obscured. Three orbits were made over the area but as no break appeared in the clouds they flew south to The Hook of Holland, where the secondary target was situated. As cloud also obscured this target, they set course back to The Hague and were fortunate in finding a small break in the cloud through which ten aircraft were able to bomb the target. Two clusters of bombs were seen to fall on the target building and smoke and debris rose to about 1,500 feet. Another cluster of bombs undershot, falling south of the canal basin, but unfortunately cloud obscured the results of the other bombs. However, it was thought that at least two bombs must have hit some of the liquid oxygen stores. The Squadrons then set course for Ursel where they landed and after re-fuelling took off once again, in sections of four to strafe three targets in The Hague. Low cloud over the whole area made this impossible, and this part of the operation was abandoned.

9 February 1945

Although scheduled to take part in another attack on the Loosduines target, the weather was unfavourable, so the Squadron was put on a state of sixty-minutes readiness for training. An extensive programme was carried out (air to air firing, dive-bombing and Balbo Formation[9] practice), a total of twenty-nine hours, fifteen minutes practice flying hours being reached.

Two aircraft were despatched as escort to Mustangs photographing the attack on the Boosduinen target, which was being carried out by 453 and 603 Squadrons. Whilst over the target, Red 1 (Australian W/O J P Ryan) was hit by light flak. Red 2 was unable to give any information apart from the fact that W/O Ryan was flying below him at a height between 5,000 and 6,000 feet, when he was hit. Thus, W/O Ryan was listed as Missing.

10 February 1945

At 11:20hrs four aircraft were airborne on a combined Jim Crow and weather recce and found the area from Den Helder to north of Texel clear of cloud, but south of this and for some considerable distance inland was covered with thick cloud for 4,000–5,000 feet. No shipping was observed when a recce of the harbour was made. However, at 12:25hrs three merchant vessels of approximately 4,000–5,000 tons were seen moored on the southern basin. All vessels appeared to be painted red and had central smoke stacks. The section proceeded to The Hague and then southward to The Hook of Holland, crossing out there at 8,000 feet.

Two aircraft of the readiness section were scrambled at 11:40hrs to make a search for pilots who had baled out of a Lancaster after colliding with a Spitfire, off Skegness. A thorough search was made but without result. The section was relieved by a Warwick aircraft at 12:55hrs, then returned

1. Squadron Leader RA 'Max' Sutherland DSO and 2 Bars of Orpington, Kent. The veteran of many attacks on VI launching sites, he is pictured as the leader of the main attacks on V2 rocket installations at The Hague, codenamed Operation Big Ben.

2. Two squadron members check a 500lb bomb before it is hooked up under the Spitfire before a mission against V2 sites at The Hague. Note that the two 250lb bombs are already hooked up. The 500lb bomb will be slung underneath the fuselage of the Spitfire.

3. A more detailed photograph of squadron members checking the fuses prior to a dive-bombing Spitfire mission. Note, the man on the right (Pertwee) looks more concerned than his boss.

4. Flight Lieutenant Raymond Baxter briefs his men prior to a dive-bombing mission. The table-top map is a detailed study on The Hague, with button pins marking the main target areas. 'Bax' will take his team into a heavily protected area; the men are therefore studying the map carefully. The lockers behind the men have the following names chalked on them (from left to right): Zuuber, Toone, Menzies, Cupid.

5. 'Max' Sutherland briefs his men before a dive-bombing mission. 'Double Whisky' from the Polish squadron is second from the right. Note the map sticking out of Sutherland's left boot.

6. A Spitfire is seen silhouetted against the smoke from its exploding bombs, as it pulls away from a dive on a Dutch V2 installation near a civilian housing estate.

7. Wrecked buildings of the Film Studios in Haagsche Bosch, used by the Germans for firing V2 rockets, seen after a dive-bombing Spitfire attack in February 1945.

8. 'Cupid' Love on joining 602 Squadron.

9. Squadron Leader 'Tommy' Rigler on joining 602 Squadron.

10. From left to right: Flight Lieutenant HRP Pertwee, Squadron Leader RA Sutherland, F.O. FW Farvan and Flight Officer GD Stephenson carry out checks before yet another sortie.

11. The crest of Fighter Command who carried out the successful dive-bombing missions against V2 rocket sites.

12. The squadron crest of 602 City of Glasgow Squadron.

13. Veteran 602 Squadron Flight Lieutenant Raymond Baxter checks his log book of events against the squadron histories during his interview in support of this book.

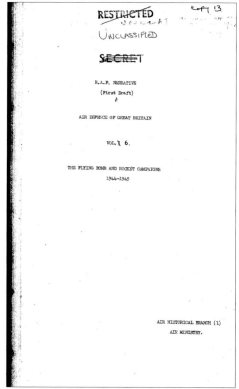

RESTRICTED   Copy 13

UNCLASSIFIED

SECRET

R.A.F. NARRATIVE
(First Draft)

AIR DEFENCE OF GREAT BRITAIN

VOL. X 6.

THE FLYING BOMB AND ROCKET CAMPAIGNS
1944-1945

AIR HISTORICAL BRANCH (1)
AIR MINISTRY.

14. A copy of the original manuscript on Air Defence of Great Britain Vol 6 (formerly Vol 7), unclassified document (formerly secret) that proved that Operation Big Ben was a major success and not a failure as noted by Alanbrooke.

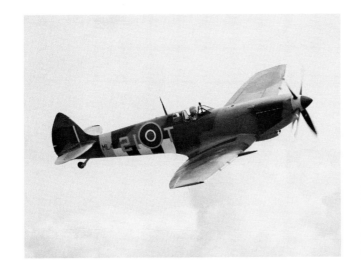

15. A clipped winged Mk IX Spitfire, typical of the aircraft used originally in Operation Big Ben.

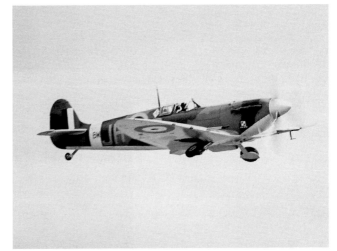

16. The Mk V Spitfire had its own small part to play during the operation. This one is seen shortly after take off.

17. 'I loved that aircraft from the word go,' said Raymond Baxter of the dive-bombing Mk XVI Spitfire.

18. Bomber Command's raids of V2 installations were not as successful as those carried out by Spitfires; however, they did have their uses.

19. Raymond Baxter OBE during his interview with the writers concerning the once covert Operation Big Ben.

to base.

A section of four aircraft took off with 250 lb bombs to attack the Staalduine Bosch target at the Hook of Holland, bombing in a south-west/north-east direction. At 8,000–3,500 feet, all bombs fell in the target area. On the recce that followed, a light motor truck was seen on the road west of Hooge Veen and was attacked. All aircraft made three attacks, and many strikes were seen. A merchant vessel of approximately 3,000–4,000 tons, possibly derelict, was seen on the river one mile west of Maasluis. A V2 contrail was reported to Controller at 15:00hrs rising vertically from The Hague from 6,000 to approximately 40,000 feet.

Four more aircraft were despatched on an armed recce/dive-bombing mission. The target was Rust-en-Vreugd and as one of the aircraft returned early, due to mechanical trouble, the target was bombed with six 250 lb bombs – the weather was perfect. All the bombs fell approximately fifty to 150 yards east of the target aiming point, four on the north side of the road and two on the south side. Meagre and inaccurate flak was encountered from the target area. The section then made a recce of Leiden, Amsterdam and Haarlem, attacking a staff car on the road south-east of Haarlem. Another V2 contrail was seen by the section, rising from 10,000 feet (to approximately 40,000 feet) from The Hague at 16:00hrs.

11 February 1945

Weather conditions over the continent prevented any operational flying from being carried out, but throughout the day the pilots were kept busy on a flying practice programme including squadron formation, cross country low flying as well as air to ground and dive-bombing practice.

12 February 1945

The continuation of bad weather again caused operations to be cancelled and made it impossible for any practice flying to be carried out. Instead, many Link Trainer hours were put in throughout the day and in the afternoon a talk on Deflection Shooting was given by S/Ldr Sutherland, which was followed by a skeet shooting[10] competition in which F/Sgt Francis showed his prowess as a marksman.

13 February 1945

The Squadron was at a state of readiness of sixty minutes for training and a very intensive programme was carried out. From 09:00hrs, when the first section of six aircraft took off on formation, dive-bombing, skip bombing and air to ground practice, until 18:50hrs, when the last section landed the pilots were kept busy on all types of practice flying and at the end of the day, forty-seven hours had been flown bringing the total for the month up to 136 non-operational flying hours.

14 February 1945

Eleven aircraft each with a 1,000 lb bomb load took off as part of a three-squadron striking force to attack The Haagsche Bosch target in the Dutch capital. The weather was perfect and after crossing in north of The Hague at 11,000 feet, they attacked the target north-east to south-west from 10,000–3,000 feet through a curtain of very accurate light as well as some accurate heavy flak. During the dive the leaders and No. 3s of each section hit the target (except one 500 lb and one 250 lb bomb which hung up), the bombs fell on and around the aiming point, leaving a red glow from the direct hits. The Squadron strafed the whole of the target area down to 500 feet, encountering much light flak but without the accuracy of that experienced during the bombing attack, when the aircraft of S/Ldr Sutherland and F/O Baxter were hit, both receiving superficial damage. The Squadron landed at Ursel at 10:40hrs and after re-fuelling were airborne again at 12:18hrs and en route to the Hotel Promenade, which they attacked with cannon and machine-gun fire from 6,000 feet to zero feet, many strikes being seen on the hotel buildings. Again, very intense light flak was encountered and the aircraft of F/O McHardy (New Zealand) was hit but not badly damaged, and the pilot was uninjured.

An entry of deep regret is made, concerning a flying accident in which F/Lt G Y G Lloyd was killed. As the Squadron came in over base they were given the order 'Echelon Starboard' and F/Lt Lloyd passing under F/Lt Waterhouse's aircraft from the port side, pulled up under his belly and collided with his aircraft. He immediately fell away, flicked, and dived down, crashing into a field adjoining the aerodrome (15:30hrs is recorded as the time of the accident). He was killed instantly. Fortunately, although part of his propeller had broken away, F/Lt Waterhouse managed to land safely without injury.

Six aircraft were despatched to bomb The Hague/Voorde target with 250 lb bombs. Three aircraft returned early with mechanical trouble but the remainder carried on to the target area, which they bombed south-west to north-east from 7,000–2,000 feet. Two bombs fell north-west of the aiming point. Due to faulty RT, Yellow 3 and 4 bombed the railway line north-east of the target and as the bombs fell on the track a large green flash was seen. The section then flew to The Hague to Gouda railway line, and sighting two stationary passenger coaches in a siding at Hooge Veen, they strafed them with cannon and machine-gun fire and left one of them smoking furiously. The other received many strikes. After a recce of the Boskoop Leiden area during which no movement was seen, the section set course for base.

15 February 1945

Low cloud and poor visibility in the Low Countries prevented any operations from being carried out.

16 February 1945

Neither operational nor practice flying was possible due to adverse weather conditions.

17 February 1945

No improvement in the weather. More Link Trainer* and some talks by the flight commanders. In the afternoon a talk to the ground crews by S/Ldr Sutherland.

18 February 1945

In the morning, the weather showed little signs of improvement, but by 15:00hrs it was possible to fly the aircraft from Swannington to Coltishall (from where the Squadron were operating until they moved to Ludham). The movement of equipment took some time and organisation, as both Matlaske and Swannington had a considerable amount to transfer to Coltishall (the Squadron had to be fully operational by first light on 19 February).

19 February 1945

Low cloud and haze prevented any flying from being carried out during the morning. By mid-day the local weather conditions had improved and two aircraft were despatched on a combined weather and armed reconnaissance. Thirty miles from the English coast, cloud became thick at 2,000–5,000 feet and, as the section approached the Dutch coast flying at 9,000 feet, they saw that the continent was obscured by cloud. Although they flew over the area for fifteen minutes, they could find no break in the cloud and set course for base.

20 February 1945

Six aircraft took off to dive-bomb the Hotel Promenade target in The Hague, but extremely poor weather conditions were met over the

*Raymond Baxter comments on the references to Link Trainer in the Squadron History: 'I am worried about the references to Link Trainer. I believe it was entered in the diary to meet statutory requirements. I have no recollection of Link time, nor does my log book record this.'

continent, and the operation was abandoned and the section returned to base, bringing their bombs back.

Operations advised that concentrated attacks were to be made on the Haagsche-Bosch target in The Hague, which had been divided into eight sections and were to be bombed by the Wing throughout the day. S/Ldr Sutherland led the first section of six aircraft to attack Section 'A' and, having crossed in south of The Hook of Holland, made a reconnaissance of the area, but no shipping or movement of any kind was seen. Flying north to The Hague, they found the area obscured by heavy cloud and returned to base.

The next section of six aircraft took off to attack Section 'D' but found thick cloud on the target area and could not attack. Crossing out, they encountered some accurate light flak from the coast south of Katwijk.

Six aircraft, two of which returned early (one with mechanical trouble, the second as escort) found the Dutch capital obscured by cloud, and after making a reconnaissance of the roads and railways to Alkmaar and Stoopdorp, they attacked the railway junction north-west of Alkmaar. Two bombs fell a few feet from the track whilst the remainder were approximately fifty yards short of the junction. On the road south of Middenmeer, two aircraft made three attacks on a stationary motor van – seeing many strikes – whilst the other two aircraft made two attacks on an open motor coach and left it in flames and smoking furiously.

21 February 1945

At 10:30hrs four aircraft, led by F/Lt Pertwee, each with 250 lb bombs fused airburst were despatched on a combined Jim Crow and armed reconnaissance. After crossing in south of Den Helder they made a recce of the straits and the harbour. In the former, two vessels of approximately 100 feet in length were seen facing west. One appeared to be of the corvette type whilst the other may have been a minesweeper. Both vessels had central smoke stacks and, although no smoke was coming from them, they appeared to be moving slowly westwards. In the Den Helder harbour, three stationary vessels of the coaster type and of approximately 3,000 tons were seen as well as ten or more barges.

After completing the Jim Crow, the section flew south to Alkmaar where a 15 cwt truck was bombed by one aircraft and strafed by two others. No results came from the bombing but after strafing – four attacks – it was left smoking. To complete the operation, the target at Haagsche Bosch was dive-bombed by three aircraft with six 250 lb bombs and strafed by four aircraft in the dive. Four bombs fell in the target area but the positions of the other two were unobserved. No flak was encountered throughout the operations.

The bombing of the Haagsche Bosch target continued throughout the day, a total of twenty-eight sorties being flown. All operations were carried out by four aircraft each of which carried two 250 lb bombs fused airburst. After the aircraft pulled out of their dive they all strafed the length of the wooded area with cannon and machine-gun fire, and in many cases the aircraft went down to deck level. They then proceeded to the Ockenburg Klinier target, which they also strafed in a similar fashion. After the attack, which was led by S/Ldr Sutherland, an explosion and fire started in the north-east quarters of the target and dense black smoke issuing to a considerable height was seen for about ten minutes. Light flak from the target area was encountered on each operation.

Two aircraft returned early from the last operation of the day, one with mechanical trouble and the other acting as escort, but the remaining aircraft, led by F/O Farrell (USA), after bombing the Haagsche Bosch made a reconnaissance of The Hague area during which they attacked three 30 cwt trucks, which were carrying many German soldiers. Prior to the attack, they were very hastily evacuated; but many strikes were seen on all the vehicles. A 15 cwt truck and trailer were attacked about a mile farther north and strikes were also seen on them.

22 February 1945

Six new aiming points in The Haagsche Bosch lent a new interest to this target, which had now been bombed for many weeks.

Ten aircraft, led by the commanding officer, S/Ldr Sutherland, took off to bomb the target at two aiming points in the centre of the wooded area. Crossing in at 10,000 feet they saw a large column of smoke rising from the film studios situated at the north-east end of the target following the attack made on this point by 453 Squadron. 602 Squadron then went in to attack, diving south-west to north-east from 9,000–2,000 feet, strafing the whole length of the target area in the dive. Twelve bombs fell on and around the southern aiming point and four or five orange coloured explosions, probably from fuel storage were seen, columns of grey and black smoke rising from them to some considerable height. Six bombs fell around the northern aiming point and two south of the anti-tank ditch that ran along three sides of the target area. Cimbing to 8,000 feet they proceeded to Ockenburg Klinier where the house at the north-east end of the target was strafed by all the aircraft. Many strikes were seen on the roof and walls of this building and smoke was seen coming from the roof and windows. Some inaccurate light flak was encountered during the dive-bombing from the target area.

Seven aircraft, each carrying two 250 lb bombs fused airburst, and one aircraft with two 250 lb fused eleven-second delay took off to bomb the targets at Haagsche Bosch and Ockenburg Klinier. After crossing in at

10,000 feet over The Hague they broke up into two sections of four and Yellow Section proceeded to Haagsche Bosch, which they bombed from 8,000–2,000 feet. Two bombs fell approximately ten yards south of the bridge at the south-west end of the target area whilst two more fell about forty yards north of the bridge. Two more fell within a 100-yard radius of the aiming point and two south of the target area on the Staats Spoor station. They re-joined Red Section north of Delft and flew to Ockenburg where Yellow Section strafed the house on the target area. The section dive-bombed and two bombs hit the base of the eastern wall. The others fell twenty and fifty yards north-east of the target (two aircraft strafed in the dive). Meagre, moderately accurate, light flak from south of Haagsche Bosch was experienced.

23 February 1945

The Squadron made its second move within six days. 'Au revoir' was said to Coltishall and by late afternoon, their dispersal to Ludham was complete, with the squadron ready for operation the following morning. 603 City of Edinburgh Squadron were to be sharing it from 24 February.

24 February 1945

The results of the first day's operations from the new station were very pleasing. The first show of the day was a combined weather and armed recce. Two aircraft crossed in north of Katwijk at 9,000 feet over thick cloud and found the target area obscured. They flew north-east towards Amsterdam where the cloud became slightly less dense, and bombed with four 250 lb bombs the railway line at Baambrugge, south to north, from 6,000–2,000 feet. All bombs fell on the railway track. A recce that followed was uneventful.

Thoughout the day, the weather over the Dutch capital was unsuitable for bombing attacks to be made on the Haagsche Bosch target, but aircraft were always able to find a clear patch somewhere in Holland and as a result the railway lines at different parts of the country suffered.

Four aircraft were despatched to bomb the target of Haagsche Bosch, but finding it obscured by cloud, proceeded to Aalsmeer where they bombed the railway east of the town with six 250 lb bombs, but poor visibility made it impossible to observe the results. Blue 4 did not bomb and jettisoned his bombs in the sea.

F/Lt Wroblewski (Polish) led four aircraft in an attack on the railway bridge over a canal and road at Koegras. Two bombs fell on west end of the bridge, two forty yards north-west and two south-east of bridge. The canal lock control building was hit and a column of smoke and debris was seen to rise from the building.

The next section of four aircraft, after making reconnaissance of the area from Ijmuiden to Den Helder (where the visibility was very poor), turned south where the weather conditions were better and attacked a railway junction seven miles north-east of Alkmaar from 6,000–1,000 feet. Four bombs fell dead on the railway lines and four about twenty yards west of it. The section then set course for base crossing out north of Egmond.

On the last mission of the day, two aircraft bombed a railway bridge over a canal half a mile east of Schagen. Four bombs fell on the railway line north of the bridge and two south of the bridge; missing the railway. The other two aircraft bombed a road canal bridge adjoining and bombs fell on the road at each end of the bridge. In the recce that followed a three ton carrying wagon was sighted travelling north from Sloopdorp. This was attacked and left smoking, troops scattering from the wagon into the adjoining woods, which was strafed by Red 2. The section then climbed to 8,000 feet and crossed out north of Bergen aan Zee.

25 February 1945

Four aircraft took off to attack the Haagsche Bosch target (aiming point D) with eight 250 lb bombs fused airburst. They crossed in north of The Hague and attacked south-west to north-east from 8,000–2,000 feet, four bombs falling in a cluster thirty to sixty yards south-west of the target aiming point and a second cluster falling seventy-five to 100 yards north-east of the point. Dense black smoke rose from both clusters to a height of 500 feet. During the dive, all aircraft strafed the length of the target area. On the recce that followed, a motor truck and trailer moving south-east from Stompetoren were attacked from 2,000 to deck level, and two aircraft made two and four attacks. The truck stopped and a number of Nazi soldiers took cover in the adjoining wood. Many strikes were seen on both vehicles, and when the section strafed the wood, two soldiers were killed by Red 4 as they ran out of the woods. During the attack on the Haagsche Bosch some 20mm tracer was encountered.

Six aircraft, led by F/O Farrell, were despatched to bomb the same target, the aiming points for this operation being 'D' and 'E'. The section bombed south-west to north-east, from 8,000–2,000 feet, strafing in the dive and all bombs fell around the two aiming points. After the attack, the aircraft made a successful reconnaissance of the Haarlem and Alkmaar area, attacking two staff cars west of Waterkant. Both cars stopped but no occupants got out and after the attack the cars were left in flames. A truck travelling on the same road was attacked and left smoking. East of Hoorn a light van was attacked by two aircraft and after strikes were seen one vehicle stopped. To complete the operation, the other two aircraft attacked a 30 cwt truck on the same road and had the pleasure of leaving it burning merrily on the roadside.

At 12:15hrs six aircraft, with two 250 lb bombs and led by S/Ldr Sutherland, took off to attack the Haagsche Bosch target. Diving south-west to north-east from 7,000–3,000 feet and strafing as they dived, ten bombs were dropped on the target within a radius of 175 yards from the aiming point. One aircraft did not bomb. During the attack some accurate light and heavy flak was experienced from the target area and from the coast at The Hague. The section carried out a recce at deck level as far as Amsterdam; then climbing to 2,000 feet proceeded to Leiden/Delft and west to Rotterdam. There they found a motor transport park in the courtyard of the two buildings forming two sides of a triangle. Approximately thirty camouflaged vehicles were parked in the courtyard and about ten along the northern side of one of the buildings. Twelve attacks were made in all and the aircraft that had been unable to bomb the primary target dropped two 250 lb bombs on one of the buildings in a shallow dive. An explosion (possibly from petrol storage) followed and dense black smoke and flames rose from the building, spreading eastwards for nearly a mile. Strikes were seen on all the vehicles and the pilot who made the last attack was unable to see the target through the thick pall of smoke that covered the area. After the first attack, both light and heavy flak was encountered over Rotterdam.

The next section to bomb Haagsche Bosch consisted of four aircraft all carrying two 250 lb bombs. Blue 2 lost the others in the cloud crossing in at The Hook of Holland, and sighted a large two-funnelled merchant vessel of approximately 10,000 tons moving westward on the river west of Maaluis. He attacked a train moving south-east in The Hague/Gouda line with two 250 lb bombs that fell only a few feet behind the last truck. He then made two strafing attacks and saw strikes on the locomotive and trucks. Meantime, the other three aircraft had successfully bombed the target and then carried out an uneventful recce. Some accurate light flak was experienced from the target and from the small village of Rijnsburg.

Six aircraft were airborne to attack the Haagsche Bosch target with twelve 250 lb bombs. Small patches of cloud interrupted the approach but all bombs fell in the target area and the length of the wood was strafed in the dive. During the recce that followed, six attacks were made on a staff car moving westward on the road south-east of Alphen. Many strikes were seen and the car stopped. Before crossing out all the aircraft strafed the target at Ockemburg and strikes were seen on the house there. A moderate amount of very accurate light flak was encountered from south-east of the Haagsche Bosch as well as some accurate heavy flak from The Hague.

Five aircraft, one of which returned early due to mechanical trouble, attacked the Haagsche Bosch. During the attack, intense accurate light flak was experienced from the target area, and on his return F/Lt Sutherland reported that at least five guns were situated along the north-west boundary and four more near the south-east corner of the target area. Flying over Rotterdam to assess the damage caused after the attack on the transport park carried out by the previous section at 12:15hrs, they found the buildings completely gutted and still smouldering and all the vehicles completely destroyed, only burnt out chassis remaining. No flak was encountered and they were able to estimate the number of vehicles destroyed as being at least forty.

26 February 1945

Two aircraft carried out a weather and armed recce, and finding the target in The Hague obscured by two layers of cloud, flew to Utrecht where a road bridge some distance from the town was bombed. Two bombs fell east and two west of the bridge. An uneventful recce followed before they set course for base.

Attacks on the Haagsche Bosch were resumed but four aircraft, which were despatched at 08:30hrs, found the target obscured by cloud. They proceeded on a recce and at Ultgeest bombed a railway junction with eight 250 lb bombs. The bombs fell on the station, two on a railway shed and two on the railway line south-east of the junction. Two near misses fell close to the rails at the junction. A staff car and a 15 cwt truck were attacked near Alkmaar, and after many strikes had been observed, both vehicles stopped (the staff car having shot off wildly along the road, ending up in a field). A V2 contrail was seen rising from north-east Holland at 08:56hrs.

Six aircraft attacked the Haagsche Bosch target with twelve 250 lb bombs all of which fell in the target area, all aircraft strafing the wood down to 500 feet. A staff car moving south on the Ijmuiden to Amsterdam road, was attacked by one aircraft and left smoking and strikes were seen on another car moving south-east on The Hague to Gouda road. Two aircraft also attacked two cars moving out of Gouda and many strikes were seen causing the cars to stop. Two more V2 contrails were seen – one moving from north-east Holland and one rising from The Hague. Another six aircraft took off to bomb the Haagsche Bosch and ten bombs were seen to drop in the target area (two bomb hang ups were jettisoned into the sea). During the dive, the section carried out the usual 602 Squadron procedure and strafed the length of the wood. A recce followed and on the Amsterdam to Ijmuiden road, a two ton truck moving towards Amsterdam was attacked by two aircraft. The vehicle stopped and its Nazi occupants took cover. Many strikes were seen and the truck was left burning. A camouflaged van was attacked north-east of Alkmaar by all the aircraft and stopped after many strikes had been observed. At a railway terminus nearby, all the aircraft attacked five carriages and eight trucks and strikes were seen all along the rolling stock.

At 13:15hrs two V2 trails were seen rising from 2,000–19,000 feet from the Texel area. The trails zigzagged slightly and were topped with a puff of what appeared to be smoke.

Six aircraft, led by S/Ldr Sutherland, attacked the Haagsche Bosch, each aircraft carrying two 250 lb bombs. A fire started near the centre of the wood and greyish white smoke, which rose steadily from it, was still seen when the section left the target area ten minutes later. The recce that followed was uneventful, no movement being seen in the Amsterdam, Hague, Utrecht, Rotterdam areas.

At 16:30hrs heavy cloud covered The Hague, preventing the next section of six aircraft from attacking the Haagsche Bosch. Instead, they attacked a bridge over a railway at Slootdijk, with eleven 250 lb bombs, diving south to north from 8,000–3,000 feet. One bomb fell on the railway track, whilst three bursts were seen around the southern end of the bridge. Two more near misses were observed just off the track north of the bridge and the remainder of the bombs fell in the surrounding fields. Throughout the recce, no movements were seen.

At 11:30hrs the Air Officer Commanding, Air Vice Marshal Baker, with Group Captain Donaldson, visited the squadron at Ludham.

27 February 1945

Four aircraft were despatched on a combined weather and armed reconnaissance, but found the continent obscured by thick cloud at 7,000 feet. They returned to base, bringing their bombs back with them. During the operation, two V2 contrails were seen, one from The Hague at 07:40hrs and the other from north-east Holland at 08:15hrs.

Another section of four aircraft on a weather and armed recce found the whole area covered by thick cloud and brought their bombs back with them

Hoping that the weather over Holland might have improved, four aircraft took off on another combined weather and armed recce. Crossing in at 7,500 feet over Zandvoort above thick cloud, they came down through it to 5,000 feet (just below cloud base) and recced to Haarlem and Den Helder. A car moving through the village north-east of Almaar was not attacked due to the proximity of the house, and other than this vehicle no movement was seen throughout the operation.

Finding the Haagsche Bosch target obscured by cloud, the next section of four aircraft flew to Assum where they bombed a railway junction scoring a direct hit on the line. A factory beside the junction was also bombed and two direct hits scored, leaving the buildings enveloped in clouds of brown smoke. Two miles south of Opperdoes, a staff car and two camouflaged trucks moving westwards were attacked. Both trucks stopped and were left smoking and the staff car disintegrated. The aircraft of F/Lt Wroblewski, who was leading the section, received superficial damage to the radiator from the debris that rose from the car. Yellow 4 then bombed a railway bridge over a canal four miles west of Obdam, the bombs falling fifteen yards north of the railway track.

Four aircraft finding The Hague obscured by thick cloud, flew towards Rotterdam, breaking cloud at 6,000 feet. They proceeded to the target area and bombed The Haagsche Bosch, north-east to south-west, from 6,000–1,500 feet with eight 250 lb bombs fused airburst. Two bombs fell about fifty yards each side of the aiming point 'B'. Other results were not observed. The section then broke port, reformed and recced to east of Leiden, Alphen and Amsterdam. Again, transport in the form of two 15 cwt trucks was seen but due to the proximity of houses was not attacked.

On their return from the last attack of the day on the Haagsche Bosch target, the pilots reported having seen six bombs fall around the 'C' aiming point area. One fell short of the canal and one fifty yards south-west of aiming point 'B'. All aircraft strafed the length of the target in their dive and after forming up, recced to Gouda east to Woerden and thence to Haarlem. At a road junction, east of Benthuizen, a three ton truck with a large trailer, which may have been used as a liquid oxygen container, was seen and attacked. After many strikes had been seen the vehicles stopped. They were smoking badly and dark brown liquid was seen pouring on to the roadway. The section then set course for base. Once again, the Haagsche Bosch was the target attacked throughout the day by all squadrons of the wing.

28 February 1945

After successfully dive-bombing the target with six 250 lb bombs and then strafing the target area, the section of four aircraft recced to north of Ijmuiden, Amsterdam and south to Katwijk, but saw no movement of any kind. Red 4 bombed a railway bridge north of Leiden, his bombs falling ten to fifteen yards north of the bridge, very close to the railway track. The other aircraft flew to Rotterdam where on the river east of the town a large concentration of eighty to 100 barges, some of which had four metal pylon-like superstructures, was seen. Intense accurate red and yellow light flak was encountered from Ijmuiden as well as intense accurate light and heavy flak from Katwijk.

Four aircraft dropped six bombs from 6,000–2,500 feet around the aiming point on the Haagsche Bosch target and two more at the anti-tank ditch north-east of the aiming point. They then proceeded on a recce of the Gouda, Ijmuiden and Leiden areas. At west of Gouda, two aircraft attacked an open truck carrying supplies. The car stopped and was left smoking. No other movement was seen during the operation.

Four aircraft took off to attack the same target and attacking north-east to south-west from 5,500 to 1,500 feet and then strafing the target, they dropped the bombs fifty yards south of the aiming point, causing an explosion from which grey and black smoke rose to 500 feet. Two bombs fell seventy-five to 100 yards east and two 100 yards north of the aiming point. The other results were unobserved. A recce was then carried out over the Utrecht, Amsterdam, Uitgeest areas, which proved uneventful.

Another section of three aircraft bombed the Haagsche Bosch target with six 250 lb bombs from 6,000–3,000 feet, strafing in the dive and saw the bombs fall fifty yards from the aiming point. Yellow 4 bombed a bridge over a canal, his bombs falling on the road fifty yards from the bridge. During the recce that followed, a three ton troop carrier with trailer and a small van travelling south-east near Assum was attacked and after many strikes had been seen and both vehicles had stopped, they were left smoking. No other movement was seen throughout the operation, and at 14:05hrs the section crossed out at Egmond.

Of four aircraft that took off to attack the same target in The Hague, one returned early due to mechanical trouble. Low cloud over the Dutch capital prevented an attack from being made and so flying eastwards to Gouda, F/Lt Pertwee, who was leading the section, saw a bridge over the railway east of the town, which they bombed from 6,000–2,000 feet, scoring one direct hit on the western end of the bridge, three on the railway twenty yards south of the bridge and two near misses on the junction north-east of the bridge. Turning north, the section recced to Opmeer and Bergen but no movement was seen, apart from some horse-drawn vehicles, all of which were loaded with hay or straw (these were particularly noticeable throughout the whole of Holland at that time).

Target area 'B' was bombed with eight 250 lb bombs and strafed with machine-gun and cannon fire. Four of the bombs fell within 100 yards of aiming point 'B' and two within fifty yards of aiming point 'D'.[11] The results of the other two bombs were not observed. Some light flak was experienced from the target area. After the attack the aircraft climbed to 6,000 feet, at which height they recced up to Den Helder. A car travelling on the road one mile west of Permerend was attacked by Blue 4 and left stationary and smoking. South-east of Schagen a three ton truck, a green 30 cwt lorry and trailer with tractor, all moving south-east, were attacked and after many strikes had been noted the vehicles stopped. Again many horse-drawn vehicles laden with hay or straw were seen.

The last attack of the day on the Haagsche Bosch target was led by F/O Baxter. Crossing in at 6,000 feet over The Hague below thick cloud, at the same height they bombed the target north-east to south-west, from 6,000–2,000 feet, strafing it in the dive. All bombs were seen to burst within 100 yards of the aiming point. A recce of the areas of Aalsmeer, Amsterdam, Edam, Alkmaar followed, during which Yellow 3 and 4 strafed a three ton covered motor truck south of Purmerend, which stopped and was left smoking. Yellow 1 and 2 strafed a tractor and trailer camouflaged mottled green on the Oosthuizen to Edam road, and these were also left smoking. At a road junction west of Alkmaar a staff car was attacked by all aircraft and left in flames. Bursts of inaccurate heavy flak were encountered when crossing in at The Hague, and also some meagre but rather inaccurate flak from the target area.

1 March 1945

The Haagsche Bosch was again the target on which all bombing attacks were to be directed. The first operation of the day took off at 07:25hrs and four aircraft soon found the target area covered in heavy cloud. So, at 08:10hrs, they preceeded to Gouda, where they attacked a railway junction west of the town. Four bombs fell dead on the junction and the others about forty to fifty yards off the railway track. Climbing to 7,000 feet, the section made a reconnaissance of the Boskoop/Katwijk area, but no movement was seen. At 08:03hrs a V2 was seen rising out of cloud at 6,000 feet over The Hague area and at 08:23hrs a V2 contrail was seen rising from the same area.

Six aircraft were despatched to attack the Haagsche Bosch target, which was found to be obscured by cloud. Flying north-east to Haarlem and breaking cloud at 3,500 feet, they attacked the railway junction at Gouda with eleven 250 lb bombs, fused airburst. Four bombs fell between the railway tracks fifty yards north-east of the bridge. Two bombs fell east of the junction and two short of the bridge on the edge of the road. One bomb, which hung up, was jettisoned into a lake. A stationary three ton truck and a 15 cwt van were attacked on the Rotterdam/Gouda road and many strikes were seen. Another 15 cwt truck was attacked east of Gouda and destroyed. North of Ijmuiden a large green omnibus travelling south on the Alkmaar/Limer road was attacked, many strikes being seen before the vehicle stopped. The section crossed out south of Egmond.

Eight aircraft carrying one 500 lb and two 250 lb bombs fused airburst attacked the Haagsche Bosch target, encountering some inaccurate light flak from the target area. Two aircraft returned early, due to mechanical trouble. Five sticks of bombs were seen to burst around the aiming points but the results of one stick were not observed. Three aircraft strafed the target in the dive. The section re-formed and flew to Ursel where they landed at 16:35hrs. After re-fuelling they took off and flew back to base.

2 March 1945

Four aircraft attacked the Haagsche Bosch with 250 lb bombs, which all fell around the aiming points. In the recce that followed, F/Sgt Zuber attacked a large truck carrying supplies and after two attacks left it smoking. He then made two attacks on a camouflaged troop-carrying omnibus, which stopped and was quickly evacuated, and saw many strikes all over the vehicle, which was left smoking. North-west of Purmerend he strafed a large camouflaged truck and saw many strikes after which the truck stopped. On the road east of Haarlem, a reconnaissance type armoured car was seen, and as by this time his ammunition was rather low, he could only make one attack, but in this he saw many strikes. He soon set course for Belgium, landing at Tilburg. After the aircraft had been examined he took off, landing at Ludham at 16:15hrs. Meanwhile, the remaining aircraft carried out an uneventful recce to south of Den Helder.

After making so many attacks on the same target, it was a pleasant change for the Squadron to be given another one in the form of the Staalduin Bosch at The Hook of Holland. Twelve aircraft, led by S/Ldr Sutherland, attacked this target south-west to north-east from 8,000–3,000 feet, some aircraft strafing in the dive, and encountering some light flak. The first section attacked the north-west end of the target, the second section the centre, and the third section attacked the south-east end. The results were extremely good, all bombs falling in the wooded area, covering the whole length of the target. One large explosion – possibly from liquid oxygen storage – was seen to come from the target aiming point, orange coloured flames spreading to nearly 100 yards, after which smoke was seen rising from the area. The squadron re-formed and flew to Ursel where after re-fuelling and re-bombing with two 250 lb and one 500 lb bomb each they took off again, intending to attack the same target, but had to abandon the operation due to the weather over the whole of Holland. All 500 lb bombs and some 250 lb bombs were jettisoned in the sea. The squadron landed back at base at 17:30hrs.

3 March 1945

At 07:10hrs four aircraft were airborne on a dive-bombing/armed recce operation. Their target once again was the Haagsche Bosch. The attacked from south-west to north-east from 8,000–2,000 feet with eight 250 lb bombs, all bombs falling around the aiming points 'E' and 'F'. Some small explosions from which smoke rose to 300 feet were seen from the target area. The section that was led by F/Lt Stephenson then carried out a recce to south-west of Amsterdam, where they attacked a camouflaged staff car moving in the same direction. The vehicle stopped and the uniformed occupants quickly took cover. After two attacks by each aircraft the car was left blazing.

Another four aircraft took off and at 12:35hrs bombed a new target south of the race course at The Hague, an area in which there were V2 storage sites. Finding the target obscured by cloud, the section orbited south-east of Leiden until the cloud cleared from over the target area. They attacked north-west to south-west from 8,000–3,000 feet and the results of the bombing were good. Four bombs fell in the centre and four along the base of the triangle, which formed the target area. On their return to base, the pilots reported having seen considerable damage and a total of eight fires burning in the built up area south-east and south-west of the Haagsche Bosch, which had been bombed by medium bombers a short time previously. Smoke rising to 7,000 feet extended as far as Rotterdam. Some inaccurate light flak was encountered from the target area.

The same target was attacked by a section of four aircraft at 13:00hrs. This was attacked through a gap in the clouds, which covered the Dutch capital. Strafing the target in the dive, six bombs were seen to fall in the target area and two a short distance north-west of it. A recce of the Gouda, Rotterdam and Delft area followed and, west of Gouda, an open truck was seen by Blue 1. He gave a short burst, but seeing that it was carrying civilians, many of which were women, his attack ceased. No strikes were seen. It is thought that these people may have been evacuees from the Haagsche Bosch area in The Hague.

Three aircraft were despatched to attack the same target, experienced intense but inaccurate flak, but saw four of their bombs fall in the target area and two a short distance south-east of it. After the attack, they carried out a recce and north-east of Leiden, a large van moving north-east was attacked by two aircraft. After seeing many strikes, the vehicle stopped and smoke started to rise from it. All the aircraft attacked a staff car moving in the same direction on a nearby road. The car stopped and was left smoking, the occupants having made a hurried escape. A fire engine proceeding towards The Hague was not attacked.

Four aircraft, which took off to attack the Staalduin Bosch target, found the area from The Hook of Holland to north of The Hague obscured by thick cloud, so the task was abandoned.

A section of three aircraft, led by F/Lt Pullman, encountered similar weather conditions and flew inland and found a large break in the cloud over Gouda. They attacked the eastern railway junction from 7,000–3,000 feet and saw two of their bombs fall on the northern and two on the southern end of the road bridge over the railway. Two more fell on the railway embankment and a column of white smoke rose from this area and continued for some considerable time. Croosing out north of The Hague, they landed at base at 17:15hrs

4 March 1945

The first mission of the day was a dive-bombing attack on the Wassenaar/ Rust-en-Vreugd target and four aircraft dropped their bombs in the target area with good results. A reconnaissance of the Leiden, Haarlem and Assum area was then carried out at 4,000 feet. A bus was attacked, which soon stopped and was left smoking furiously. No occupants were seen to get out of the vehicle. Very intense and damnably accurate light flak was experienced from the north-east end of Rust-en-Vreugd, and also some very intense accurate light flak from Bergen aan Zee, when the section crossed out.

Four aircraft, each carrying one 500 lb and two 250 lb bombs, were airborne at 10:15hrs to attack the Staalduin Bosch target, and crossed in at The Hook of Holland at 13,000 feet over heavy cloud. The whole area so far as they could see was completely obscured and cloud base was found to be less than 5,000 feet. They set course for Ursel and jettisoned their 500 lb bombs in the sea, landing at Ursel at 11:40hrs. After re-fuelling, they took off again with their two 250 lb bombs but the area was still obscured by thick cloud. The section then set course for base, landing at 13:30hrs with their bombs.

Again, a section of four aircraft carrying a full bomb load found the target area covered by thick cloud and jettisoned the 500 lb bombs in the sea. They landed at Ursel, re-fuelled and took off again only to find that there had been no improvement in the weather over the target area. The section landed at base with the 250 lb bombs at 14:15hrs.

5 March 1945

Weather conditions over Holland had not improved when the first section of four aircraft led by F/Lt Pullman crossed in south of The Hague. Heavy cloud at 7,000–4,000 feet obscured the target area and the aircraft flew north-east where they found favourable conditions. A railway junction at Kortrijk was bombed from 7,000–3,000 feet, and two bombs were seen to straddle the junction whilst the others fell along the embankment farther south. Blue 3 (P/O McHardy) developed engine trouble and with Blue 4 (W/O Crosland) as escort, proceeded to B77 where they landed safely. The remaining aircraft recced to south of Amsterdam where they strafed a three ton truck moving north-east. Eight attacks were made and the vehicle was left in flames.

Encountering similar weather conditions over the target area, the next section of four aircraft flew to Delft where F/Lt Wroblewski, who was leading the section, noticed a concentration of sixty to eighty box trucks in the southern end of Delft station. Although cloud base was less than 5,000 feet, the section dived to 1,500 feet, strafing in the dive, and the section leader had the pleasure of seeing his two 250 lb bombs fall on two rows of trucks causing an explosion from which smoke and debris arose. Two bombs cut the track south of the junction and the others fell on open ground to the south. The leader and his No. 2 then made a strafing attack seeing many strikes along the two rows of trucks from which much smoke was steadily rising, and it is estimated that at least six trucks were totally destroyed, six more probably destroyed and approximately thirty damaged by strafing.

New target material in the form of a photographic mosaic showed that a track through the wooded area south of the race course at The Hague was being used for the transportation of V2 rockets to the sites around this area. S/Ldr Sutherland briefed the pilots on the method of attacking this target, stating that after releasing bombs all the aircraft would strafe the length of the track in the continuation of the dive.

Six aircraft led by F/O Baxter were despatched to attack this target but one returned early due to mechanical trouble. At 11:45hrs ten 250 lb bombs straddled the target length of the track and many strikes with cannon and machine gun were observed along the length of the ride. Successful recces of the Amsterdam, Zaandam, Haarlem areas were then carried out, during which one three ton truck and trailer was attacked and the truck left in flames and the trailer smoking. Another three ton truck was left smoking and an open truck carrying supplies received much of the ammunition from F/Sgt Zuber's aircraft.

During the dive-bombing attack, much more accurate flak was encountered from the north-west end of the target and Blue 1 and Blue 6 were hit, the former suffering superficial damage to his aircraft, the latter coming back to base with a considerable piece missing from the elevator of his machine.

One aircraft of the next section returned early due to mechanical trouble. The remainder led by W/O Toone employed the same tactics and saw their bombs fall in pairs about 100 yards apart along the length of the ride. Many strikes were seen from the strafing. Throughout the recce which followed, many covered horse-drawn vehicles were seen in the Leiden/Haarlem areas. Moderate accurate flak was again encountered from the north-east of the target area.

Crossing in over heavy cloud, which totally obscured the target area, F/Lt Pullman pressed on and was fortunate in finding a very small break in the cloud, which allowed him to attack the railway junction at Kwakel. Three sticks of bombs fell along the railway embankment on either side of the track. The bombs on one aircraft hung up, and were jettisoned in the sea.

6 March 1945

Owing to unfavourable weather conditions over Holland, no operational flying took place. The Squadron was put to sixty minutes readiness and an extensive programme including squadron 'Balbo' dog fights and air to air firing was carried out.

7 March 1945

Bad weather conditions over Holland continued throughout the day and no operations were carried out. The Squadron did practice flying in the morning and were released at midday.

8 March 1945

Take off time was postponed from 07:15hrs because of the weather forecast. At 08:30hrs F/O Baxter led a section of four aircraft on an armed weather recce, returning at 10:00hrs, having been unable to bomb the target. Heavy cloud from 5,000–2,000 feet covered the whole of Holland. There was no improvement in the weather and no other operational flying was carried out during the day.

9 March 1945

A training day. A very extensive programme was carried out and a total of sixty-one sorties flown. The pilots were pleased to note that the total days flying time for practice was 46 hours, 45 mins.

10 March 1945

A section of four aircraft despatched on an armed recce found the area covered with thick cloud, the base of which was at 2,000 feet. Flying north to Ijmuiden brought no improvement in the weather and the aircraft set course for base.

Again, the weather over the target was unsuitable for an attack to be made and the section flew to Alphen where better weather conditions allowed them to bomb the railway junction with eight bombs, fused eleven seconds delay. All bombs straddled the railway approximately ten yards from either side of the track. Blue 1 (F/O Baxter) developed engine trouble and set course for Belgium, landing safely at B56 airfield. The remainder recced to Hillegom where they attacked a three ton truck and trailer. The vehicles stopped and after the first attack an explosion was seen causing oil, debris and red and green minor explosions to rise from the trucks. Four attacks were made by each aircraft and the truck was left with flames belching from the engine, whilst from the remainder of the body and the trailer a considerable amount of smoke was rising. It is thought the vehicle was carrying ammunition. No other movement was seen throughout the recce.

As the next section was approaching the Dutch coast, a large explosion was seen from the Ijmuiden area. Low cloud made it impossible to attack on the Wassenwaar/Ravelijn target, and after making an uneventful reconnaissance of the Alkmaar/Den Helder/Amsterdam areas, the section attacked a railway junction at Uitgerest, diving down from 5,000 to 1,500 feet. Four 250 lb bombs fused eleven seconds delay fell on the railway track at the junction. Two fell twenty-five yards south-east of the junction and the results of the others were not seen. The section crossed out north of Ijmuiden.

Cloud base was still at 5,000 feet when the next section of four aircraft led by F/Lt Wroblewski took to the air. They crossed in over The Hague and continued inland to Gouda where they made the road bridge over the railway their target. Bombing from cloud base at 1,500 feet, they straddled the bridge with four 250 lb bombs fused eleven seconds delay, the bombs falling next to the railway track. The other four bombs fell on open ground nearby. In the recce that followed, a small van was attacked south of Amsterdam and left in flames. A 15 cwt van with a large trailer was also moving westward on the Amsterdam to Haarlem road and, after many strikes had been seen on it, both vehicles were left with much smoke rising from them. Continuing the recce to Medemblik, a 30 cwt covered truck was seen five miles west of the town. After W/O Ellison had made his attack, the vehicle was seen to be badly damaged and smoking. The section crossed out north of Bergen aan Zee. No flak was encountered throughout the attack.

11 March 1945

Owing to a report of bad weather over the target area the section of four aircraft, which were despatched to bomb The Hague/Duindigit targets, were recalled by the Controller fifteen minutes after take off.

Because of the low cloud over Holland, it was decided to despatch sections of four aircraft, without bombs, to carry out armed reconnaissance.

The next section, led by F/Lt Pullman, recced to the south of Amsterdam where a 15 cwt lorry carrying supplies was strafed and left in flames. A three ton covered truck moving towards Haarlem was attacked by two aircraft and after the second attack an explosion was seen to come from it. A third attack caused considerable damage to the vehicle, which was left smoking. As the section crossed out south to Katwijk, the leader saw a vehicle with an exceptionally large trailer moving north-east on a small road near the coast. Before he could position himself for an attack, the vehicle disappeared into what appeared to be an opening in the hillside. Some moderately accurate flak was encountered from Katwijk.

No movement was seen throughout the next reconnaissance but a number of pontoons with bridges fitted were seen lying on either side of the Amsterdam/Limuiden canal.

Of the seven aircraft that took off on the next armed recce, one returned early, due to mechanical trouble. The remainder, because of bad weather conditions, split up into sections of three, one making a recce of the northern half of Holland, and the other the southern half.

F/O Farrell, leading one section, apart from seeing an E boat moving into Ijmuiden harbour, saw no movement throughout the northern area.

F/Lt Wroblewski, flying with the other section, when fifteen miles from the Dutch coast, saw the periscope and part of the conning tower of a midget submarine. He immediately positioned for attack, but the submarine hastily submerged and disappeared before an attack could be made. Apart from this incident, the recce over the Maasluis, Rotterdam, Leiden and Delft area led by S/Ldr Sutherland and executed at deck level, was uneventful.

The next section of four aircraft met with more success, and after a recce of Katwijk, Leiden, Zaanwijk, Utrecht and Gouda at 2,000–3,000 feet, they returned with a good mechanical transport score. One stationary staff car and two 30 cwt covered trucks seen south-east of Katwijk were attacked and left smoking, and north-east of Leiden another 30 cwt was left severely damaged.

The last section of four aircraft to be despatched carried out a recce from Leiden to Boskoop thence to Utrecht and Katwijk during which they strafed one three ton and one 30 cwt van moving south towards Gouda. Both vehicles were left badly damaged and smoking profusely. The section landed at 19:10hrs and in landing W/O Menzies unfortunately overshot the runway but was uninjured.

12 March 1945

Owing to low cloud over Holland, the first section to take off did not carry bombs. Led by F/Lt Pullman, they crossed in at 5,000 feet and broke cloud at 3,500 feet over Gouda. Flying north they observed a stationary 30 cwt truck near Hootdoorp, which after being attacked by two aircraft was left smoking. Apart from an unusual amount of horse-drawn vehicles, no other movement was seen throughout the recce, which covered the Amsterdam, Harlem, Leiden and Utrecht areas. A V2 contrail was observed rising from The Hague at 07:13hrs.

Although there was no improvement in the weather conditions the next section of four aircraft, led by F/Lt Wroblewski, carried 250 lb bombs fused eleven seconds delay, their intention being to attack interdiction targets inland. When over Delft, a three ton truck was observed and after a quick attack by two aircraft was left smoking furiously. Continuing to Woerden, the section bombed the railway junction there in a shallow dive from 3,000–2,000 feet, two bombs cutting the railway track west of the junction and two more falling alongside the track nearer to the junction. The other bombs fell near the track, but on open ground. Flying north, a large tank and a three ton truck, with trailer, all stationary, were attacked by all aircraft and many strikes were seen on all vehicles. On the second attack made by F/Lt Wroblewski, fragments of metal rose from the tank, one piece lodging in the radiator of his aircraft.

The last section of four to take off carried 250 lb bombs and finding no cloud over the target area, bombed The Hague/Duindigit target from 9,000–5,000 feet. Four bombs fell on the race course, which formed part of the target, and two in the wooded area south of the area. The position of the remaining two bombs was unobserved. Throughout the recces of the Amsterdam, Schagen, Alkmaar, Ijmuiden areas, which followed the attack, no movement was seen.

13 March 1945

Since the Squadron had no commitments until 12:30hrs, the morning was spent in the station lecture room where a number of combat films were shown, after which the station armament officer talked to the pilots about the fusing of the six-hours delay bombs, which were to be used in the afternoon's operations.

602 Squadron was one of the four squadrons that were despatched to attack The Hague/Duindigit target with 500 lb bombs fused six-hour delay and 250 lb bombs fused airburst. Ten aircraft took off and crossing in over The Hague in a shallow dive, the squadron, led by S/Ldr Sutherland, climbed and at 13:04hrs attacked the target from 10,000–3,000 feet, from north-east to south-west, through a curtain of light flak. Bombing results were excellent, the majority of the bombs falling around the south-east aiming point, and three or four along the ride, which runs from the Leiden road to the southern end of the race course. Breaking inland, the aircraft climbed to 10,000 feet and proceeded to Ursel where they landed at 13:50hrs. After re-fuelling and re-bombing with 500 lb and 250 lb bombs fused airburst, the squadron took off again, leaving WO Menzies at Ursel with the commanding officer's aircraft, which had undercarriage trouble. Attacking the same target south-west to north-east from 10,000–3,000 feet, two sections of three aircraft concentrated their attack on the same aiming point as before, whilst the section led by F/O Baxter bombed and strafed gun positions in the area from which the majority of the flak encountered on the previous mission had been seen to come. Although the guns in this area did not fire, there was still extremely intense and accurate light flak encountered during the attack. Again the bombing was excellent and bombs from the two sections of three fell around the south-east aiming point. Two large explosions were seen in this area, and as the squadron climbed after the attack, palls of smoke were seen along the 'ride' and over the aiming point. The squadron landed at 17:10hrs and from the enthusiasm shown by all the pilots

afterwards there was no doubt that the operation was one of the best ever carried out by the Squadron.

Group Captain Dunn of No. 12 Group visited the station and accompanied the pilots of both Squadrons (including 603 Squadron) to a nearby country club where a very pleasant evening was spent.

14 March 1945

Two aircraft were despatched on an armed weather recce, and on approaching the Dutch coast, found the whole of Holland covered in very thick haze, which rose to heights varying from 7,000–5,000 feet. They attacked The Hague/Duindicht target with four 250 lb bombs, which fell on the race course and then, climbing to 5,000 feet, recced north to south of Den Helder only to find that north of Haarten the haze became thicker.

Group Captain Dunn attended the briefing of the six pilots who were to make a low level attack on a new target at The Hague. A very careful briefing was carried out as the timing had to coincide with the diversionary dive-bombing attack to be made on another target by 603 and 124 Squadrons. Unfortunately, the operation had to be cancelled due to weather conditions over the Dutch capital.

It was decided to despatch a section of four aircraft to attack The Hague/Duindicht target throughout the day. Visibility was extremely poor and at times the target was difficult to find. The first section dropped their bombs around the southern aiming point and on their return it was noted that that part of the target had been completely devastated as a result of the previous day's bombing, and that the flak opposition, usually very strong, was very meagre.

In a recce of the Gouda, Amsterdam and Haarlem area which followed, a stationary car was attacked south of Wesserluis by the leader F/O Baxter, and many strikes were seen.

Two aircraft returned early from the next operation, one due to mechanical trouble, and his No. 2, because of the thick haze into which the leader and his No. 2 had disappeared when the first aircraft set course for base. The remaining aircraft attacked the Duindicht target, all bombs falling in the target area, but because of the extremely poor visibility, no recce was carried out after the attack.

On approaching the target, the next section found that it was being attacked by another section of aircraft, so proceeded inland and recced to Amsterdam and north, bombing a road bridge over a railway east of Purmerend. Two bombs fell on the northern end of the bridge and four others nearby. The results of the two bombs were unobserved.

15 March 1945

Thick haze covered the aerodrome during the morning, and it looked as though the six aircraft due to carry out low level attacks would not fly. Again, the pilots spent part of the morning in the lecture room where combat films were shown and a lecture on low level bombing attacks was given by the commanding officer.

One or two weather recces were carried out by other squadrons, and the Squadron was anxious that if the weather conditions improved, target areas should be attacked. S/Ldr Sutherland suggested that 'provided visibility below cloud – which is low – is good enough, I will take six aircraft across the North Sea and make the attack at deck level.'

Six aircraft took off at 15:05hrs, carrying one 500 lb and two 250 lb bombs fused eleven seconds delay 'skip bomb', the new target being the Bataafsche Petrol Co. at The Hague. It proved to be abortive as the weather was extremely poor the whole way. After flying a short distance at deck level, forward visibility became nil and it was necessary to climb to 1,000 feet. Heavy cloud formed forty miles from the English coast, the tops being 800 feet high and it was estimated that the base was 300 feet or less. When the aircraft got to within ten miles of the Dutch coast, there was still no improvement and the operation had to be abandoned. All 500 lb and four 250 lb bombs were jettisoned in the sea. On returning to base the section split up to land. Red 1 saw a bomb on the port side of the runway and warned flying control, which in turn warned the remainder of the section to keep airborne. F/Lt Wroblewski, who was approaching to land at 300 feet with flaps and wheels down, retracted his undercarriage, and prepared to go round again. He could not, however, obtain any boost from the throttle and the aircraft commenced losing height and speed. When over the hangar and the main camp buildings, he realised he'd have to force land. He decided not to jettison his bombs and land straight ahead with wheels retracted, because of the danger to personnel and buildings, from the jettisoned bombs. Instead, he decided to complete a very tight 180 degree turn at low speed and land down wind on the runway in use. He put his wheels down at 150 feet and just got in line with the runway in a steep bank and a very low speed when the port wheel struck the ground and the wing tip grazed the grass. This exhibition proved the pilot to have outstanding courage and exceptional flying skill.

16 March 1945

Thick local haze made operational flying impossible during the morning, but by midday there was a distinct improvement and it was hoped that a section of four aircraft would take off during the afternoon. A weather recce carried out by one of the other squadrons dashed all hopes and, again, practice flying was the order of the day.

The readiness section of two aircraft was scrambled to search the area north of Skegness where a Lancaster was believed to have ditched. After carrying out an uneventful square search northwards from Skegness, they were directed to Spilsby where they landed at 19:20hrs.

17 March 1945

Once again, the low level attack on the target in The Hague was postponed, because of low cloud in that area.

Four aircraft, carrying one 500 lb and two 250 lb bombs fused eleven seconds delay, took off to bomb railway targets of opportunity. F/O Farrell led the section to the Leiden/The Hague railway tracks. The other bombs fell alongside the track about three yards distant. During the attack intense accurate flak was encountered from the vicinity of the race course at The Hague. The aircraft then proceeded to Ursel where they re-fuelled and re-bombed with the same bomb load. At 12:50hrs they took off again and flew to Gouda where they dropped their bombs on and around the railway junction situated west of the town. The two 250 lb bombs on F/O Campbell's aircraft hung up during the attack, but were successfully dropped on the railway junction at Alphen scoring two direct hits. The section landed back at base at 14:30hrs.

However, at 11:25hrs a section of four aircraft took off, led by F/O Baxter. They carried the same bomb load as Farrell's section and dropped them in a shallow dive from 3,000 feet to deck level along the east side of the railway track south of Boskoop. The embankment crumbled, the railway tracks were seen to be broken and the north end of the bridge undermined. In the recce to Gouda and The Hague, which followed, a medium tank was attacked (west of Gouda). All aircraft took part and the tank was left smoking after many strikes had been seen on the body and tracks. The section landed at Ursel, and after re-fuelling and re-bombing, took off again and proceeded to Gouda where three aircraft bombed a road bridge over the railway lines no more than thirty yards north of the bridge. The other aircraft bombed a nearby railway line and these also fell on the lines. The section landed at Ludham at 15:50hrs. No flak was encountered throughout the mission.

F/Lt Stephenson led a section of four aircraft, armed with one 500 lb and two 250 lb bombs each, which attacked Gouda/The Hague railway line from 7,000 feet to deck level. One cluster fell on the track and two more within ten yards of it, whilst the fourth cluster fell on the road running parallel with the railway. The tank which had been attacked by the previous section was seen to be smoking furiously. Climbing to 9,000 feet, the section crossed out at Katwijk, and proceeded to B67 where they landed, re-fuelled and re-bombed, taking off again at 15:35hrs. This time they selected as their target a railway bridge over a road south-east of the Dutch capital. F/Sgt Zuber (who according to the Squadron history was 'quickly proving himself to be one of the Squadron's marksmen') was successful in dropping his bombs on the southern end of the bridge and completely destroying it. The other four clusters of bombs fell on and around the railway track just south of the bridge.

After completing a successful mission, the section set course for base, where they landed at 17:15hrs. Again no flak was encountered.

When the next section (each carrying two 250 lb bombs, led by F/Lt Pullman) was taking off the leader's engine cut. He quickly retracted the undercarriage and was fortunate enough in coming to a stop on the grass beyond the runway. Both bombs came off, one of them being found with the fuse torn off, some distance behind the crashed aircraft. The pilot was uninjured. The leader's No. 2 landed fourteen minutes later and the other two aircraft did not take off.

18 March 1945

At 08:50hrs four aircraft, each carrying two 250 lb bombs and led by F/O Farrell, took off on an armed recce and bombed the Haarlem/Leiden railway lines. Diving slowly from 5,000–1,000 feet they were successful in securing three direct hits on the track, while one stick of bombs fell only a few yards from the track. The section proceeded to Leiden and Gouda, and thence to Amsterdam and Haarlem but no movement was seen. They crossed out north of Katwijk.

At 10:15hrs a section of four aircraft, led by F/O Baxter, were airborne and proceeded to Gouda where they bombed the road bridge over the Leiden/Gouda railway line, north-west of the town. They used eight 250 lb bombs fused eleven seconds delay. One cluster of bombs fell on the side of the bridge and three clusters were near misses, one falling on the embankment at the base of the bridge. A recce of the Boskoop, Amsterdam and Egmond area carried out at 4,000 feet proved uneventful and the section crossed out at Egmond.

Two aircraft rendezvoused with PRU Mustangs over Ludham and escorted the two Mustangs to The Hague, Delft and Leiden at 7,000 feet. After escorting them back to Felixstowe, the section set a course for base.

At last the weather was suitable for the low level attack by six aircraft of 602 Squadron.

After a very careful briefing, the section, each carrying one 500 lb bomb and two 250 lb bombs fused eleven seconds delay, took off. Led by S/Ldr Sutherland, the section consisted of F/Lt Pertwee, F/Lt Pullman, F/Lt Stephenson, F/O Baxter and F/Sgt Zuber.

The section rendezvoused with 124 Squadron over Ludham. Both 124 and 453 Squadrons were to make diversionary attacks on the target of the race course in The Hague, whilst 602 Squadron made a low level attack on the Bataafsche Petrol Co. building, which was situated in the built up area north of the Haagsche Bosch, two miles from the coast.

Whilst 124 and 453 Squadrons were making their attack on the race course, 602 Squadron, having crossed in at 2,000 feet and dived at roof top level approaching the target from the north-west, released their bombs in straight and level flight below the level of the roof of the target building, at a range of approximately fifty yards, four of the six aircraft strafing the face of the building in the approach. F/Sgt Zuber's aircraft was hit in the starboard mainplane just prior to the release of his bombs, which fell fifty yards to port of the building. As the section broke to clear the roof of the target, S/Ldr Sutherland's aircraft was hit by flak which was considerable and the starboard elevator was destroyed. Red smoke and flames were seen to roll from the eastern face of the building from bombs, which must have penetrated inside and smoke and debris rose to a considerable height. White smoke rose from the western side and the target was last seen enveloped in dense black smoke. The roof of the building, however, appeared to be intact, but from the clouds of red smoke, which were seen just after the attack and the heavy pall of smoke that later obscured the target, it was considered that the interior of the building had been completely destroyed.

All aircraft landed at Ursel where, after re-fuelling and re-bombing, four took off to bomb interdiction target at the leader's choice. Crossing in at Maasluts at 10,000 feet, he selected the Delft/Rotterdam railway line and bombed it from 8,000–3,000 feet, but unfortunately no results were seen.

S/Ldr Sutherland returned to base at 18:25hrs, thirty-five minutes after the others, having flown back in F/Sgt Zuber's aircraft, leaving his own to have a new elevator fitted and to be brought back by F/Sgt Zuber.

19 March 1945

At 08:40hrs four Spitfires, each carrying two 250 lb bombs fused eleven seconds delay, took off to bomb interdiction targets. Crossing in north of The Hague, they flew to Utrecht and bombed the railway junction north-west of the town, with all bombs, from 8,000–3,000 feet. A thick haze over the area made visibility extremely poor and only one cluster of bombs were seen to fall a few yards east of the railway lines. The section recced to Amsterdam/Haarlem at 3,000–2,000 feet and west of Alsmeer a stationary staff car and a small van were attacked by all aircraft and many strikes were seen. No flak was encountered throughout the operation.

Weather conditions steadily got worse and the next section of six aircraft were recalled by the Controller after twelve minutes' flying.

20 March 1945

Except for the last mission of the day, the aircraft were kept busy bombing railway interdiction targets.[12]

Four aircraft, each carrying one 500 lb and two 250 lb bombs fused eleven seconds delay, took off and set course for Katwijk. After crossing in they proceeded towards Haarlem, bombing the Haarlem to Leiden railway lines from 7,000–2,000 feet. An exceptionally strong wind made bombing somewhat difficult and one 250 lb bomb fell on the track. The remainder of the bombs fell from up to thirty yards of it.

The section landed at Ursel, but two aircraft were unserviceable due to mechanical trouble. Whilst waiting for those aircraft to be made serviceable the remaining two aircraft were scrambled on an air-sea rescue patrol. They patrolled an area eight miles north of The Hague for sixty minutes. The pilot was seen sitting in his dinghy and later a Walrus aircraft landed about 100 yards from him, having encountered some flak from the coast. It taxied around the dinghy during which time coastal batteries opened up on it. 602 Squadron pilots last saw the aircraft taxiing westwards about two miles from the dinghy. They made many unsuccessful attempts to contact the Walrus by R/T and attract her attention by diving towards the dinghy, but it was later learnt that the aircraft had damaged its rudder when landing on the very rough sea. On returning to Ursel, 602 Squadron aircraft re-fuelled and re-bombed and took off at 14:15hrs. They bombed the same target as before from 7,000–2,000 feet, scoring a direct hit on the track with one cluster, whilst the other bombs fell about twenty yards away from the track. The remaining two aircraft after being made serviceable flew directly to base.

At 10:10hrs four Spitfires, each carrying a 1,000 lb bomb flew to Leiden where, three miles south of the town, they bombed the railway from Leiden to The Hague. They scored one direct hit with a cluster of three bombs and two near misses. The position of the fourth cluster was unobserved.

After completing their mission, they flew to Ursel where they re-fuelled and re-bombed, and at 12:35hrs took off and proceeded to Delft where they bombed a road junction north of the town. Two clusters of bombs fell on the road and one cluster on a canal bridge. The position of the fourth cluster was not observed. Although no flak was seen throughout the operation, on return to base it was found that F/Lt Stephenson's aircraft had been hit by flak.

Two aircraft carried out an uneventful escort to two PRU Mustangs to The Hague and back to Felixstowe (commencing 14:30hrs).

Four aircraft, each carrying one 500 lb and two 250 lb bombs, were despatched to attack a new target – a V1 launching site[13] and surrounding buildings situated on the Ypenburg airfield south-east of The Hague. As they approached the target, they saw a large fire already burning after an attack made by four aircraft from another squadron. After their attack, which was made south-east to north-west from 7,000–1,500 feet, another large fire was seen to be burning. Having completed their mission, the section recced to Alphen where north-west of the town a car was attacked by all aircraft and left damaged. A large troop carrier was seen moving north-east on the same road and troops scrambled for shelter when the vehicle stopped prior to the section making its attack. It was left badly damaged. With the exception of some inaccurate light flak encountered as one of the sections crossed out south of Katwijk, no flak opposition was met throughout the day.

21 March 1945

The Squadron was at a state of sixty minutes readiness for flying training and throughout the day the pilots were kept busy carrying out an extensive practice flying programme. Forty-one sorties were flown and by the end of the day a total of thirty-three hours had been completed.

22 March 1945

Three aircraft armed with two 250 lb bombs took off at 07:55hrs and bombed The Hague to Gouda road, six miles west of Gouda from 7,000–1,000 feet, from west to east. One cluster of bombs fell dead in the centre of the road and two clusters along the side of the road. An uneventful reconnaissance of the Leiden, Haarlem and Egmond area followed.

At 10:55hrs S/Ldr Sutherland led a section of six aircraft armed with one 500 lb and two 250 lb bombs, which made low level attacks on a railway junction south-east of Voorsburg, from 5,000 to less than 1,000 feet. One cluster of bombs fell dead on the junction, two clusters on the line east of it and two more on the road running parallel to the railway.

The position of one cluster of bombs was not observed. The section flew to Ursel, crossing out over The Hook of Holland, landed at 12:20hrs, and one hour later was airborne; armed with the same bomb load they proceded to the same target. Again, this was attacked from 5,000 feet to less than 1,000 feet, and another cluster of bombs was seen to burst dead on the junction. Two more clusters cut the lines north and south of the junction and one of the pilots scored a direct hit on the railway bridge, severely damaging it. One 250 lb bomb hung up, but was brought back to base. On the return flight, the aircraft of F/Sgt Love developed mechanical trouble and the pilot had to bale out about sixty-five miles from the English coast. He was seen to get into his dinghy and, operations having got a very good fix of the position, at once set the wheels of air-sea rescue in motion and a short time later advised the squadron that F/Sgt Love had been picked up by a Catalina and was on his way back to 'terra firma'.

At 14:20hrs two aircraft on readiness were scrambled to carry out an air-sea rescue patrol over the area where F/Sgt Love had ditched. Directed by the Controller, they were soon over the spot and saw the Catalina land and pick up the pilot.

The last mission of the day took place at 16:00hrs, and was a railway interdiction operation carried out by six aircraft armed with two 250 lb bombs each. At 16:40hrs they bombed the Gouda to Alphen railway line north of Boskoop, cutting it in two places with two clusters of bombs and seeing two near misses with the other two clusters. Another cluster fell approximately twenty yards west of the track and one 250 lb bomb was seen to fall on the track farther north. The section then recced to Amsterdam and Haarlem and thence to Edam, but no movement was seen. Much smoke was seen rising from the target at the Kurhams garage in Scheveningem after the dive-bombing attack made by 453 Squadron. No flak was encountered in any of these operations.

23 March 1945

The squadron were advised by the controller that they would fly a maximum of thirty-two sorties a day. From 09:10hrs sections of four aircraft armed with one 500 lb and two 250 lb bombs, attacked interdiction targets landing at Ursel and re-fuelling and re-bombing there.

Four aircraft, led by F/Lt Stephenson, took off (also at 09:10hrs) and thirty-five minutes later bombed The Hague to Gouda railway, south of Hoorn from 6,000–1,000 feet, scoring two direct hits on the railway lines with two clusters of bombs. The section landed at Ursel at 10:35hrs north of Boskoop from 6,000–1,000 feet.

The next section attacked a road bridge over the railway junction west of Gouda from 8,000–1,000 feet. One cluster of bombs fell on the road at the north end of the bridge. Two clusters fell on the railway east of the bridge and another on the railway embankment.

After re-fuelling and re-bombing, the section took off and flew to east of The Hague where they bombed a stretch of The Hague to Gouda railway line, cutting it in two places with two clusters of bombs, whilst two clusters fell on the roadway running parallel to the railway.

Four aircraft bombed the Leiden to Alphen railway line at 11:50hrs, from 4,000–1,000 feet, scoring direct hits with two clusters of bombs and causing the embankment to collapse with the other two clusters. On the return flight from Ursel, they bombed The Hague to Gouda railway line from north-west to south-west from 5,000–1,000 feet. All bombs burst on the railway lines and the roads running parallel to them. In the short recce that followed, two very large green canvas covered trucks were stationary north of Rotterdam. After two attacks had been made and many strikes seen on both vehicles and smoke from one, the section climbed to 6,000 feet and crossed out at Katwijk. Another similar sortie from another flight of four Spitfires of 602 Squadron followed.

At approximately 18:00hrs F/Sgt Love returned, having spent a day in hospital at Haleworth aerodrome. He was none the worse for his recent experiences.

24 March 1945

More attacks on railway lines were successfully carried out, but it was noted that the Nazis were not repairing the considerable damage to lines inflicted by Spitfire squadrons. Similar observations and attacks were carried out on 25 March. It appeared that the Nazis were buckling under the intensity of the attacks.

26 March 1945

Poor weather conditions kept the aircraft grounded all morning and the Squadron was put to a state of sixty minutes readiness.

Good news was received of the immediate award of a bar to the DFC of S/Ldr Sutherland. A release was granted in the afternoon and the squadron celebrated the award in a 'fitting manner'.

27 March 1945

Bad weather conditions prevailed and only a few practice flying sorties were carried out during the morning.

28 March 1945

No offensive operations were possible owing to the continuation of adverse weather conditions. Two aircraft were despatched on a combined Jim Crow and weather recce but were forced to return owing to low cloud base, which was down to 2,000 feet thirty miles from the English coast.

In the afternoon, the new sector commander, Group Captain Hawtry, visited the Squadron and spoke to the pilots and ground crews.

29 March 1945

Bad weather conditions over Holland prevented any show. Combat films were shown in the lecture room.

30 March 1945

Mustang escort for photo reconnaissance over target areas in The Hague. A small amount of light flak was experienced.

More bombing of railways and bridges. After the operations at approximately 17:10hrs, Group Captain Hawtry informed the squadron that S/Ldr Rigler was relinquishing his command of 603 City of Edinburgh Squadron and had been awarded the DFC. More good news followed that F/Lt Pertwee was to take command of 603 Squadron. The double event called for a 'celebration' in which congratulations were offered to S/Ldr Rigler for the successful completion of his many operations and to S/Ldr Pertwee for every success in his new command.

31 March 1945

Sorties against railway lines and bridges were carried out by the Squadron. Also, many motor vehicles were attacked and left badly damaged. The last entry in the Squadron History for March 1945 states proudly: 'The score of mechanical transport destroyed or damaged today amounts to nine.'

A comprehensive log of 602 Squadron is the only way to highlight for the reader the amount of difficulties – frustrations – Spitfire squadrons went through during Operation Big Ben. Very bad weather conditions were sometimes overcome despite a severe winter and some tenacious attacks on V2 sites were executed. As importantly, the supply chains for V2 activity (by road and rail) were also heavily attacked and the Nazis could not repair/rebuild as quickly as the Spitfires damaged them; this must have had an effect on the number of rockets fired on London.

If we also observe the more than occasional full-blown assault on Nazi personnel and their hardware, the many aspects of countering the V2 threat were tackled in a very intense and broad way indeed, especially when we consider how much training time was given to flying clipped wing Mark XVI Spitfires and executing dive-bombing exercises.

DFCs, promotions and other awards were not presented willy-nilly and the expertise and derring-do of the pilots was fully recognised at the time.

It is, of course, difficult to ascertain from a Squadron History what significance the bombing raids on The Hague had in countering the direct attack of V2 rockets on London. However we shall look at evidence in Chapter V concerning this. Suffice to conclude here that a definite warm feeling is achieved by reading the Squadron History and the observations noted.

Every squadron naturally believed that they were making a significant contribution to the war effort in countering the V2 threat. Indeed veteran pilots such as Raymond Baxter are convinced of the success of Operation Big Ben. So, in order to announce it an official success, let us now look at the success rate of V2 rockets during the Spitfire raids and measure the trends of intensity and conclude if Operation Big Ben was successful or not.

NOTES

1   The historical details of 453 Australian squadron and 603 City of Edinburgh Squadron operations are also highly relevant stories. Indeed, both squadrons played important roles within Operation Big Ben. However, it has not been possible in this modest volume to include every squadron history, so the detail of 602 Squadron (along with an Appendix featuring elements of the sister role of 603 Squadron) is deemed to be comprehensive enough, providing the key issues that have in some areas received public attention (mainly through the memories of Raymond Baxter in his own writings). To ignore these important moments would have been a foolish oversight by the authors however, something had to give and it is regretted that 453 Squadron are not as well documented as their British or Polish counterparts. But their contribution is by no means overlooked and is documented in part within 602 Squadron's history. As for 603 Squadron's intense and accurate activity – as laid down in their Squadron History – repetition was a problem but key issues can be found in Appendix D.

2   Mostly 250 lb two and one 500 lb bombs.

3   The format of Squadron History is more laboured in this chapter to show the frustrations experienced by a highly trained squadron. It is deemed important that a full understanding of all aspects of Operation Big Ben is appreciated in this chapter.

4   This was typical of Sutherland who was a tenacious foe.

5   RAF Matlaske.

6   During the 1930s, an American, Edward Link, operated a flying school. Because of the economic depression at the time, he had the idea to decrease the expense of flying lessons by using a ground aviation trainer. Link constructed an aircraft, which could imitate the flying pattern of an aircraft. During the Second World War, half a million pilots got their flying training on the Link Trainer.

7   As quoted in Squadron history, more likely one 500 lb bomb and two 250 lb bombs.

8   F/Lt Raymond Baxter wrote of this sortie in his log book: 'Attacked secondary target. 12 aircraft through cloud gap.' He then explained that, 'you take your only opportunity'. This log book entry and explanation enhances the perception of the accuracy of the 602 Squadron history used.

9   Balbo Formation: a standard formation of Spitfires in the air.

10 A competitive target shooting competition invented in America during the 1920s by several Massachusetts men who wanted to improve their aim before the hunting season.

11 No maps detailing the aiming points of each target were located in the research of this book.

12 F/Lt Raymond Baxter explained: '20 March 16:20hrs, we struck the railway, but I mentioned in my log book that it was "getting monotonous". The armament was generally reliable but occasionally let us down . . . someone

said that the delay mechanism we used on some of the bombs consisted of a vial of acid, which was broken when the spinner on the bomb came off. The acid then slowly dripped through a piece of copper and then the bomb went off. I wasn't that happy sitting on top of a 500 lb bomb with acid dripping through a piece of copper.'

13   It must be stressed that Operation Big Ben (as its names suggests: Big Ben being the codeword for V2 rocket) dealt specifically with V2 rockets. However, it did, as this reference in the Squadron history clearly states, deal with attacks on the odd V1 rocket site. This has been an overplayed aspect of Big Ben and, as a consequence, confused Big Ben with Operation Crossbow, which it had nothing to do with.

CHAPTER V
Success or Failure?

'... I reached the end of my time in the RAF. At such a time
one looks back and wonders "what was it all for?" I had
made so many good friends in my early days, only to lose
them so quickly ...'

My Autobiography
Dennis 'Hurricane' David

It is now important to lay down the detail that supports our claim that
Operation Big Ben was successful. The detail of this can be found largely
in '*Air Defence of Great Britain Volume 6 (formerly Volume 7) – The Flying
Bomb and Rocket Campaigns 1944–45*'.[1] This document, formerly Secret,
then down-graded to Restricted and finally Unclassified, was written for
the Air Ministry by an unnamed RAF officer and makes many ibid
references. The copy used for research in this book is marked 'copy 13' (by
hand).

With the intensity of Big Ben operations some success there had to be
and the following detail heaps high praise indeed upon the men who flew
counter-measures against V2s and casts doubt upon Alanbrooke's
opinion of a glorious failure.

A summary of Big Ben flights is showcased in this chapter to provide a
summary that works well in juxtaposition to the detail of the effect V2
rockets were having on Britain. Apologies are made for any repetition of
the Squadron Histories; it is done purely to highlight the success rate of
Operation Big Ben and clarify the subtleties and details of the sorties
flown.

On 8 November 1944 the German Home Services for the first time
announced that V2 attacks were being made on London. Two days later
Churchill made his long-delayed announcement, without specifying that
London was the Nazi target. So the government decided not to warn the
general public of the threat of attack? For one thing, nine GI Mark II sets,
which were part of the system that rocket warnings might have been
given, were transferred to SHAEF (mid-November) to provide radar

cover for Brussels and Antwerp. But even if they had remained in the UK the prospects of establishing within a short time an efficient warning system were not good. The difficulty was not that particular rockets might escape observation, but that a large number of unnecessary warnings would have been sounded in London.

By mid-November the general position was such that when AOC-in-C, Fighter Command again raised the question of direct attacks on the launching areas near The Hague, the response was more favourable than before. Air Marshal Hill wrote to the Air Ministry on 17 November, making his letter the occasion for a thorough review of the difficulties under which Fighter Command had been operating. He pointed out that armed reconnaissance had to be carried out by Spitfires in daylight whenever weather permitted, and as winter approached their scale of effort was being seriously affected (all this was true enough but there was an urgency in the need for counter-measures and this is where the frustrations crept in). The majority of sorties had to be flown at low altitudes if the pilots were to identify suitable targets and attack them with cannon and machine-gun fire; and in an area where the Germans had deployed a large number of light anti-aircraft guns this was a dangerous procedure. Altogether, armed reconnaissance seemed to Hill to be ineffective unless combined with other forms of offensive action.

Bomber Command and 2nd Tactical Air Force could assist here, though so far they had done very little. A number of sorties were also being flown by bomb-carrying Spitfires of Fighter Command whose pilots were, however, under strict instructions not to bomb if there was any risk of causing civilian casualties (not something the Nazis were particularly concerned about, but of course the Spitfire squadrons adhered to it).

Air Marshal Hill wanted a revision of policy. He maintained that the positions of certain targets were known accurately and that the civilian population had been moved away from the rocket launching points. In his view, therefore, it was 'a question of balancing the certain injury to British civilian life and property against the possible injury to Dutch civilian life and property'. He asked that bombing attacks should be permitted in spite of the risk. He also asked for suitable rocket targets and for the airfields used by aircraft launching flying bombs against the UK to be placed on a higher priority for attacks by Bomber Command.

The whole question was considered at a conference on 21 November under the chairmanship of the Deputy Supreme Commander. Air Marshal Hill and members of the Dutch Government were present. The latter agreed that if bombing attacks on launching points and storage sites were indeed considered necessary and likely to prove effective, they would raise no objection at this stage. Air Marshal Hill was therefore given authority to undertake such attacks even against targets near built-up areas, provided he considered them 'reasonably discriminating'.

This applied only to Fighter Command and its fighter bomber aircraft. No alteration was made in 'Crossbow' policy and it affected 2nd Tactical Air Force and Bomber Command. Air Chief Marshal Tedder put the claims of the battle on land on 2nd Tactical Air Force higher than the needs of rocket counter-measures. However, the current operation of this force included attacks on the railway bridge at Deventer, Zwolle and Zutphen, which carried communications to The Hague.[2] 2nd Tactical Air Force was therefore considered to be making a contribution to defence against rockets.

As for Bomber Command, their operations were to continue to be governed by the instruction from the Combined Chiefs of Staff whereby the greatest possible effort, particularly by visual bombing, was to be made against oil targets and communications, especially those affecting the Ruhr. This did not absolutely rule out attacks against other targets. But these would obviously not be attacked if conditions were favourable for attacks on targets within the scope of the directive from the Combined CoS. In any case, according to Air Intelligence at this time, the scale of flying bomb attacks on Britain was likely to remain low!

Although the medium and heavy bombers thus remained inoperative against both rocket and flying bomb targets, the decisions of 21 November marked the beginning of more active counter-measures, as well as a new interest on the part of Fighter Command in the rocket attacks. Hitherto, apart from its comparatively small effort in armed reconnaissance, its task had been largely passive, that is to utilise its system of intelligence and communications for the warning system, which in one important respect, the warning of the general public, had not been put into operation. Henceforth, it was to attempt a specific task, one which was unique in the history of the Command and one more usually undertaken by a bomber force, namely the attack at its source of an organisation itself attacking the UK.

For the fortnight after Fighter Command had been given greater liberty of action, the weather was poor and only spasmodic attacks could be made. Conditions improved during the first week in December and a more sustained offensive was undertaken.

No. 12 Group of Fighter Command, being more suitably located than No. 11, had by now been made responsible for operations against The Hague area, and a list of targets suitable for attack by fighter bombers was issued to it on 29 November. It included a suspected storage area and a depot for motor vehicles in the Haagsche Bosch, suspected storage areas near Wassenaar, at Voorde and Huis-te-Werve, and a vehicle park and storage area and billets believed to be occupied by rocket firing troops in the Hotel Promenade at The Hague. Light attacks had been made on some of these targets on 21 November; and between then and 4 December, thirteen and a half tons were dropped in small bombs of 250 lbs.[3]

However, weather was a large issue, as mentioned in the operations log book of 602 Squadron:

'1 December 1944. 10.00hrs. A combined 453 and 602 Squadron dive-bombing show on which six aircraft were to take off at 10.00hrs led by S/Ldr Esau, DFC of 453 Squadron was postponed due to adverse weather conditions. Later in the morning the weather had improved somewhat and the 12 aircraft took off at 11.55hrs with two 250 lbs bombs and one 500 lb bomb, only to find the target obscured by thick cloud. After jettisoning their bombs in the sea, all the aircraft landed at Maldecen aerodrome, where unfortunately on landing F/Lt Pertwee (602 Squadron) hit a jeep that was crossing the runway, thereby damaging the starboard mainplane of his aircraft. Fortunately neither he nor the driver of the jeep was injured.'

Raymond Baxter (602 Squadron) plays down the bad weather by saying: 'Every now and again we were affected by bad weather but that was the exception rather than the rule, because you see Maxie Sutherland would fly round and round and wait for a hole. We were very determined.' He concluded by saying of the above entry: '. . . Flt Lt Pertwee hit a jeep that was crossing the runway? I don't remember that.'

The accuracy of the bombing missions was considered very high; but many of the targets were well concealed, particularly in the Haagsche Bosch, and observation of results was often difficult. Nevertheless, the early consensus was: the enemy was at least being harassed, and many targets, which had hitherto enjoyed complete immunity, were now being attacked for the first time.

Raymond Baxter gave his philosophy of conducting operations over Holland at this time: 'The Germans originally released their V2s from a suburb in The Hague – the corner of a street – but they gave that up. I knew that part of Holland like the back of my hand. We studied the maps very carefully, and actually, one target, the oxygen plant, which we called the 'Winegar Works', was actually in a built up area, but mostly, the sights were rural. They would set up their V2 – which was mobile – fire it and bugger off. So it was very difficult from our point of view. We needed a lot of luck but our philosophy was to make life as difficult as possible for the enemy and, invariably, we would do an aggressive reconnaissance over the area, and shoot anything that moved, because it would either have to be German or a collaborator. The great goal was to find a train, but we never did [sic[4]], because we had blown up virtually every bridge we saw. And railway embankments were good to skip bomb with 11 seconds delayed action bombs, but one of my bombs didn't delay and my poor little Spitfire had a rough ride as a consequence.'

An attack was made on 10 December against the main railway station at

Leiden, through which rocket supplies were known to pass; four Spitfires dropped eight 250 lb bombs of which at least four hit the target.

The Hotel Promenade in The Hague was also hit (as detailed in the Squadron History of 602 Squadron):

'10 December 1944. 10.00hrs. F/Lt JCR Waterhouse led the first dive-bombing section . . . to dive-bomb the target at the Hotel Promenade in The Hague. Crossing in over The Hague they pin-pointed their target and bombed it from 11,000–3,000 ft, two bombs were seen north of the hotel whilst two others exploded east of the building – the other results were not observed, due to cloud obscuring the target, as their aircraft pulled out of their dive. No flak was encountered from the target area or during the recce of the Leiden/Amsterdam area which followed.'

Altogether, between 25 November and 17 December[5] nearly three hundred sorties were flown by Fighter Command over Holland and twenty-five tons of bombs were dropped.

2nd Tactical Air Force was also indirectly assisting in the offensive against The Hague area by attacking German communications south of the Zuider Zee. Railway lines were cut south-west of Zwolle by fighter bombers, a bridge north-east of Rotterdam was destroyed, and Leiden station was bombed by Typhoons. The important communications points at Deventer, Zwolle and Zutphen were attacked by medium bombers.

Offensive action by Fighter Command during these three weeks was small in weight of bombs dropped, and by that token alone not much could be expected from it in reducing the scale of German attack. But it was in this way that the new policy of counter-measures could be most strikingly justified, and there was, therefore, no little interest in the size of the German effort at this time.

In the first week of the period 25 November–2 December, forty-five rocket incidents were reported in the United Kingdom. In the next week, thirty-five, and in the next, twenty-nine. Activity, therefore, decreased as Fighter Command's efforts increased. But whether the two were directly connected was not demonstrable. It was perhaps evidence against it that the scale of rocket attack against Antwerp increased as the Ardennes offensive gathered strength. In other words, it was possible that in order to increase the rate of fire against the main Allied base in Belgium while the German offensive was in progress, the scale of attack on other targets had to be reduced. However, it was also noticeable that the accuracy of attack against London fell away after Fighter Command began regular bombing. In the first week of the period over half the incidents occurred in the London Civil Defence Region; in the next two weeks, only a third. Perhaps most significant was the fact that whereas up to the beginning of December the enemy effort was fairly equally divided between day and night, in the following fortnight only about one-fifth of the incidents were by day. It seemed fair to assume, therefore, that the more determined efforts of Fighter Command in daylight had forced the Germans to fire mostly at night.[6]

All rockets launched against the UK continued to come from the general area of The Hague, but a wider dispersal of launching points was discerned at this time. Three districts were in use: one south of Leiden, one in The Hague (Wassenaar district), and one three or four miles east of the Hook of Holland. It was thought that supplies of rockets were brought to Leiden by rail, and were then taken by road to field storage depots near the launching areas for final assembly. Liquid oxygen was believed to be conveyed by rail as far as The Hague itself. Intelligence on the German field organisation made it fairly clear that operational control was being exercised by the SS, which was known to provide at least one of the eight firing troops in action. Certainly two, and possibly three of these were thought to be firing against England, the others at Antwerp.

Fog affected operations in the week 17 to 24 December and only eighty-three sorties were flown over The Hague by Fighter Command. They included, however, the heaviest single attack that had yet been mounted. This was the work of thirty-three Spitfire XIV and XVI aircraft of Nos 229, 453 and 602 Squadrons against Marlot, a block of flats near the Haagsche Bosch, which was believed to be the headquarters of the rocket firing troops in the district. The Spitfires each carried one 500 lb bomb in addition to two 250 lb bombs. Photographs were taken during the attack, which was made on Christmas Eve, from an accompanying Mustang, but they showed only one direct hit. Later photographs, however, showed that considerable damage had been done and shortly after the attack the building was evacuated. One Spitfire was destroyed by anti-aircraft fire.

The German effort against London during this week was also low. There were only twenty-eight incidents, seven in the London area. As in the previous fortnight most of the firing was at night. There were no incidents that caused heavy casualties.

However, on 22 December the Home Secretary, Herbert Morrison, suggested to the Chiefs of Staff that more powerful counter-measures should be applied against The Hague area. His was the main responsibility for the security of the civilian population and certain developments in that sphere threatened an effect out of all proportion to the moderate scale of rocket bombardment. These originated from doubts which had been expressed about the safety of the London underground railways under rocket attack. It was feared that rockets might penetrate the tunnels running under the Thames and cause flooding with heavy loss of life (especially at night when thousands of people were sheltering in 'tube' stations). Accordingly, during December the transmission of special warnings to the London Passenger Transport Board was considered so that the under-river floodgates of the 'tubes' could be closed during attacks.

Herbert Morrison was anxious, therefore, that rocket attacks should be reduced below even the present low effort. He recognised that the scale of attack had fallen during the first three weeks of December, and this he credited to the attacks of Fighter Command and 2nd Tactical Air Force; but he suggested that heavy bomber attacks upon The Hague launching areas would reduce it still further. He also argued that as, according to the Air Ministry, the morale of all the German firing troops, not only those attacking England, was being affected by the attacks of Fighter Command and 2nd Tactical Air Force, heavy bomber operations against rocket targets would contribute to the security of the lines of communication of the Allied forces in Belgium as well as to the defence of the UK.

The Home Secretary's views were considered at a meeting of the Chiefs of Staff on 23 December, who strongly recommended that heavy bombers should not be employed against targets near The Hague. Their reasons were two-fold: first, they were sure that the attacks would mean heavy loss of life amongst Dutch civilians and the destruction of much Dutch property without achieving anything more than a temporary interruption of rocket firings; second, for the eight to ten known or suspected targets to be attacked effectively some 1,200 to 1,500 sorties by Lancasters would be needed, and this effort, it was felt, could not be justified.

Nevertheless, the possibility of widening the scope of counter-measures by bombing was much to the fore at this period. During December the Deputy Chief of the Air Staff asked the Economic Advisory Branch of the Foreign Office and the Ministry of Economic Warfare to review again the liquid oxygen factories that might be providing fuel for rockets. A detailed paper was prepared and circulated on 18 December 1944. It emphasised that Germany required liquid oxygen for industrial purposes and for high-altitude flying as well as for rockets and that it was impossible to say what were the requirements for each purpose or what factories provided them. There were indications that the Germans would probably rely for liquid oxygen for rockets on plants producing at least fifteen to twenty tons a day, supplemented by deliveries from such of the smaller plants as lay within fifty miles of rocket launching points. There were in Holland eight plants that the Germans might be using, five in western Germany and five elsewhere in Germany. None of the German plants, however, could be positively identified as producing for rockets and, consequently, none were attacked. Those in Holland continued to be studied and one, at Loosduinen, was eventually bombed by Fighter Command, but the evidence was never conclusive that the Nazis used these plants for rocket fuel.

Another type of target, which if successfully attacked might affect the scale of attack from The Hague, was studied in January 1945. This was the road and rail communications system between Germany and western Holland. A report on the subject by the Deputy Chief of the Air Staff was presented to the Chiefs of Staff on 13 January. Leading from northern Germany to enemy-occupied Holland there were four main railway and four main road bridges, all of which crossed the Ijssel river between Doesberg, near Arnhem and Kampen, near Zwolle. All were strongly constructed, some 4,000 yards in length, and heavily defended by anti-aircraft guns. For their destruction, the employment of the tactical air forces appeared most suitable; and it was estimated that about 600 sorties by fighter bombers or 400 by medium bombers would be needed to destroy the railway bridges and a similar effort for the road bridges. Even then, the interdiction would be complete. It would be necessary to prevent attempts to repair the bridges or to convey supplies across the Ijssel by pontoon bridges or barges. The possible diversion of road traffic to the northern route across the Zuider Zee causeway would also have to be reckoned with. For such extensive operations the approval of the Supreme Commander was necessary, and neither the Air Staff at the Air Ministry nor SHAEF considered that they were justified. Consequently, plans for the full interdiction of supplies to The Hague were left at the paper stage against the possibility that their execution would be necessary if rocket attacks substantially increased.

Niedersachswerfen was also re-examined during January 1945, as a possible target. By this time German jet-propelled aircraft were considered to present a real threat to Allied superiority; and it was as a producer of jet engines rather than rockets that the factory was placed on the current target lists for Bomber Command and the 8th Air Force on high priority. It was felt that although to destroy it would probably be impossible, damage to the approaches and to the storage sheds and workers' dwellings on the surface, might disrupt production. For two months the best method of attacking it was examined.

A detailed model of the target area was constructed and studied by officers of Bomber Command and the 8th Air Force, who concluded that the output of the factory could not be stopped with existing types of bomb. It might be reduced by continued attack of the railway system in and near the target area; but this would have meant a very considerable diversion of bombing effort from targets more profitable to the general offensive. On 8 March the Chiefs of Staff finally agreed that attacks upon the factory would not be worthwhile. So, no radical change was made in the policy of counter-measures, which remained those carried out by Fighter Command, supplemented by 2nd Tactical Air Force. This applied until all attacks upon Britain, both rockets and flying bombs, had ceased.

Up to the middle of January the striking force that Fighter Command maintained for attacks against The Hague amounted to four squadrons of Spitfires (453, 229, 303, 602). All operated under No. 12 Group, chiefly from the Coltishall sector. No operations were flown against the area at night. The intruder resources of the command were at this time fully committed to the support of Bomber Command; and although the question of using intruder pilots under training was considered, nothing came of it.

During the first month of this period operations were affected by the weather; only some 300 sorties were flown, of which nearly one-third had to be abandoned. As this was also the period in which there was heavy fighting in the Ardennes, the effort of 2nd Tactical Air Force was largely confined to the support of the Allied ground forces and few operations were carried out which might have affected The Hague area.

Attacks were carried out, as weather permitted, in accordance with a list of targets agreed upon between Air Intelligence and the Director of Operations (Air Defence) at Air Ministry and Fighter Command. The list initially comprised eleven targets: seven wooded areas near The Hague, Wassenaar and Hook of Holland, which were in use for storing rockets preparatory to firing, one headquarters building at The Hague, one supply depot (the Leiden goods station) one liquid oxygen depot (the Staats Spoor station at The Hague) and the billets and vehicle park at the Hotel Promenade at The Hague. The list was supplemented during the next two months as intelligence indicated fresh targets; and by the middle of February there were seventeen targets between Hook of Holland, The Hague and Leiden, which were judged to be connected with rockets and an attack on which had been approved. The main consideration in clearing a target for attack, when its connection with the German organisation had been established, was the danger to Dutch civilians. Very great care had to be taken in briefing pilots, selecting aiming points and planning the method and direction of attacks in order to minimise possible civilian casualties.[7]

During November 1944 there had seemed to be a possibility of carrying out attacks on particular launching sites at times when rockets were about to be fired. It was hoped to make use of the wireless traffic between the headquarters and sub-formations of the German rocket batteries, which was being intercepted by 'Y' units in Belgium, to obtain warning of attacks by individual launching sites. A study of the intercepts up to the end of November indicated that a warning of about an hour would usually be obtained, which was sufficient for aircraft either of Fighter Command or 2nd Tactical Air Force to be over the site at the time of firing. Further study showed that there would be little or no indication of which of the sites within a battery would be firing; and while the wireless traffic proved a valuable source of information on changes in the disposition of the German firing troops, it was never used as a basis for operations against particular sites.

During the weeks 17 December–16 January, Fighter Command only operated on fifteen days and a high proportion of the sorties that were flown had to be abandoned, in which case bombs were either jettisoned in the sea or brought back to Britain. Altogether, 258 fighter bombers were despatched of which ninety-two were unable to find their targets. In addition, sixty-eight armed reconnaissances were flown in which machine-gun and cannon attacks were made on rocket storage areas and rail and road transport near The Hague. A small number of bombing attacks, four in all, were made at squadron strength (twelve aircraft); but the normal strength both for bombing attacks and armed reconnaissances was four aircraft. There was also the attack by three squadrons on the Marlot flats, which were in use as headquarters.

With the exception of the latter attack and four attacks upon the Hotel Promenade at The Hague, all bombing was against storage areas. The Haagsche Bosch, where enemy activity was believed to be heaviest and where rockets were actually photographed from the air during December as they lay in side roads cut through the trees, was attacked on five occasions. Four attacks were made on two more storage areas at The Hague – Voorde and Huis-te-Werve; three areas at Wassenaar, north-east of The Hague, received nine attacks. Altogether, just under fifty tons of bombs were dropped during the period, mostly consisting of 250 lb bombs.

It was very difficult for the fighter bomber pilots to assess results at the time of attack. The Hague area was heavily defended (at the end of January 1945, the position of 105 light anti-aircraft guns and forty-four heavy had been identified in the area of the Hook of Holland), and while losses due to enemy fire during the month amounted to only one Spitfire, it was highly dangerous for pilots to come below 3,000 feet[8] either to bomb or to observe results. Nor, since most of the bombs were dropped in wooded country, was photographic reconnaissance after an attack really fruitful. What appeared undeniable, however, was that the effort against launching areas ought to be sustained at least throughout the hours of daylight, and, if possible, by night also. Night sorties, as we have seen, were not possible at this time owing to the commitments of Fighter Command in support of Bomber Command's attacks against Germany. Moreover, a sustained effort by day during the winter months meant that a large number of sorties against specific objectives would be failures owing to bad weather and obviously poor visability.

The scale of attack during the second half of January remained low. Only nine bombing attacks were carried out, all of them against rocket storage areas. A tenth attack was attempted but had to be abandoned owing to cloud. Armed reconnaissances fared no better; seven were attempted but only two were carried out. The weather was particularly bad towards the end of the month and no operations were carried out during the last week. The most notable attack on a suspected rocket target during this period was in fact not the work of Fighter Command but of 2nd Tactical Air Force which, on 22 January, sent four squadrons of

Spitfire fighter-bombers to attack a liquid oxygen factory at Alblasserdam. The target was destroyed. 2nd Tactical Air Force was more active at this time against communications east of The Hague than it had been at any time since the middle of December 1944.

However, the first half of February 1945 saw these attacks, and those of Fighter Command, increase in response to a decision of the War Cabinet on 27 January that Fighter Command should intensify its attacks on The Hague area and that 2nd Tactical Air Force should supplement the attacks on communications, which Fighter Command was already planning. Two more Fighter Command squadrons (603, 124) began to participate in the offensive and a list of secondary targets, more suitable for attack in bad weather than the targets near The Hague, was prepared. These were stretches of railroad and railway junctions in the rear of The Hague, in the Gouda, Uttrecht and Amersfoot areas: the junction at the latter place was particularly important.

The results were apparent from 3 February, which was the first clear day for nearly a fortnight. In the succeeding two weeks (3 to 6 February), thirty-eight attacks, involving 286 sorties, were attempted against targets near The Hague, compared to sixteen attacks and seventy-four sorties in the previous fortnight. With the exception of three armed reconnaissances all were bombing sorties; forty could not be carried out, some through mechanical troubles but most because of bad weather.

Altogether, thirty-one bombing attacks were carried out, mostly against rocket storage areas. The Haagsche Bosch was attacked on seven occasions, the Staalduine Bosch, near the Hook of Holland, on five, and Rust-en-Vreugd at Wassenaar on three; four more attacks were carried out on storage areas at The Hague and Wassenaar, and the Hotel Promenade at The Hague was attacked three times. In accordance with the new policy four attacks were made on secondary railway targets.

But the target against which the greatest effort was made was of a type that had not previously been attacked by Fighter Command – a suspected liquid oxygen plant in a former tramway depot at Loosduinen, south-west of The Hague. As a result of the close study of the possible sources of liquid oxygen supply that had been made in 1944, it had appeared that no major offensive against likely plants was possible, but in December Fighter Command had been asked to consider the attack of three factories in Holland which held promise as targets. One of these – Alblasserdam – was attacked by 2nd Tactical Air Force on 22 January, with great success. Another, at Ijmuiden, consisted of two buildings in the middle of a large factory area and precision attacks upon it would have been exceptionally difficult. The third possibility – Loosduinen – was a difficult target so long as care was taken to avoid Dutch casualties (as there was civilian property on three sides of the factory). It was, therefore, with some reluctance that Fighter Command undertook its attack, especially as there was no reliable evidence that even complete success would affect rocket supplies: the intelligence officers at Fighter Command believed that all the oxygen that was required for the existing scale of rocket attack could be transported from Germany.

Two attacks were made upon Loosduinen on 3 February, one on the 8th and two on the 9th. In all but one attack the bombing runs were made over one side of the factory that was free of housing; and the technique of the pilots has been well described as 'trickling their bombs towards the target'. For this reason five attacks had to be made. Altogether, seventy-eight fighter-bombers, carrying nearly thirty tons of bombs, attempted to attack the factory but only about one third of their bombs were released. However, with the last attack the factory was sufficiently badly damaged to be ignored in the future.

In attacks on other targets, fifty tons of bombs were dropped, chiefly on the two storage areas most used by the Germans, the Haagsche Bosch and the Staalduinsche Bosch, at which over thirty tons were aimed. The accuracy of bombing was high: only seven tons of bombs were estimated to have fallen outside the areas. Moreover, 500 lb bombs were frequently dropped, whereas previously, loads had consisted almost exclusively of 250 lb bombs. The change had been made possible by an arrangement with 2nd Tactical Air Force that Fighter Command aircraft could land to re-fuel and re-arm at an airfield at Ursel, near Ghent.

But what damage had been done was hard to estimate. Occasionally, heavy explosions in the woods indicated that rockets had been detonated; and it was known that even slightly damaged rockets had to be returned to Germany for repair before they could be fired. What the number of these was, however, was not known. It was, in fact, rather from the indirect evidence of changes in the scale and character of attacks on London than from direct evidence or damage in and near The Hague that the effect of the offensive could best be assessed.

With the exception of the fighter-bomber attack on Alblasserdam and two unsuccessful attempts by medium bombers to deny communications across Ijssel at Zwolle and Deventer, the efforts of 2nd Tactical Air Force over the period 17 January–16 February took their usual form of attacks on communications south of the Zuider Zee. Over 3,000 sorties were flown and impressive numbers of barges, railway locomotives and rolling stock, and motor vehicles were destroyed, and railway lines were cut at no fewer than 139 points. But as in the case of the operations of Fighter Command, the precise effects of this upon the enemy's position in Holland could not be estimated, nor upon his rocket organisation in particular. Again, it was in the attacks upon Britain that any evidence of success would be apparent.

During the last fortnight of December 1944, the scale of rocket attack on London remained low. Only fifty-seven rockets were reported compared to eighty during the first half of the month and eighty-six in the second half of November. The majority of rockets continued to be fired at night, only fourteen incidents occurring during daylight. This alone meant some relief for London as casualties from rockets falling at night tended to be lower than in daylight incidents. The accuracy of the German fire also remained poor: only fifteen rockets fell within the London Civil Defence Region. Casualties were, in fact, slightly higher than during the first half of the month – 176 killed and 352 seriously injured compared to 128 and 310 – chiefly because of two serious incidents in Islington and one in Chelmsford in which 124 people were killed and 168 injured.

On the continent, in contrast, the scale of rocket attacks increased, especially during the last week of December when the Ardennes battle was at its height. Altogether, 217 rockets were reported, all fired at Antwerp, compared to 143 in the first half of the month, a small number of which had been fired at Brussels and Liège.

The comparative lull in the attack on London was soon broken. Beginning with the first week in January 1945, the number of rockets reported weekly in the United Kingdom jumped from an average of thirty-four for December to fifty-nine. There was no decline during the rest of the month when 167 incidents were reported, making a total for the month of 226, compared to 137 for December. On 26 January there were seventeen incidents, thirteen of them in the London area, the highest so far recorded in one day. The first half of February saw still heavier attacks. Up to and including the 16th, 145 rockets were reported; and again on one day, the 13th, there were seventeen incidents, eleven in the London area. With this increase in fire there was, for most of the period, an improvement in accuracy. During December 1944, only one-third of reported incidents were in the London area. During January 1945, the proportion rose to exactly a half; and this was maintained during the first few days of February. Then however, during the week 10 to 16 February, which saw the heaviest week's activity since the rocket attacks had begun, only a little over one third of the incidents were in the London area.

Where the total number of incidents was comparatively small no great significance was attached to these variations in accuracy. What was undoubtedly significant, however, was the change in the distribution of the German fire between day and night. Whereas in December only one third of the incidents in the United Kingdom had occurred during daytime, in January nearly sixty per cent were in daylight, with a similar percentage in the first half of February. It appeared, therefore, that despite the greatest activity of Fighter Command over The Hague area, the Germans were not restricted to the hours of night for firing so much as they had been when the fighter-bomber offensive opened.

With the improvement in accuracy, the higher rate of fire and the increase in daylight attacks, casualties during this period sharply increased compared to December. Between 1 January and 16 February, 755 people were killed and 2,264 seriously injured by rockets, a weekly casualty rate twice as high as that of December. There were thirteen incidents, mostly in east and north-east districts of London, in each of which more than twenty people were killed.

The greater weight and effect of the attack during these first weeks of 1945 must be placed against the background of the counter-offensive. During January, the Operation Research Section at Fighter Command Headquarters carefully collated the scale of rocket attack and of the fighter-bomber offensive against The Hague. A simple balancing of the two sets of data was hardly sufficient evidence to support any positive conclusions about the effect of the offensive. It did appear, however, that it was only in the period 4 to 15 December, when Fighter Command had been able to make sustained attacks on The Hague, that the weight of German fire had been affected. Moreover, during that period the accuracy of fire by day had been considerably, and by night slightly, affected; though on the whole it seemed that neither sporadic nor sustained attacks by day had much effect on the enemy's scale of effort or accuracy by night. What was needed was a sustained effort both by day and night, and a recommendation to this effect had been made by the Chief Intelligence Officer of Fighter Command on 22 January 1945.

The shortage of suitable night fighters made it impossible to conduct a continuous counter-offensive, but, as we have seen, from the beginning of February the weight of attack by daylight against The Hague area was markedly increased. Even so, the scale of rocket attack remained higher than at any time previously. This was not to say that the counter-offensive was failing. At the least it might be saving London from still heavier bombardment; for even though assessment of the results achieved was not easy, it was beyond doubt that damage was being caused to targets in The Hague area that were known for certain to be connected with rocket attacks. However, it was not certain which targets, or what type of targets, were most precious to the enemy.

On 15 February 1945 the Chief Intelligence Officer of Fighter Command recommended a new target policy which entailed concentrating for a week on one of the three main targets – Haagsche Bosch, the woods near Oakenburg, and Staalduinsche Bosch – rather than spreading the effort of the Command over a dozen targets. The recommendation was accepted and the new policy was applied from 20 February. Its results will be tackled presently.

In the more clearly defensive aspects of counter-measure there were some notable developments between the middle of December and the middle of February. By this time the radar stations in the UK, through No. 105 Mobile Air Reporting Unit at Malines, were detecting a large number of rockets sufficiently early for warnings to have been sounded in the

London region. If a warning of fifty to sixty seconds had been acceptable to the Civil Defence authorities the existing system would have sufficed. But something better would be required if ever the scale of attack became such that public warnings were essential, and at a meeting on 15 January, Sir Robert Watson Watt's Interdepartmental Radio Committee was asked to investigate what would be required to permit warnings of up to four minutes. In the meantime no public warnings were sounded in London.

However, on 2 January the War Cabinet decided to put into operation the scheme for issuing special warnings to the London Passenger Transport Board so that the floodgates of the 'tube' railways could be closed. Warnings began to be given on the afternoon of 8 January. During the ensuing months 201 warnings were passed, of which only nine were false; and only four rockets fell in the London region without warning.

The reliability of the warning system also came under review in connection with a project of Anti-Aircraft Command to attempt the destruction of rockets by gun fire. The question was first raised outside Anti-Aircraft Command at a meeting at Fighter Command.

Heavier attacks against The Hague were required, and bad weather during the third week in February coincided with the change in target policy of Fighter Command, whereby bombing was to be concentrated on a small number of targets; and it was not until 21 February that the Haagsche Bosch came under heavy attack. Ten attacks had been attempted on the previous two days, nine against the Haagsche Bosch and one against the Hotel Promenade; but only two were carried out. In one case the primary target could not be bombed and instead attacks were made on road and rail transport in north Holland along the line of communication between the causeway over the Zuider Zee and The Hague area. In the other, six Spitfires of 124 Squadron successfully dropped their bombs in the Haagsche Bosch in a typical attack in which the pilots dived down from 11,000–5,000 feet before bombing.

Late on the 20th, the weather began to clear and the next two days were fine. Fighter Command made the most of them. Twenty-two bombing attacks were carried out on the 21st, and seventeen on the 22nd; only five attacks were against areas other than the Haagsche Bosch. The total number of sorties flown on the two days was 214 and forty tons of bombs were dropped. Only one aircraft was lost.

Bombs were dropped in all parts of the forest, which was nearly two miles long and half a mile wide at its widest point, but particular attention was paid to the north-west corner, where a group of buildings known as the Filmstad was in use as a storage depot. It was first attacked on the morning of the 22nd by twelve Spitfires of 453 Squadron. Most of the bombs hit the target and very heavy explosions were caused; and when 602 Squadron attacked shortly afterwards the pilots were assisted by a column of smoke rising from the buildings. Their bombing was also accurate. The buildings continued to burn throughout the day and photographs taken later from a Mustang of 26 Squadron showed that about eighty per cent of them had been destroyed.

The following day, the 23rd, the weather was bad and only one sortie, on which no bombing was possible owing to cloud, was flown. It was very gratifying, however, after the efforts that the Command had made on the previous two days, to observe a marked decline in the scale of German attack. From 17 to 23 February the attack on London had continued on just as heavy a scale as in the first two weeks of the month: seventy-one rockets were reported in the United Kingdom of which thirty-one fell in the London region. But then, between dusk on the 23rd and the morning of the 26th, only one rocket fell in the United Kingdom – on the morning of the 24th. Photographic reconnaissance on that day showed that, for the first time since December, when photographs first revealed rockets in the Haagsche Bosch, there were no rockets to be seen in it. The same photographs showed four rockets in the Duindigit area contingent to the Haagsche Bosch to the north, where there was a race course from which rockets were known to have been fired. When firing was resumed on 26 February, after the sixty-two hour lull, radar evidence indicated that the rockets had come from this area; while on the same day a photograph taken from a Mustang of 26 Squadron showed a rocket in position for launching in the woods east of the race course. It seemed a fair enough inference, therefore, that storage facilities in the Haagsche Bosch had been so badly damaged that they had been vacated at least temporarily, and that while new arrangements were being made, launchings had had to cease.

It was some days before this evidence had been sufficiently studied for a new target policy to be formulated. Meanwhile, the main target remained the Haagsche Bosch, particularly the northern part near the race course. From 24 to 28 February, eighty-eight attacks were attempted, involving 400 sorties, all with the Haagsche Bosch as the primary target. The weather was cloudy and twelve operations had to be abandoned. Twenty-eight others were made against secondary railway targets, widely dispersed over the communications system between Gouda, east of The Hague, and Alkmeer in the north of Holland. Three attacks were made on the Ockenburg storage area at The Hague and one on Rust-en-Vreugd at Wassenaar, north-east of The Hague. Four attacks on the Haagsche Bosch and Ockenburg were made with cannon and machine-gun fire. The rest, forty in all, were against the Haagsche Bosch. In many of these attacks, after bombing the primary target, squadrons carried out low level reconnaissances over western Holland, attacking road and rail transport. The most successful was by No. 602 Squadron who, on the 25th, destroyed a large number of vehicles in a park north-west of Rotterdam. The total weight of bombs dropped in all these operations was seventy tons, of which forty were dropped on the Haagsche Bosch and twenty-five on railways. Bombs of 250 lbs were exclusively employed.

On 28 February the Chief Intelligence Officer at Fighter Command recommended certain alterations to targets. He did not suggest that the Haagsche Bosch should be removed from the list although there was still no sign that rockets were being stored there. The aiming points for attack, however, were so selected that the northern portion of the area, including part of Duindigit, would be covered.

There was photographic evidence available by this time that a limited number of rockets – up to six, compared with twenty to thirty that had sometimes been seen in the Haagsche Bosch – were being stored under camouflage netting in Duindigit. This area was to be one target. A second was to be the rest of Duindigit, and a third was to be the storage and maintenance area of Rust-en-Vreugd. Fifty per cent of the effort of Fighter Command was to be devoted to the first, thirty per cent to the second, and twenty to the third. In the event of bad weather, railway targets were to be attacked rather than other storage areas. This policy was approved and all concerned were informed on 1 March 1945.

It was recognised by the Intelligence section at Fighter Command that there was an element of doubt about the Haagsche Bosch target; and strenuous efforts were made to identify another storage depot, which might have taken the very important place which the Haagsche Bosch had hitherto occupied in the German organisation. For, even if the Germans had completely evacuated the Haagsche Bosch, which was not absolutely certain, they had found other means of maintaining the scale of attack on London – in the week following the resumption of firing, 26 February to 5 March, seventy rockets were reported in the UK, thirty-three of them in London, compared to seventy-one and thirty-two in the week before the lull. But until new storage areas were found it was considered worth while to maintain the attack on the Haagsche Bosch. It had certainly proved very useful to the Germans in the past and it might be possible to damage its facilities to such an extent that it could not be brought into use again. The northern portion of the area, where there was a network of roads and also a bridge across a wide and deep anti-tank bridge between the forest and Duindigit, in particular offered good opportunities for denying it to the Germans. This reasoning was not unopposed. According to the officer in charge at this time of Intelligence 3F at Fighter Command (the section responsible for the recommending of targets), officers of the Allied Central Interpretation Unit at Medmenham, which was responsible for the study of reconnaissance photographs, protested against the continued attack of the Haagsche Bosch on the grounds that photographs showed no rockets there after 24 February.

Consequently, on the first two days of March, attacks continued to be made almost exclusively against the Haagsche Bosch. Thirty-four attacks were attempted, of which eight could not be made because of the weather; twenty-three were carried out against the Haagsche Bosch and three against other storage areas, including Rust-en-Vreugd. On the 3rd, half the twenty-eight attacks that were aimed at the Haagsche Bosch, the rest at Rust-en-Vreugd and Staalduinsche Bosch, the latter being the storage area for rockets fired from the neighbourhood of the Hook of Holland.

But the 3rd was the most remarkable for one of the rare interventions of 2nd Tactical Air Force directly against a rocket target. Arrangements had been made during February that this force should attack the Haagsche Bosch with medium bombers when it had the aircraft to spare; and between 09:00hrs and 09:20hrs two wings, 137 and 139, of Mitchells and Bostons bombed the area.

There was much to be said for such an attack. A much heavier weight of bombs could be dropped simultaneously than by fighter bombers: heavier bombs could be used and the area deeply and extensively cratered. Altogether, fifty-six aircraft were employed and sixty-nine tons of bombs were dropped. Unfortunately, the bombing was very inaccurate. As far as could be judged the nearest bombs to either of the two aiming points were some 500 yards away, and the biggest concentration of bombs was over a mile away in a densely populated area. Severe damage to Dutch property and heavy civilian casualties were reported and a strong protest was lodged by the Netherlands Embassy in London. The cause of the accident appeared to be the application of an incorrect allowance for wind, which resulted in abnormal bombing errors. Instructions were given by AOC-in-C, 2nd Tactical Air Force that no further attacks by medium bombers were to be made against The Hague.

Nor was the Haagsche Bosch again attacked by Fighter Command. All the intelligence at this stage pointed to Duindigit as the only profitable target, though it was also clear that extensive storage facilities did not exist there. There was some evidence that Staalduinsche Bosch; Rust-en-Vreugd and Ockenburg were being used, but not extensively. A target of a different character that was also selected early in March was the headquarters of the Bataafsche Petroleum Company which was believed to be in use as billets and offices by the firing troops in The Hague area. One attack was made upon it on 4 March, by four Spitfires of 602 Squadron. It was a difficult target – there was much property on two sides of it – and no bombs hit the building. More successful attacks were to be made later. Otherwise, from the 4th to the 8th of the month the effort of the Command was devoted to the three storage and firing areas mentioned above, with secondary railway targets being attacked when the weather was poor. Altogether, forty-seven operations were flown, twenty against Rust-en-Vreugd, twelve against Duindigit, and the rest against Ockenburg and the Staalduinsche Bosch. Weather, as had been only too often the case during the last four months, seriously interfered.

None of the operations on the 6th, 7th and 8th could be pressed home and sixteen of those attempted on the 4th and 5th had to be abandoned. On eight occasions the primary target was obscured by cloud and the railway system in the triangle Hague/Rotterdam/Utrecht was attacked instead.

On 8 March, in the light of the latest intelligence, a new list of priorities was issued by Fighter Command. The first target was to be Duindigt, which remained the only area on which satisfactory information was available; the second was a wood at Ravelijn, a mile to the north of the race-course at Duindigt, where recent photographic reconnaissances had revealed a small number of rockets; the third was the Bataafsche Petroleum Company's building in The Hague. These were the only targets selected; the railway system east of The Hague was to provide secondary targets. Seventy per cent of the effort of Fighter Command was to be the object of a single attack, if possible by a full squadron, which would see its destruction. In fact, it was not attacked until the second half of March, by which time the target policy of Fighter Command had again been altered; and from 9 to 16 March inclusive, with the exception of three attacks on Rust-en-Vreugd on the first day of the period, all attacks were against Duindigit, Revelijn and railway communications.

A considerable effort was brought to bear during the week, many aircraft landing at Ursel, near Ghent, after a first attack, re-arming and re-fuelling there, and carrying out a second attack before returning direct to Britain. Altogether, 108 bombing attacks and twenty-six armed recon-naissances were attempted, involving 586 sorties, and 110 were carried out, though not always against primary target. Secondary railway targets, particularly between Gouda and Utrecht, were attacked as much as the storage area at Ravelijn, nearly twenty tons of bombs being dropped on each. Some seventy tons of bombs were dropped on the Duindigit area, and it was that location that proved to be the most obvious success story for the efforts of the Command. Much of the target area was heavily pitted with craters (it was remarked at the time that it looked as if Bomber Command not Fighter Command had been attacking it) and on several occasions heavy explosions followed bombing. To crown it all, from 13 March there was evidence, which was confirmed by photographs on 18 March, that the enemy had abandoned the area.

Throughout all this period, 16 February–16 March, 2nd Tactical Air Force had been supporting operations on land, and apart from the ill-fated attack on the Haagsche Bosch on 3 March their efforts had only indirectly affected the German rocket organisation. Nearly 1,500 sorties had been made against communications in Holland leading to The Hague; a railway bridge between Zwolle and Enschede had been destroyed and over fifty cuts in railway lines had been made. The usual extensive toll of railway and road transport vehicles was claimed.

During the four weeks in which so much thought and effort had been devoted to the counter-offensive against The Hague a dividend seemed to be discernible not only in the photographic evidence of the evacuation of, first, the Haagsche Bosch and, second, the Duindigit area, but also in a reduction in the scale of attack on London. This was not apparent in the first week, 17 to 23 February, when the comparatively heavy attacks of the first half of the month were maintained: seventy-one rockets fell in the United Kingdom that week, thirty-one of them in the London Civil Defence Region. But in the next week, during which a lull was forced on the Germans by the bombing of the Haagsche Bosch, the number of rockets reported in the United Kingdom fell to fifty-seven. There was something of a recovery in the week 3 to 9 March, when sixty-five rockets were reported; but in the week 10 to 16 March, during which Duindigit was abandoned, there were only fifty rocket incidents, the lowest weekly total for over a month.

For the whole period just under half of the rockets reported fell in London. In the week 3 to 9 March, the percentage rose to as high as sixty, only to be followed in the next with a fall, coincident with the fall in the scale of attack, to forty.

It was perhaps not significant that, whereas in the first week of the period two thirds of rocket incidents occurred during daylight, the proportion fell as the counter-offensive against The Hague continued. In the second week only forty per cent of rockets were launched in daylight, in the third thirty-seven, and in the fourth twenty-six. Moreover, the hours of heaviest activity were in the early morning before dawn, and the lightest the last hours of daylight and the earliest of the night. The implication was not that the presence of Fighter Command aircraft over The Hague almost throughout the day was forcing the Nazis to fire at night – this had seemed a fair enough inference in December but had been invalidated in January and February when the majority of rockets had been fired in daylight despite the fighter bomber offensive – but that the enemy's storage facilities had been so affected by the counter-offensive that rockets were having to be brought up to launching points during the night and fired as quickly as possible. In other words, no reserves of rockets were being held in the field.

The perceptible slackening in the Nazi offensive was not accompanied by a relief in the number of casualties. The fall of rockets in London was, as before, chiefly in eastern and north-eastern districts – the point of greatest concentration during the period was in East Ham – and a number of serious incidents swelled casualty lists to figures comparable with those of previous weeks. In the four weeks preceding 14 February, 473 people had been killed and 1,415 seriously injured by rockets in the United Kingdom, of whom only seventeen were killed and 107 injured outside London. In the four weeks following that date 580 were killed and 1,220 seriously injured, of whom fifty were killed and 121 injured outside

London. How much depended on freedom from really serious incidents was underlined by the fact that, whereas 114 rockets fell in London during the four weeks, six rockets alone killed 308 people and seriously injured 318. The heaviest casualties were caused by a rocket which fell on Smithfield Market in Farringdon Road, EC1, at 11:10hrs on the morning of 8 March: 110 people were killed and 123 seriously injured.

No alterations were made to the warning system during the period beyond the deployment near Lowestoft of an extra GL MK II radar set. Sir Robert Watson Watt's committee continued its examination of what an effective public warning would entail but the only warnings that were given were to the London Passenger Transport Board[9]

The month of March 1945 saw the end of the rocket bombardment of London.

Fighter Command had recently completed heavy bombing of the storage areas at Duindigit and Ravelijn and aerial photographs strongly suggested that the Nazis had abandoned the site.

Secondary measures now came into vogue: in the form of attacks on the railway lines that fed The Hague area, particularly those stretches between Haarlem and Leiden, Utrecht and Leiden, and The Hague/Gouda/Alphen area, along which rocket supplies were known to pass. The policy was not rigidly applied. The large building of the Bataafsche Petroleum Company at The Hague remained on the list of targets; and a garage – the Kurhaus – at Scheveningen, where *meilerwagen* (the long vehicles specially constructed for carrying rockets by road), were believed to be housed, was also selected for attack. Also, Duindigit and Ravelijn received a small number of attacks between 17 and 19 March, as an insurance against resumption of activity there, and from the 24th, by which time there was evidence that firing, though not storage, had been resumed in the Duindigit district, armed reconnaissances were flown daily over the area. However, during the rest of March, no other targets associated with either the storage or the firing of rockets were bombed. There was a report late in the month that a large hall at Rynsburg, near The Hague, in happier times a flower market, was being used for storage; but the evidence was not held to be sufficient to justify its attack.

The Bataafsche Petroleum Company's building was attacked on 18 March by six Spitfires of 602 Squadron. The pilots reported the attack to be very accurate. Six 500 lb and twelve 250 lb bombs were dropped and only one cluster missed the target. Later, photographs indicated that the damage was not as great as had been thought; though an intelligence report of 25 March stated that the Nazi organisation occupying the building had been evacuated. A further and heavier attack was made on 30 March by 603 Squadron. Twelve Spitfires took part, each re-fuelling and re-arming at Ursel after the first attack and then bombing again on the homeward journey. Over ten tons of bombs were dropped; at least six direct hits were scored on the building and eight near misses.

The Kurhaus garage at Scheveningen was also accurately bombed in the heaviest single attack made by Fighter Command during the whole of its offensive against The Hague. This took place on 22 March when twenty-four Spitfires of 603 and 453 Squadrons, each carrying one 500 lb bomb and two 250 lb bombs, attacked the garage section by section. The squadrons re-fuelled and re-armed at Ursel and attacked again just over three hours later. In all, over twenty tons of bombs were dropped. The full extent of the damage was not apparent; but a ramp leading from the roadway to the first floor of the garage collapsed under the bombing and the approaches were heavily cratered. A nearby transformer station was also hit. Intelligence officers at Fighter Command doubted whether the Nazis had been driven out of the garage but no more attacks were made upon it.

With these exceptions the efforts of the Command were entirely directed against railways. Between 17 March and 3 April, which was the last day on which any bombing attacks were made, a total of 1,572 sorties were flown by Fighter Command against western Holland. Nearly 1,400 were against railway targets, the rest, including the attacks on Ypenburg, were against specific objectives directly connected with the Nazi firing troops. Against the latter targets some seventy tons of bombs were dropped compared to over 400 tons on railways. The weight of bombs dropped in this period of less than three weeks was in fact higher than at any other stage of the offensive, partly because the weather was better and partly because more use was made of Ursel airfield for re-fuelling and re-arming, which allowed double attacks to be made and 500 lb bombs to be carried.

The effect of the offensive was next to impossible to estimate. Many cuts were made in stretches of track – according to the interpretation of photographs no fewer than 220; three railway bridges and two road bridges were destroyed and fourteen more damaged. But little movement was taking place on Dutch railways at that time (it was significant that while 84 M/T vehicles were claimed as destroyed by Fighter Command during that period, the total of railway vehicles was fourteen) and it was hard to say whether that was because the Nazis did not need or want to use them or because they could not. Certain stretches of railway remained unrepaired after being broken; others were repaired shortly after bombing.

There was, however, some evidence that the Nazis were at least inconvenienced by the attacks. Since the autumn of 1944 the intelligence officers concerned had accepted that Leiden was the only railhead for rocket supplies; and the stations there had not been attacked only because of the congestion of civilian property in the neighbourhood.[10] But on 18 March 1945 photographs taken by 26 Squadron of Fighter Command revealed both at Leiden and The Hague the easily recognisable long railway wagons on which rockets were transported. Five days later a similar train was photographed in Rotterdam station, and others were seen at Amsterdam in the latter part of March. The evidence was slight enough but it bore the interpretation that the direct lines from western Germany through Amersfoort and Utrecht to Leiden were being interrupted and that other routes and, possibly, railheads additional to Leiden, were being improvised.

On the basis of the intelligence the effort of Fighter Command during the last few days of March and the first three days of April was concentrated on the railways Leiden/Woerden, Hague/Gouda, Amsterdam/Hilversum and Amsterdam/Utrecht. Special attention was paid to a bridge at Elinwijk, which carried the Utrecht/Woerden railway over the Merwede Canal and to a junction of tracks on the line Woerden/Brendijk. Repair work was vigorous at both places, and although many hits were scored, photographs taken on 2 April, when the offensive was almost over, indicated that the lines were still serviceable.

Throughout this period 2nd Tactical Air Force was operating farther to the west in support of the advance across the Rhine and also scored many hits on railway communications. Again, the damage that was caused would not make the Nazis' task in bringing up rockets for firing any easier; but to what extent the rate of fire was affected by these attacks, as by those of Fighter Command, is still not known.

After the abnormally low scale of attack during the week 10 to 16 March, when fifty rockets had fallen in the UK, there was a slight recovery: between 17 to 23 March sixty-two rockets were reported. 24 March was a day free of incident. On the 25th, 26th and 27th, seven, nine and two rockets fell, the last at 16:45hrs on the 27th in Kynaston Road, Orpington, making it the 1,115th rocket to be reported in the UK. And that was the end.

All of this is incontrovertible evidence of the success of dive-bombing Spitfire attacks on Big Ben targets. It shows clearly the level of accuracy in knocking out major sites and ostensibly the decrease in successful offensive rocket launches against London. It also shows that Spitfires were the only aircraft suitable for the delicate operations; bombers had taken civilian lives and their use was quickly stopped.

It can obviously be argued that V2 rockets still murdered British civilians, but how many more would have been killed if Operation Big Ben had never taken place? It is obvious from the amount of successful hits on UK that missile manufacture was quick and the Nazis aware of the small opportunities open to them in successfully firing them (mainly during the night), but it is not right to state that the horror of the V2s was only quashed when ground troops went in – confirmed to be quashed maybe.

The pilots of Operation Big Ben – most named in the Annexes of this book – saved the lives of many people in London because of their skill, bravery and tenacity. It is a shame therefore, that their achievements have been largely forgotten until now – the 60th anniversary of the mission.

NOTES

1   All quotes and personal perceptions presented in this chapter were sourced from this official document.
2   All of this, as we have seen in the previous chapter, was carried out to the letter.
3   Dive-bombing sorties were mostly flown by Spitfire XVI aircraft; occasionally the Spitfire XIV and standard bombing in the early stages of the operation by Spitfire IXs. Each type usually carried two 250 lb bombs in wing racks and a jettisonable petrol tank under the fuselage to increase its range. This bomb load was eventually increased on occasion by one 500 lb bomb when arrangements were made for aircraft operating from the United Kingdom to re-fuel in Belgium.
4   Baxter explained after consulting his log book that he did actually attack a train.
5   Entries for 13, 14 and 15, 16 December in Operations Record Book of 602 Squadron explain that weather conditions were so poor ('thick mist and rain') that the Spitfires remained on the ground.
6   This was where it was assumed incorrectly that Spitfires dive-bombed at night; as Raymond Baxter also confirmed to me: 'We never dive-bombed at night. Total waste of time. Extremely dangerous. It was a close formation exercise and we bombed in sections of four.' However, it must be observed – see Appendix D – that 603 Squadron did do some, albeit very little, night flying training.
7   This is clearly demonstrated in the Squadron Histories (especially when Spitfires pull away from emergency vehicles or anything that appears to include civilians).
8   Anytime they did, it was almost exclusively Sqn/Ldr Sutherland leading.
9   The details of how a public warning system worked are as follows: Number of incidents in the UK: 243, Number of incidents in London: 123, Warnings Given: 228, False Warnings: 8, Incidents in London without warning: 3.
10 Leiden main station was flanked on one side by a hospital and on the other by houses.

CHAPTER VI

Where was the Luftwaffe?

The question the German anti-aircraft crews, troops and scientists working on the V1 and V2 rocket programmes might well have asked was: where is the Luftwaffe?

As Spitfire squadrons dive-bombed targets throughout Holland, the once mighty German air force was nowhere to be seen. By the end of 1944 and beginning of 1945 what was left of the Luftwaffe was defending Germany any way it could but, even then, the dog fights of a year before were few and far between.

Unlike the British, the Germans did not rotate their pilots by moving entire squadrons away from the fighting for a rest and rehabilitation. Instead, the German pilots remained fighting and dying. It was not uncommon for experienced pilots to rack up scores of more than 100 kills. Several pilots reached scores of more than 200 before they were shot down and two German aces shot down more than 300 enemy aircraft before they in turn were shot down.

The Germans had excellent fighters in the nimble ME109 and the mighty FW190, which was highly manoeuverable, fast and well-armed. But there weren't enough of the FW190 to make a difference. However, the world's first operational combat jet fighter, the ME262, could have made a big difference. As the daylight bombing raids of 1943 increased, the fast swept-wing jets could have stemmed the tide of the bombing, being virtually impossible for bomber crews to shoot down. But Hitler declared the Luftwaffe should be an offensive not a defensive weapon and ordered the production of bombers to take precedence over fighters.

The magnificent ME262 began its career as a bomber along with the FW190 and other fighter aircraft. The Luftwaffe's bomber fleet tried in vain to stem the growing tide of Allied air supremacy in 1943. At night, ME110, JU88s, ME210s, ME410s and Heinkle fast twin-engined fighters inflicted heavy losses on British Lancasters and Halifaxes flying deep missions into Germany. The technical edge see-sawed back and forth with each side outdoing the other in the night skies over Germany.

The Germans created an intricate system of ground radar to identify the British bombers at night, which for a time gave the Germans the edge.

Then the British created Windows, long strips of aluminum foil released in bundles by the bombers as they passed through German air space that completely confused German radar operators. Airborne radar on German and British aircraft became more and more sophisticated. To counter Windows the Germans flew Wild Boar fighters, fitted with radar over the target to intercept bombers as they came across.

On both sides losses were heavy. But as the Germans lost each pilot they lost his experience and knowledge. Rather than move their most experienced pilots to training schools they kept them in the front line. Much of the experience of aerial combat went down with these pilots so the newly trained pilots coming into the battle had no idea what to expect and didn't last long.

But Hitler's decree of keeping the Luftwaffe as an offensive tool only gradually began to change as the Germans were forced to defend their skies on the Western Front against the daylight bombing missions by the Americans. At first, in 1943 the bombers would come in alone over Germany, their fighter escort unable to fly that far. That's when the Germans would strike, inflicting appalling losses on American bomber crews. But with the introduction of the magnificent P51B Mustang and American airframe with the British Rolls Royce Merlin engine, that situation changed. The Mustang was able to escort the bombers all the way to Germany with drop tanks under the wings and challenge the German fighters. The P47 Thunderbolt and P38 Lightning fighters joined the Mustang all with long-range capability. These fighters took air supremacy over Germany away from the Luftwaffe, and often they would fly ahead of the bomber stream seeking out the defenders and destroying them before they could get to the bombers.

Only the ME262 could have countered this threat but Hitler remained adamant that it must be used as a bomber. By the time it was released as a fighter it was too little too late.

Another major factor that kept the Luftwaffe away from the British dive-bombing Spitfires was fuel. The round the clock bombing of Germany was slowly destroying Germany's oil industry and its ability to provide fuel for the Luftwaffe. Consequently, there were entire squadrons that remained on the ground for days waiting for a fuel delivery whilst the Allied bombers droned overhead.

Again, had Hitler used the ME262 jet fighter to its full advantage, the fuel crisis would not have affected the jet as much as it did the rest of the airforce. Unlike the Luftwaffe's piston-engined fighters, such as the ME109 and FW190 that needed scarce high octane fuel, the ME262 flew on low octane fuel which was easier to come by. If Hitler had had the foresight to make the ME262 his main fighter force in 1943 the outcome of the air battles over Germany could have been very different.

On top of fighting on the Western front the Luftwaffe was also fighting a losing battle against the Russians where their losses were appalling. They could easily match the losses in aircraft but not in pilots and that was the crux of the problem. By the end of the war the Luftwaffe had lost 62,500 aircraft and crew and they had shot down some 70,000 aircraft.

As Operation Big Ben got underway it is no surprise that the poor German troops, gunners, scientists and even civilians must have cursed the absent Luftwaffe, wondering where they were and why they weren't there to shoot down the 'Tommies'. But by the end of 1944 and early 1945 the Luftwaffe was incapable of shooting down any Allied aircraft as they had done only a year before. They had no pilots, no fuel and they had lost air supremacy over Europe. Essentially, a series of bad decisions made by Hitler and Goering, coupled with the relentless bombing of Germany's oil and aircraft production capability, the lack of trained pilots and the crippling losses over Germany spelled the end for the Luftwaffe.

Though they fought for a cause that the rest of the world viewed as evil and morally bankrupt, the quality of the Luftwaffe and its pilots cannot be in doubt.

CHAPTER VII

The Men Who Flew

'He, he. Well it was all good clean fun!'

Raymond Baxter, 602 City of Glasgow Squadron

The one thing we were keen to do when writing this book was to document the men who flew the Spitfires during Operation Big Ben. Not just their achievements but their own characters.

When one reads through the Squadron Histories, one is presented with names on a piece of paper and the basic facts of a story. Indeed, all that is there for posterity in simple black and white; but what about the colour: what did those men look like, what were they passionate about – what made those men tick?

If we are to document duty, then we owe it to the pilots who flew an opportunity to show something of themselves.

The only way we could get under the skin of a Big Ben squadron was to interview one of the men who flew in it and ask him about his colleagues.

It was in February 2004 that ex-F/Lt Raymond Baxter (602 City of Glasgow Squadron) granted some quality time for the preparation of this book, to put flesh back on the bones of the men he flew with:[1]

You became the F/Lt of 602 City of Glasgow Squadron did you not?
'I took over A flight from Dickie Pertwee and became a F/Lt. Jack Ames was my No. 2.'

There is a famous incident where one of your squadron actually shot at a V2, what was your reaction to this?
'Cupid Love. He shot at a V2. Probably the first man to ever shoot at a ballistic missile from close range. We were amazed.'

Polish pilots took part in Big Ben, can you tell us about any of them?
'F/Lt Wroblewski, or as we called him: Double Whisky. A hell of a nice guy. He would sculpt the most beautiful little heads out of the top of a piece of chalk. So detailed.

'Both on the ground and in the air the Polish were full of passion. I was very passionate. But the best story of Polish passion was told to me by Michael Bentine – who was a great friend of mine – he was an intelligence officer to a Polish squadron of Wellingtons. And the adjutant came over and said "we have a problem with these guys and their air stands". And what was found was when they had dropped their bombs they would then throw the toilet out afterwards.'

In fact you were a mixed bag. You had Canadians too?
'Royal Canadian Air Force, yes. Flying Officer Jimmy Farrell. Jimmy-Farrell-the-human-barrel, from-Jersey-City-New-Jersey. That was his nickname. Then there was Parfan. He was from somewhere like Bermuda and he became the boss of Caribbean Airlines.'

What about the British?
'Fearless. He got killed. Yes, Fearless Pullman had an airforce moustache and accent.'

You had nicknames for each other. What other terminology did you use?
'The Germans originally released their V2s from a suburb in The Hague – the corner of a street – but they gave that up. I knew that part of Holland like the back of my hand. We studied the maps very carefully, and actually, one target, the oxygen plant, we called the "Winegar Works".'

Tell me about Max Sutherland, as you seem to remember him with great fondness.
'Max Sutherland was the most dangerous man I've ever known. And I loved him. Actually we thought he was a lunatic – quite literally – he went barmy when the moon was full. And when I say barmy I mean even more fearless than normal. He was a great leader.

'He was extremely aggressive. He was 27 and we thought that it was amazing that an old guy of 27 could fly as good as him – seriously, because we were all in our early 20s.

'He was very imaginative too. He put red pepper on his Guinness. He ate flowers. He would see a bowl of tulips in a pub and eat them. So that was him.

'Then there was Cupid Love. He was a little Scotsman. He said that on one occasion he was taxiing his Spitfire and the tower radioed through and said that there was a Spitfire taxiing about without a pilot in it. But he was in it!'

You remember them with great fondness.
'They were a great bunch and we were a very tight team . . .
'VE Day was amazing for us. We went down to the local pub and we

went in our uniforms. These old guys stood up and declared, "these are boys that done it." And they picked the boss and me up and put us on their shoulders and into the pub we went. Unfortunately, the ceiling in the pub was very low and we were nearly brained. I don't remember much after that!

'The significance of VE Day was just out of this world. But shortly afterwards 602 Squadron was disbanded (19 May 1945). *Shame.* We were furious. And they sent ATA girls to take away our aeroplanes and we were so pissed and angry, we didn't even make a pass at them. They were lovely ladies too.'

NOTES

1   To get a very frank and realistic picture of the men who flew and their characters I have transcribed my interview segment with Baxter regarding his colleagues question/answer style, so the nuances of his words can be appreciated by the reader.

Afterword

Those Magnificent Men

'Operation Big Ben was one of the most demanding, probably *the* most demanding operations I took part in.'

F/Lt Raymond Baxter (interviewed February 2004
concerning his role in Operation Big Ben)

Operation Big Ben was a highly dangerous but successful mission, involving many pilots and aircraft. Some pilots were decorated and promoted largely in recognition of their courage and determination whilst completing Big Ben missions.

Pilots endured horrendous weather conditions, which severely restricted the number of sorties Spitfires could execute. As we have seen, the efforts made by the Spitfire squadrons *were very* successful despite the weather restrictions.

Inevitably, some Big Ben pilots were lost, but their contribution has been highlighted in this book, and it is to them most of all that we dedicate this work.

Today, aerial warfare is conducted from a distance. Technology has advanced so much over the past sixty years, due in part to the work of the captured Nazi scientists who had worked on V1 and V2 rockets (information concerning this falls under the generic heading 'Operation Paperclip'). We will never see a war like the Second World War again. It has its place in 20th Century history. However, it is important at the beginning of the new millennium to publish works that highlight the courage and determination of the Allied world and include as much first-hand information from the veterans as possible. At last, Operation Big Ben has been presented in such a way.

Appendix A

303 Polish Squadron History

A faithful record of 303 Polish Squadron has been included as an appendix to this book to showcase the Squadron's contribution to Operation Big Ben and its tireless dedication to the liberation of their own people.

The Polish would throw anything including the kitchen sink at the Germans, the reason simply being that their country was occupied territory and they were freedom fighters. In short, they were fighting for their loved ones back home.

What follows are the details of the passionate Polish.[1]

(For the most part, F/O J A Nicholls, the Intelligence Officer of 303 Polish Squadron, wrote the facts and details outlined in the Squadron History. They have been edited for clarification purposes by the authors.)

4 December 1944

December 1944 began with a splutter for 303 Squadron. The first few days flying was kept to a minimum by bad weather. Aside from some practice flying no operational flights took place until the 4th when F/Lt Socha led a section of Spitfire IXFs on an armed recce over Holland. They took off at first light (08:20hrs) and climbed to 10,000 feet. They crossed over land at Egmond and spotted their primary targets in the Wassenaar area. Dropping to 5,000 feet, the Spitfires dived on the target strafing it with cannon and machine-gun fire. Socha climbed quickly away as his shells hammered into buildings, he released his drop tanks and followed by the other three Spitfires climbed the section back up to 10,000 feet. Moments later, he reported seeing a Big Ben contrail at 15,000 feet, three miles north-east of The Hague. The object was thick and shorter than the drawings he had seen. Slowly rising into the sky he watched the rocket gain height; he lost sight of it at approximately 40,000 feet. This time he'd actually seen the thing and not just the contrail. Although the ground was obscured by cloud he reported that the firing point must have been somewhere near The Hague. The patrol landed back at base at 10:20hrs.

Ten minutes later, another section, led by F/Lt Malarowski, lifted off the runway at Coltishall. The drop tanks under the wings had been re-fuelled and the aircraft climbed to 10,000 feet, heading for Holland. The four Spitfires crossed land at Westhoofd and turned north to Egmond then turned again towards The Hague area where they pinpointed their targets. Dropping down to 4,000 feet Malarowski ordered the section to go into line astern formation. Jettisoning their fuel tanks the four fighters roared down on their targets, strafing buildings with cannon and machine-gun fire. Climbing rapidly away Malarowski turned the section towards the North Sea and headed for home. They landed back at Coltishall at 12:35hrs. Another armed recce took place that day, this time led by P/O Maksymowicz, but it was uneventful and clouds obscured the targets.

5 December 1944

In the early morning light, four Spitfire engines roared into life as ground crew strapped the pilots into the cockpits. Quickly going over their pre-flight checks the pilots one by one waved away the ground crew, opened the throttles and taxied out of dispersal towards the runway. At 09:00hrs the four fighters lifted off into the morning sky, F/O Szpakowicz leading. They crossed the North Sea at 10,000 feet, making landfall at Egmond then Szpakowicz turned the section south, orbiting The Hague area until spotting the target at Wassenaar/Rust-en-Vreugt. Dropping their underwing fuel tanks, the Spitfires moved into their diving positions and tore down on the targets raking them with cannon shells. Levelling out at 2,000 feet, Szpakowicz pulled the control column back hard, pulling the Spitfire into a steep climb to avoid light but accurate flak now coming up from the ground. Glancing into his mirror he saw the remaining three Spitfires coming up rapidly behind him. At 7,000 feet the flak was out of range and the section turned towards home. They landed at 11:00hrs.

While Szpakowicz's section was attacking its targets two more Spitfires were scrambled on an Air-Sea Rescue (ASR) search for a Mosquito. One Spitfire had problems, having engine failure on the runway, another Spitfire managed to get airborne at 11:15hrs. Steering 100 degrees then 140 degrees to meet up with a group of Mosquitoes already searching for downed aircraft, but made no contact and was recalled to base by Control.

This was a busy day for 303 Squadron as they made the most of the good visibility. F/Lt Szalestowski led a section of Spitfires on another armed recce mission. The four fighters left the runway at 12:30hrs and climbed to 10,000 feet. Half an hour later they were orbiting The Hague. At this point, Szalestowski dropped his tanks and dropped down to 7,000 feet while the rest of the section remained above him. Then peeling into a dive he tore down on the target strafing it with cannon and machine-gun fire. Seeing bits fly off the buildings and vehicles in the target area, he levelled out of his dive at 10,000 feet and climbed quickly away, forming up with the Squadron minutes later. The section continued their patrol and spotted four ships at Rotterdam. One ship of approximately 400 to 500 tons was seen stationary in the harbour. Another larger ship was also spotted in the same area. The pilots believed the ships to be flak ships. The patrol touched down on the runway at Coltishall at 14:35hrs.

Twenty-five minutes later, F/Lt Kedzierski led another armed recce over Holland and the Spitfires attacked targets in The Hague area before landing back at base at 16:45hrs. It had been a long day for the pilots of 303 Squadron.

6 December 1945

The first patrol spotted a Big Ben contrail that appeared to come from The Hague area. F/O Maksymowicz took off at 09:30hrs with three other Spitfires in tow. Climbing to 10,000 feet they crossed land at Egmond and headed for The Hague. Moving into a line astern formation, the four Spitfires dropped their fuel tanks and dived down on their targets near Wassenaar using machine-gun and cannon fire. Climbing to 8,000 feet Maksymowicz suddenly spotted the contrail high above him. Sure it was the contrail left by a rising V2, he reported the sighting. He'd seen it at approximately 30,000 feet but lost sight of it a few moments later. The section returned to base and touched down at 11:25hrs.

At noon the same day F/Lt Malarowski led another armed recce over Holland. Strafing their targets the four Spitfires ran into heavy and accurate flak over the Hook as they headed for home. Fortunately, the cloud base was at 2,000 feet and none of the aircraft were hit as they flew into the cloud. They emerged from the cloud at 10,000 feet and headed for home.

7 December 1945

The following morning, Maksymowicz's section had great success over Rotterdam. The four Spitfires took off at 08:20hrs, heading for Holland in good visibility. Crossing at Egmond several minutes after being airborne Maksymowicz spotted a train with two covered wagons leaving Rotterdam. This was too good to miss. Calling his section to a line astern formation he ordered them to jettison their drop tanks. Peeling off, the four fighters dropped to 4,000 feet then one by one dived on the unfortunate train, hammering it with cannon fire. Each pilot watched his shells hit the trucks and locomotive as the aircraft strafed the train one after the other.

As he climbed away, Maksymowicz circled, watching the rest of his section dive on the train, their shells hitting the target. Steam and flame poured from the locomotive now stopped dead on the tracks. They landed back at base at 10:14hrs.

8 December 1945

The Squadron was only able to launch one armed recce patrol led by F/Lt Socha. Taking off just after first light at 08:12hrs they headed towards The Hague but were unable to find the target due to thick cloud that started at 2,000 feet and ended at 12,000 feet. Bad weather stopped any more operational flying that day.

9 December 1945

Squadron formation flying was carried out on the 9th and would have been uneventful but for F/Lt Kedzierski who made a heavy three-point landing near the perimeter of the airfield. His aircraft jumped slightly then rolled forward then turned sharply to the right. At that moment, his starboard undercarriage leg collapsed and the aircraft spun to the left damaging the propeller and the main plane. As Kedzierski climbed out of the cockpit he saw that his starboard tyre was caught in a deep track that accounted for the violent stop.

10 December 1944

Both armed recce flights launched from Coltishall on the 10th were unable to pinpoint their targets in The Hague area because of thick cloud cover. The base was as low as 2,000 feet making any form of attack very difficult. The late morning patrol, led by F/Lt Szalestowski, had some excitement when two aircraft of the section of four reported engine and drop tank trouble. Over Rotterdam, Glencoe 19 and 29 reported their technical problems announcing they needed to land quickly. The two good Spitfires escorted their colleagues to Ghent where the stricken fighters were able to land safely. The rest of the section crossed over the sea at Ostend and headed home.

11 December 1944

One patrol managed to get airborne on 11 December. F/Lt Malarowski led a section of Spitfires towards The Hague area. Taking off at 14:15hrs they climbed to 10,000 feet and crossed land at Westhoofd. Pinpointing their targets over the Wassenaar area, Malarowski led the section in on their attack run, strafing the buildings and vehicles in the area. Flak burst all around him and he could see the tracer shooting up from the ground as his Spitfire dived. The fighter rocked as the flak burst around him. Pulling out of his dive at 2,000 feet he climbed rapidly towards The Hague area, and the rest of the section formed up behind him. Climbing rapidly away they headed for base but over the Hook heavy, intense flak rose up to meet them. This was much greater than the flak over The Hague. Red balls burst all around them. They climbed to 12,000 feet, finally leaving the deadly anti-aircraft out of range. They landed back at base at 15:45hrs.

12 December 1945

Two Spitfires took off from Coltishall at 08:15hrs on a weather reconnaissance mission. Led by P/O Martens they crossed land at Egmond and headed towards The Hague. Cloud base here was as low as 3,000 feet and the tops 13,000 feet. They landed back at 10:25hrs.

Flying was scrubbed for the next five days due to bad weather and poor visibility. Some practice flying was done but no operational flying took place.

18 December 1944

Four Spitfires left Coltishall at 11:00hrs on an armed recce. They crossed in at Westhoofd flying at 10,000 feet and headed up towards The Hague but the mission was aborted and they turned back for home. Thick cloud cover over the target made attack impossible.

Later in the afternoon, S/Ldr Drobinski led a section on an armed recce. Four Spitfires leapt into the air from Coltishall at 15:00hrs and climbed to cruising altitude. In formation they crossed land at Ijmuden and turned north to The Hague but were unable to see the primary target because of thick ground mist. Heading towards The Hague/Voorde area Drobinski spotted the secondary targets and attacked but they saw no results. They ended their patrol by heading out over the Hook towards home. The four Spitfires landed at 16:50hrs.

Thick fog and other adverse weather conditions ensured no aircraft from 303 Squadron would be flying operationally or on training for the next few days.

23 December 1944

The morning of 23 December, four Spitfires roared into the air at 10:35hrs on a search and rescue mission for survivors of a downed Heinkel bomber. For nearly two hours the aircraft searched but nothing was found. The Spitfires landed back at Coltishall at 12:15hrs.

F/Lt Socha led the armed recce mission that afternoon with a section of four Spitfires taking off at 15:00hrs. They climbed to their usual altitude of 10,000 feet and crossed land at Westhoofd then turned north towards The

Hague. Socha spotted the targets in the Wassenaar area and, unable to drop his extra fuel tank, he detailed two Spitfires to attack with cannon and machine-gun fire. Two aircraft peeled away from the section, dropped into their dives and strafed buildings, sheds and warehouses in one pass, then quickly climbed back up to the section. Visibility was fifteen miles. As they ended their patrol they spotted a large grey merchant ship stationary near Maassluis. They landed back at Coltishall at 16:45hrs.

24 December 1944

The first patrol of the day started at 08:20hrs when four Spitfires led by F/Lt Szpakowicz took off and headed towards the continent. Over Wassenaar they strafed and attacked their targets but saw no results and headed back home.

Later that morning, two Spitfires, led by F/Lt Bartys, took off from base in the company of a Mustang at 10:05hrs. They were to escort the Mustang that would be photographing bombing results in The Hague/Manlot area. Over the target area, the Mustang flew at 6,000 feet. 303 Squadron's intelligence officer related that the bombing appeared to be well concentrated. But over the target the aircraft experienced R/T interference and at the same time ran into light but intense and accurate flak. They managed to get back to base at 12:20hrs. More targets in The Hague area were strafed during the patrol that afternoon but no results were seen.

28 December 1944

For the next three days fog kept 303 Squadron firmly on the ground. Then on 28 December, shortly after first light, four Spitfires took off from Coltishall heading towards Holland. Led by F/Lt Rzyski, the fighters crossed land at Den Helder and roared south towards Ijmuden. Spotting a train with three wagons moving south-east, Rzyski rolled his aircraft into a dive, flicked the firing button and waited as his height wound down. Behind him, he knew the other three Spitfires were doing the same. Levelling out he pressed the firing button and watched his shells rake the trucks and locomotive. Then, before the flak could open up, he pulled the stick back and the Spitfire shot into a steep climb. Turning quickly, he looked down at the scene below as the other Spitfires attacked. Flame and steam belched from the locomotive that was now stationary. Satisfied, they formed up and continued the patrol. Crossing over water at Westhoofd the four Spitfires landed back at Coltishall at 10:50hrs.

Before Rzyski and his section landed, S/Ldr Drobinski took off at 10:30hrs with three other Spitfires behind him. He led the section in at Westhoofd flying at 10,000 feet before heading towards their primary target at The Hague/Langenhorst. Wheeling the section around Drobinski dropped into a dive strafing buildings and sheds at 2,000 feet. He could see shells hitting the walls and smashing windows as he shot over the targets. Behind him the rest of the section laid down a hail of shells before climbing away to join up with their leader and head for home. Over The Hague, as they roared for home, heavy intense and accurate flak burst all around them. The fighters were rocked and buffeted by the blasts and they managed to climb above it. They landed back at Coltishall at 12:15hrs.

Two Spitfires from 303 Squadron were detailed to escort a Mustang on a photographic mission over The Hague. While the Mustang flew at 5,000 feet busy photographing, the two Spitfires stayed high at 9,000 feet.

At 13:30hrs F/Lt Maksymowicz took off from base with three other Spitfires on an armed recce over The Hague. They crossed land at Westhoofd and turned towards The Hague. Over The Hague the section split into two with one strafing the Hotel Promenade. The two Spitfires roared down on the buildings and other general posts belching tracer from their machine guns and cannon. The other two aircraft attacked a locomotive moving east. They swarmed over the target, shells hammering into the locomotive. Within minutes it was disabled, belching steam and smoke. The two sections formed up, under heavy, accurate flak and began the quick dash at full throttle out to sea towards home and safety.

31 December 1944

For the next two days the squadron was idle as bad weather kept them on the ground. But on 31 December two Spitfires were detailed to escort a Mustang on photographic duty over The Hague. For a short while the Spitfires lost contact with the Mustang but they all breathed a sigh of relief when they picked it up again just over the Hook on its way home.

In the month of December 1944, 303 Squadron flew 237 hours of operational flying by day. They flew thirty-five hours of training on the Spitfire IXFs and twenty-two hours on Spitfire Vbs.

1 January 1945

For 303 Squadron the New Year began with a bang. On New Year's Day, S/Ldr Drobinski led a section of twelve Spitfire IXFs on a raid over Holland. But unlike other missions of the previous month, this time the fighters carried something different: bombs. They flew into the sky at 12:45hrs and Drobinksi climbed to 10,000 feet. They crossed land over Katylik then turned south to The Hague. It was here that they pinpointed their targets. Peeling off into their bombing runs, Drobinski led the rest of the squadron in from north to south. As he did so, flak began shooting up at the aircraft. Taking evasive action he kept the target in sight as it rapidly loomed in his sights. He glanced at the altimeter watching the needle wind quickly down as his height dropped away. His thumb hit the firing button and the two bombs under his wings dropped from their moorings. He pulled back on the control column and the lightened fighters quickly responded. Below, he could see his bombs had hit the target. As the flak burst around him, Drobinski climbed and circled watching the rest of the Squadron. In all, ten direct hits were made on the target. The runway was hit, and several buildings in the target area exploded into flames. One strike hit a building that erupted in a huge explosion. Cloud cover was 6,000–10,000 feet as the rest of the Squadron formed up on Drobinski and climbed away out of the sight of the flak-gunners below. They landed back at Coltishall at 16:40hrs.

But S/Pt Bisanz made a rough landing on the return. Coming in with a second formation of four Spitfires he hit the ground hard, tearing off his tail wheel. His aircraft came to a sudden stop after some heavy bumping resulting in extensive damage to the tail unit. His aircraft was Spitfire IXF MA 763.

Though the first day of the New Year began well the next two days brought 303 to a standstill as poor weather kept the Spitfires on the ground. But on 4 January 1945 they took to the air once again.

4 January 1945

The first operational flight of the day was an armed recce with F/Lt Malarowski leading three other Spitfires. The four fighters took off at 11:25hrs from Coltishall and climbed to 10,000 feet. Visibility at the time was only five miles with the cloud base around 1,500 feet and the tops as high as 15,000 feet. The four Spitfires crossed land over Egmond and headed south towards The Hague. These aircraft carried no bombs so strafing was the order of the day. Pin-pointing their target they dropped in line astern on the buildings beneath them and sprayed the area with cannon and machine-gun fire, but flying in only one pass they didn't see any strikes and climbed rapidly away. Two aircraft landed at Brecles airfield to re-fuel and returned to base. The remaining two Spitfires continued on their patrol and Malarowski quickly contacted Control, reporting a Big Ben contrail rising rapidly. He'd seen it at 8,000 feet and watched it climb into the sky and lost sight of it around 20,000 feet. The two Spitfires were north-east of The Hague. Moments later as they turned back towards base, they spotted another Big Ben contrail. Both these sightings seemed to come from The Hague area. They landed back at base at 13:25hrs.

A little more than an hour later four more Spitfires put their noses into the air and lifted off from Coltishall on another armed recce. F/Lt

Salestowksi led the section climbing hard to 12,000 feet. They crossed into Holland over Westhoofd then turned north to The Hague. The target was in The Hague/Haagsche Bosch area. Seeing the target Salestowksi led the other Spitfires strafing the target area. They climbed away without seeing any hits at all. They spotted a Big Ben contrail (first seen at approximately 7,000 feet) fifty to sixty miles east of Leiden. Salestowski reported it in, losing sight of it around 35,000 feet. The time was 15:31hrs when Salestowski reported the sighting and the aircraft were flying at 10,000 feet. Five minutes later Salestowski was excitedly reporting back to Control as another Big Ben shot up into the sky. This time, they could see the actual rocket itself. Describing it as short and thick in shape he'd caught sight of it around 3,000 to 4,000 feet and the two pilots watched it rise at great speed into the sky until they lost sight of it at 25,000 feet. These sightings had also come from The Hague area. Visibility for this mission was good over the target. They landed back at Coltishall at 16:30hrs.

5 January 1945

Shortly after dawn, 303's first armed recce of the day took to the skies at 08:45hrs. Led by F/Lt Szbikowicz they headed for Holland. Crossing land at Westhoofd the four fighters turned south to Egmond following the coastline towards The Hague. In The Hague/Huis (Werve area) they strafed their target, raking it with machine-gun and cannon fire but observed no hits as they pulled out of their dives into tight climbing turns. The flak was light but accurate so they quickly climbed above it. They had been in the air for forty-two minutes when Szbikowicz reported seeing a Big Ben contrail rising out of the Litrees area and they lost sight of it at approximately 20,000 feet. The cloud base was 4,000 feet and the tops 5,000 feet. The visibility over Holland for that patrol was ten miles.

Malarowski was up again in the early afternoon leading three Spitfires on an armed recce. They took off from Coltishall at 13:40hrs and headed for The Hague area. But this patrol would prove to be uneventful. Even though they strafed their target, coming out of their shallow dives at 600 feet and spraying cannon and machine-gun shells all over the target, none of the pilots reported seeing any hits on the target as they roared overhead and climbed quickly away. They saw no Big Ben contrails that day and returned to base at 14:30hrs, frustrated and ready for tea.

For nearly ten days adverse weather kept 303 Squadron's pilots grounded. Only on 7 January did they manage a weather recce but it was aborted three quarters of the way to the Dutch coast because of poor visibility.

14 January 1945

It was the 14th when the weather cleared enough to fly. At 13:55hrs four Spitfires, with F/Lt Rzyski leading, took off from Coltishall and headed for the Dutch coast. Climbing to 11,000 feet they crossed land at Westhoofd and turned towards The Hague area where the targets were. Once identified the Spitfires dropped to 5,000 feet. Peeling off, Rzyski led the formation in a line attack on targets in a wooded area near The Hague. Strikes were seen from their cannon and machine-gun fire as they climbed away. Heading for home, Rzyski reported sighting a Big Ben contrail. It was seen approximately sixty miles east of The Hague at 10,000 feet rising rapidly. Within seconds it was lost in the clouds. Rzyski turned his patrol towards the sea and headed for home. The four Spitfires touched down again at Coltishall at 15:40hrs.

17 January 1945

Poor weather stopped flying for the next two days. But on the 17th the weather had cleared enough for five Spitfires, led by F/Lt Socha, to roar off the runway and head towards Holland. Their objective was to attack targets in the Hook/Staalduine Bosch area. Socha aborted the mission because of adverse weather conditions. (The armed recce left the base at 08:30hrs.)

The next armed recce launched by Coltishall fared a little better. It was Malarowski again leading a section of Spitfires on an armed recce to attack targets in The Hague/Laneibwerst area. Four Spitfires raced down the runway at Coltishall and climbed into the morning sky. It was 11:00hrs and they pointed their noses towards Europe. Malarowski climbed the section to 10,000 feet where they levelled out. They crossed at Egmond then turned south to The Hague and then north. They flew above the tops of the clouds. The cloud base itself was at 2,000 feet with visibility at ten miles. Unfortunately for Malarowski and the three other Spitfires the weather obscured the targets below and he had to abort the mission. Turning back, there was a sudden shout over the R/T as someone had spotted a V2 contrail rising quickly. Estimated to have come from nearly forty miles inland of The Hague the rocket shot high into the morning sky and they quickly lost sight of it. Malarowski radioed Control as the four fighters left the continent behind them and roared over the North Sea towards home. They landed safely back at Coltishall at 12:45hrs.

Twenty minutes after Malarowski's section took off, two more Spitfires, with F/Lt Frainkiewicz leading, left the base and climbed rapidly away towards the sea. The time was 11:20hrs. At Den Helder they saw an 'N' class minesweeper with no steam up. The two Spitfires dropped down to 4,000 feet as they searched for their targets. This was an armed recce so the two Spitfires searched for something to shoot up. Twenty miles off the English coast they spotted a V2 contrail shooting up into the sky. They lost sight of it between 15,000 and 20,000 feet. They were back at Coltishall by 13:05hrs.

The last armed recce of the day was led by F/Lt Maksymowicz. They climbed rapidly away from Coltishall at 15:30hrs and crossed into enemy air space over Egmond. They then turned towards the Hook of Holland/Staalduine Bosch area, where they sighted their targets. Raking the buildings and vehicles with cannon and machine-gun fire, the four Spitfires one by one pulled out of their dives at approximately 1,000 feet. Intense flak coming from the south-west of the target burst all around them as they pulled rapidly away. Climbing above the anti-aircraft fire the four fighters turned for home; it was then that they sighted a V2 contrail in the distance. They touched down at Coltishall at 17:30hrs.

The following day the first and only sortie of the day was at 09:40hrs (armed recce). Four Spitfires roared off the runway heading for Holland again. But they were back in little more than an hour, the mission scrubbed because of bad weather.

20 January 1945

The day was a little better than the previous one, when bad weather had kept the Squadron grounded. The first flight of the day climbed into the morning sky at 08:20hrs heading once again for Holland. Their mission was to attack targets in The Hague/Roogsche Bosch areas. Flying above the cloud tops at 14,000 feet, the Spitfires could not see their targets because of the thick cumulus cloud below them. But shooting out of the cloud cover they spotted a V2 contrail rising vertically. Checking the map reference, F/Lt Szrakswicz checked to find the firing point of the rocket. They concluded it had come from The Hague area. Over the target cloud tops were at 11,000 feet and the base at 3,000 feet with visibility just three miles. Realising the mission was scrubbed because the targets could not be identified let alone attacked, Szrakswicz turned the section for home, reporting the V2 sighting at he did. They landed back on terra firma at 09:50hrs.

For the rest of January 1945 there was no operational flying due to adverse weather conditions over the targets in Holland.

1 to 3 February 1945

February 1945 was an intense time for 303 Squadron, but for the first two days of the month the pilots were grounded by bad weather. The morning of 3 February however, two Spitfires took off from Coltishall at 09:45hrs. The leader of the two aircraft was F/Lt Bartes. They were to escort two

Mustangs for photographing V2 sites at The Hague. They made contact with one Mustang and headed for Holland; contact with the other Mustang was lost. While the two Mustangs went in over The Hague taking photographs, the Spitfire patrolled five miles away waiting for the other fighters to return. Suddenly, Bartes radioed his wingman. His engine was running rough. He would have to land. Turning away from The Hague, Bartes made an emergency landing at Ghent, an airfield in Allied hands. With the Mustangs back with the final Spitfire, the patrol received suspected false emergency vector 110 degrees from Kenway whilst at the Hook, which was challenged with a scramble code. Kenway replied, but he did not understand the message (a strange voice gave a vector of 250 degrees).

Turning on a course of 111 degrees half an hour later, the patrol sighted a V2 contrail rising high into the sky. It appeared to be coming from The Hague. Visibility on this sortie was between five and ten miles.

Later that morning, 303 pilots were detailed to escort a Halifax patrolling over the Dutch coast. Blue Section, four Spitfires led by F/Lt Franckiewicz, took off first at 11:50hrs. They contacted the big bomber as it made its way across the North Sea. Red Section, led by F/Lt Zdankowski, took off at 13:20hrs and made contact with the Halifax, while Green Section, led by S/Ldr Drobinski, took off from Coltishall at 14:50hrs to form up with the Halifax on the last leg of its patrol. While Blue and Red Sections patrolled with the Halifax they landed for re-fuelling at Ergel and then headed for home. Drobinski led his section along the southern point of the Halifax patrol line where they contacted the bomber and escorted it to Ostend. Before landing for re-fuelling, Franckiewicz reported seeing a V2 contrail at 13:12hrs coming from The Hague area. The Spitfires were flying between Antwerp and Nijmegen at 20,000 feet. Blue Section touched down at Coltishall at 17:20hrs, Red landed at 18:05hrs and Green Section landed back at base at 17:21hrs. The next two days, bad weather kept 303's pilots on the ground.

6 February 1945

F/Lt Malarowski was up with another Spitfire at 12:20hrs. Leading a section of two fighters, Malarowski's patrol was to escort two Mustangs to photograph V2 sites at The Hague. The Mustang pilots' task was to photograph the sites before and after bombing raids. The photographic mission was successful and Malarowski remained in constant contact with the two Mustangs all the way back to base. They touched down on the runway at 14:15hrs.

Later that afternoon, two Spitfires were scrambled to escort a Fortress in distress. They had been airborne for thirty-five minutes when they were recalled by Control. The fortress had landed safely.

8 February 1945

Just after first light F/Lt Socha's engine coughed, spluttered and roared into life. Moments later he was rolling down the runway and into the air leading three other Spitfires on an armed recce to V2 rocket sites in The Hague. Climbing to 10,000 feet they crossed over land at Westhoofd and turned north towards The Hague. Spotting their targets in a wooded area below, they prepared to dive. One by one the Spitfires jettisoned their fuel tanks; except Socha whose tank remained firmly stuck to his aircraft. Nevertheless he ordered the rest of the section to attack. Three Spitfires peeled off dropping down to 6,000 feet when they went into their strafing runs, raking the target with cannon and machine-gun fire. As each pilot attacked he could see shell strikes from their tracers in the woods. But the men did not wait around. Conscious of the danger of flak from the target they climbed quickly back up to 10,000 feet and rejoined their leader. At 09:00hrs Socha reported seeing a V2 contrail. The visibility on this flight was at five miles with a low cloud base of 3,000 feet. As the Spitfires returned to Coltishall the airfield was covered with thin mist. They landed at 09:50hrs.

Later, Socha was back in the air. Leading Green Section he took off with three other Spitfires at 12:10hrs. Before, at 11:30hrs, Blue Section with Malarowski leading, had taken off. The mission for these eight aircraft was to escort a Halifax on patrol. The patrol went according to plan with Green Section relieving Blue Section over Noorderhoofd at 20,000 feet. Malarowski reported seeing a V2 contrail twenty miles north-west of Noorderhoofd (which appeared to have been fired from The Hague area) shoot up into the sky. His section picked up the contrail at 6,000 feet but lost it at 30,000 feet as the rocket entered cloud. The visibility was ten to fifteen miles.

9 February 1945

The next day, 303 Squadron was up in force, four sections of Spitfires IXFs (a total of twelve aircraft), with staggered take off times, escorting a Halifax bomber patrolling over Holland. They saw no sign of any V2 rockets on that sortie but the flight was not without excitement. Red Three had to land at Antwerp with engine trouble, while Red One and Red Two landed at Ghent to re-fuel before returning to base. Blue section led by F/Lt Franckiewicz landed at Ursel in the middle of their patrol to re-fuel. The four Spitfire IXFs spent forty-five minutes on the ground and resumed patrolling with the Halifax at 15:45hrs. The first section to take off from Coltishall was Red Section at 11:45hrs, three Spitfires with F/Lt Szelstowski leading. They landed back at base at 17:35hrs. The next section was Blue Section who took off at 12:40hrs and returned at 18:30hrs.

Then F/Lt Malarowski, leading White Section (only two Spitfires), took off at 13:45hrs and returned at 16:35hrs. Green Section was the last to leave Coltishall at 14:40hrs. Its three Spitfires, with F/Lt Rzyski leading, climbed to the standard height of 20,000 feet to escort the Halifax over Holland. They returned at 17:20hrs.

10 February 1945

The morning's sortie was another escort mission that saw most of the Squadron in the air taking it in turns to accompany a Halifax bomber on patrol over Holland. This time three sections of two aircraft carried out the escorts. P/O Martens led Blue Section (the first to take off at 11:50hrs). Both aircraft landed at Ursel with engine trouble and did not complete their escort duties. Red Section left Coltishall at 12:50hrs but only one returned at 17:45hrs. Red Two suffered a damaged prop and had to land at Ursel, while Red One continued the patrol until recalled by the Controller. Green Section, led by F/Lt Bartkowiak, ran into R/T trouble and aborted the mission. They landed back at base at 15:15hrs. No one that morning saw enemy activity.

However, later in the day the story was a different one. Three Spitfire IXFs, with S/Ldr Drobinski leading, roared away from base at 14:00hrs and climbed rapidly to 10,000 feet on an armed recce. Their target was The Hague/Woorde area. Crossing over land at Westhoofd, the section turned north towards The Hague and began losing height. They flew in a loose formation rather than tight on each other's wing. This way they could cover each other in case they were bounced by enemy fighters or more importantly, if they were hit by flak. Pin-pointing the target, Drobinski brought the three fighters down to 6,000 feet, then wheeled over diving on the target strafing it with cannon and machine-gun fire. The Spitfires attacked from north-east to south-west, levelling out of their dives at 2,000 feet then quickly climbed away. That day the sky was clear and visibility was thirty miles. They landed back at base at 16:05hrs.

14 February 1945

Poor weather and very low visibility kept 303 Squadron on the ground until 14 February when twelve Spitfire IXFs, with S/Ldr Drobinski leading, took off from Coltishall (13:15hrs). Under their wings they carried two 250 lb bombs. Climbing rapidly to 11,000 feet, they crossed over land north of The Hague and turned towards their targets: several buildings in The Hague/Rust-en-Vreugd area. Over the target the cloud base was 9,000 feet and the tops around 12,000 feet. Drobinski could see the targets ahead and below and wheeled the squadron around into diving formation, losing altitude quickly. Drobinski led the squadron on their bombing runs from north to south. He pulled out of his dive at 3,000 feet, released his bombs and climbed rapidly away as flak opened up. Seconds later, his bombs hammered into the target area. As the rest of the aircraft attacked he counted nine more strikes in the area. Two buildings received direct hits and were left burning fiercely. One of the pilots still had a bomb hung up under his wing and Drobinski ordered him to jettison it at sea. The squadron landed at Ursel at 14:50hrs and took off at 16:00hrs heading for Coltishall where they landed at 17:05hrs.

15 February 1945

The only mission on this day was escort duties for 303 Squadron. Eight Spitfire IXFs in four sections of two took off at staggered intervals to escort the Halifax to the patrol line over Holland. The first was Red Section, led by F/Lt Zdanowski, who took off at 13:20hrs and 15:50hrs. Then thirty-five minutes later, Blue Section led by Sgt Janicki took off from Coltishall and arrived back at base at 16:20hrs. Yellow Section, with F/Lt Franckiewicz leading, climbed into the sky over Coltishall at 14:30hrs and were back at base at 17:00hrs. Finally, Black Section, with P/O Martens leading, were airborne at 15:15hrs and were back at base at 17:05hrs. Blue and Red Sections carried out their escort duties with the Halifax, but Black and Yellow Sections turned back early because of adverse weather conditions. It was on this sortie that Sgt Janicki leading Blue Section reported seeing a V2 contrail rising rapidly into the sky having come from somewhere in The Hague area.

For the next three days bad weather kept the Squadron on the ground.

19 February 1945

With good weather, escort duties were again on the cards. Four of 303 Squadron's pilots were soon airborne (in staggered take offs) to escort a Halifax while on patrol over Holland. Two Spitfires, with F/Lt Szpakowicz` leading, left the base at 12:45hrs and returned at 15:20hrs. F/Lt Bartys, leading Red Section, took off at 13:30hrs and the two fighters returned to base at 15:10hrs. Blue Section made contact with the Halifax as they climbed to 20,000 feet and escorted the heavy bomber for twenty minutes before being recalled due to bad weather. Red Section never did rendezvous with the Halifax as they were ordered to return because of the worsening weather situation. But as Blue Section were heading out to sea, they spotted a V2 contrail that appeared to have been fired from The Hague area. Red Section at the time was on its way home at 20,000 feet between Antwerp and Nijmegen.

20 February 1945

At 11:40hrs Spitfires from 303 Squadron began escort duties for a Halifax bomber patrolling the Dutch coast. Two Spitfire IXFs of Red Section, led by P/O Krzeptowski, took off first. Forty minutes later, two more Spitfires, this time from Blue Section, led by Rzyski climbed away from Coltishall and headed for the rendezvous point. Over the next three hours, Spitfires from Yellow, Green, White, Black and another two from Red Sections would take to the air (the last two leaving at 15:40hrs). Only the first two aircraft from Red Section and the later two Spitfires from Green Section managed to make contact with the bomber and carry out their escort duties. Green Leader F/Lt Socha spotted a V2 contrail rising out of the area near The Hague and reported it as being like a large, squat shell. He caught sight of the rocket at 17,000 feet but lost sight of it around 35,000 feet. The escort duties were the only operational flights carried out that day. Cloud cover was up to 18,000 feet and patchy as high as 35,000 feet.

21 February 1945

The pilots of 303 Squadron escorted a Halifax bomber patrolling over Holland. Red Section was the first to claw its way into the afternoon sky. Taking off at 13:00hrs, W/O Sznapka led another Spitfire IXF towards their rendezvous point. Two aircraft from Blue Section, led by P/O Corecki, also took off at 13:00hrs. They were followed twenty minutes later by Green Section, led by F/Lt Szpakcwicz. Two aircraft from Yellow Section, led by F/O Maksymowicz, took off from base at 14:20 hrs. Red Section flew direct to Ursel where they landed at 14:15hrs and waited on readiness until 15:30hrs. They took off and made contact with the Halifax carrying out their duties until 17:10hrs when they peeled away heading for home. Blue Section headed towards Antwerp and proceeded to try to make contact with the Halifax but was unable to, so landed at Ursel at 14:50hrs. They took off at 17:10hrs and returned to base. In the meantime, Green Section had a bit more excitement. They caught up with the Halifax and patrolled with the bomber as planned. Like the other aircraft they landed at Ursel joining other Spitfires from their squadron. They all took off at 15:45hrs heading back to base. On their way home, the Spitfires rolled into a shallow dive as they strafed a trailer in The Hague area. Yellow Section carried out their patrol and landed at Ursel as well. They left there at 17:45hrs heading back to base.

The afternoon sortie was different. This time six Spitfire IXFs, led by F/Lt Szpakowicz, took off on an armed recce mission at 14:00hrs from Coltishall. Their target was Ockenburg. The six fighters climbed rapidly away from base up to 10,000 feet where they remained. Sighting the target, Szpakowicz led them in their bombing runs. He started his dive at 8,500 feet flying from the south-east to the north-east. He could see the rocket installations rapidly getting larger in his sights as the height dropped away. His thumb rested on the release button. Flak now poured up from the target area but it was inaccurate and burst around him. Finally he pulled out at 5,000 feet but he released his bombs. Climbing away to avoid flak he watched the rest of the flight go into their bombing runs. The other pilots scored two hits but three overshot and one bomb was hung up and the pilot had to head out to sea to jettison it. Forming up again, the fighters headed out to sea over The Hague and followed the coast to Ostend where they crossed back in again and landed at Ursel. Green Section, from the Halifax escort duties, joined Szpakowicz's flight as they took off from Ursel at 16:36hrs. Spotting a five ton lorry pulling a trailer, Szpakowicz led the eight aircraft down onto the vehicle. They strafed it with cannon and machine-gun fire. All of the Spitfire pilots scored hits on the vehicle which burst into flame as the British fighters sped away towards home. They all landed at Coltishall at 18:05hrs.

22 February 1945

The day was set aside for practice formation flying and practice bombing. Using practice bombs, six Spitfires carried out the various drills, obtaining good results on their bombing runs.

23 February 1945

No operational flying took place for 303 Squadron pilots due to adverse weather conditions.

24 February 1945

At 11:05hrs four Spitfire IXFs, led by F/Lt Socha, took off on an armed recce heading towards The Hague area, but eighty-five miles out the third of four aircraft developed engine trouble and returned to base (escorted by the fourth). The two remaining aircraft flew on, crossing land at Katwljk then heading for The Hague area. Below them cloud covered the land as far as they could see. Spending only five minutes over The Hague, Socha and his wingman headed for home. Crossing the coast over the North Sea they spotted two American Thunderbolts circling over an oil patch on the cold water. They landed back at Coltishall at 12:40hrs.

The armed recce that left Coltishall only thirty minutes after Socha's flight saw nothing and returned without firing a shot.

Even S/Ldr Drobinski's armed recce was uneventful that afternoon. Bad weather hampered visibility over the target areas so no attacks were made.

25 February 1945

Early morning, the sounds of Spitfire engines running up split the quiet air. F/O Zdanowski, plus three others, rolled down the runway and clawed into the air at 08:35hrs (three Spitfire IXFs and one Spitfire XVI). Their mission was to attack targets in The Hague/Haagsche Bosch area. Twenty miles off the Dutch coast they split into two sections. The first section crossed over land at 8,000 feet over The Hague and flew straight to the target at Haagsche Bosch, where they strafed buildings and installations on the north side of the target with machine-gun fire and cannon. Climbing to 8,000 feet the two Spitfires rolled into their dives, their guns pouring shells into the target. Pulling out at 2,500 feet, the fighters turned sharply and climbed up to 8,000 feet.

The second section crossed over land south of The Hague and headed towards Ockenburg climbing to 7,500 feet. Over the target, the Spitfires rolled into their dives, cannon and machine-gun fire strafing buildings, vehicles and personnel. Pulling out at 800 feet they rapidly climbed away from the carnage up to 5,000 feet where they headed back to sea, rendezvousing with the first section off the Dutch Coast. All four fighters landed back at base at 10:25hrs.

While Zdanowski's armed recce was busy over the continent, four more Spitfires, led by F/Lt Szpakowicz, left base at 10:00hrs. Their targets were in The Hague/Ockenburg area. Climbing to 10,000 feet the Spitfire IXFs roared out to sea, heading for Holland. They crossed over south of the Hook and turned inland dropping to 6,000 feet. Over the target, Szpakowicz called out the attack code, flipped his aircraft over and dropped into a dive, sending cannon and machine-gun shells into the targets below as he pulled out at 2,000 feet. Each aircraft attacked in the same way, coming in from the south-east and the north-west. Szpakowicz reported to Control that there was no movement on the ground and climbed the section to 10,000 feet.

Crossing out over the Hook, several loud bangs filled his ears, as his Spitfire was hit by heavy and accurate flak. Behind him, his No. 2 was also hit. Szpakowicz ordered the formation to brake then began a large orbit over the sea to assess the damage to his and the other aircraft. He soon realised his radiator had been hit. The controls heavy in his hands, he struggled to maintain height but to no avail. The altimeter needle slowly wound down as he lost height his engine running rough. Soon he knew it would stop altogether. The water was rushing up to him as he lost more and more height. Above him, the remaining three Spitfires watched their leader skim the waves then hit the water. Several seconds passed as they anxiously watched for Szpakowicz to climb out of the Spitfire, but the aircraft sank below the waves with no sign of the pilot. The remaining aircraft landed at Ursel, their fuel very low. Szpakowicz was reported missing, believed sunk.

The next armed recce that took off from Coltishall at 11:55hrs managed to find their target in the Haagsche Bosch area and strafed it with machine-gun and cannon fire. All aircraft returned safely to base. That afternoon's armed recce at 13:40hrs was forced to turn back after forty minutes' flying due to bad weather.

26 February 1945

Early in the morning six Spitfires in three sections of two took off from Coltishall at 07:10hrs on anti-midget submarine patrols. However, each patrol was uneventful and the aircraft returned to base without sighting the enemy or firing their guns.

Later (12:55hrs), an armed recce of four Spitfire IXFs, led by F/O Zdanowski, roared into the grey afternoon sky heading for The Hague/Haagsche Bosch area. Climbing to 8,500 feet they headed for Holland crossing over land north of The Hague. Turning, Zdanowski led the section into strafing runs from south to north, ripping up buildings and ditches with machine-gun and cannon fire. Flipping the aircraft into a dive he dropped down to 3,000 feet watching strikes from his guns peppering the target area. Pulling out quickly, he climbed away and turned to watch shells from the rest of his formation hit the target. They saw no movement on the roads or in the woods they had been attacking. Heading for home, they crossed out north of The Hague at 3,000 feet. All aircraft landed safely back at base at 14:35hrs.

27 February 1945

A dreadful accident happened on this day. Sgt/Pt Prusak, who had been posted out of the Squadron, got airborne from Coltishall on his way to the Polish Record. He landed at Harrington, a US Air Force base, and later, when he took off in his Spitfire MA814 at 14:24hrs, he decided to perform a roll at low altitude and his aircraft hit the ground and caught fire. Prusak was burnt to death.

There was no other flying from Coltishall that day.

28 February 1945

The first armed recce of the last day of the month took off from Coltishall at 09:30hrs. F/Lt Franckiewicz (Red One) led three other Spitfire IXFs of Red Section into the morning sky and headed for Holland. Beneath their wings the Spitfires carried fuel tanks. They crossed land over the continent at 10:55hrs. Flying at 5,000 feet the aircraft headed for the target near The Hague.

They could see the target clearly, but as Franckiewicz was preparing to dive he flicked the switch to jettison his external fuel tanks but nothing happened. The R/T crackled as Red Three reported the same problem. For fifteen minutes they circled over the area, watched by the enemy below. Franckiewicz desperately tried to jettison his tanks but to no avail. Finally, he turned away from the target area, pushed the throttle forwards and headed for home with the rest of the section in a line abreast formation. Not one shot had been fired by the four Spitfires. They all landed safely back at base at 11:00hrs.

While Franckiewicz and his section were reaching their target over Holland, the second armed recce patrol of the day took off from Coltishall at 10:05hrs. The Spitfire IXFs, led by F/Lt Szelestowski, climbed into the air and headed for the continent. Their target was also The Hague area but it was partially obscured by cloud so they turned and crossed land north of Katwlik flying at 5,500 feet. In the Leiden/Hague/Rotterdam area they orbited waiting for the target to clear of mist and looking for other targets of opportunity. They got lucky. On The Hague to Gouda road they spotted a three ton lorry moving towards The Hague. It stopped suddenly as four people jumped out and ran for roadside cover. Szelestowski watched them run away from the truck and take cover; then he called to the other two aircraft to follow him down. Kicking the rudder he rolled his Spitfire into the top of his dive flicked the firing button and watched the ground come racing up to him. The aircraft dropped from 2,000 to 200 feet where they levelled out, their cannon and machine-gun shells ripping into the lorry.

As Szelestowski climbed rapidly away, the truck below was a flaming wreck with grey smoke pouring out of it. Moments later, they spotted twenty to thirty troops marching in single file along a road heading towards The Hague, and all three aircraft attacked, strafing the troops as they dived for cover. There was more activity than usual on all the roads that morning, all of it heading towards The Hague. Turning the aircraft away, Szelestowski led them back over their primary target that was still covered in mist and cloud. Reluctantly, he turned the section, heading out to sea for home.

Eighty miles from Coltishall, the three pilots spotted a large explosion in the sea that sent plumes of water and grey smoke rising fifty feet into the air. All three aircraft landed safely back at Coltishall at 12:00hrs.

In the early afternoon, Franckiewicz was airborne again leading another section of Spitfires on an escort of a Mustang. Four Spitfire IXFs shot off the runway at 13:30hrs and climbed rapidly away into the grey winter sky. They formed up with the Mustang over the North Sea and escorted it all the way across towards The Hague. While the Mustang took pictures, the four Spitfires orbited off the coast. After several minutes they picked up the Mustang again and headed home. This was the last flight of the month of February 1945. Flying time during that month was as follows: the

Spitfire XVIs flew twelve hours in total and the Spitfire IXFs 418 hours for the month.

1 March 1945

According to the Squadron History written by F/O J A Nicholls, intelligence officer for 303 Squadron, March 1945 began with an armed recce led by S/Ldr Drobinski. Eight Spitfires climbed into the afternoon sky on the first day of the month at 14:45hrs. Seven were Spitfire IXFs and one was a Spitfire XVI, each aircraft carrying one 500 lb air burst bomb. The target was again The Hague/Haagsche Bosch. Climbing to 19,000 feet over the North Sea the fighters crossed over land north of The Hague at 15:30hrs. They flew direct to the target dropping down to 10,000 feet. Approaching the target, Drobinski watched it getting closer then, in the right position, signalled to the rest of the formation to begin their attacks. Pulling the stick back a little and pushing the rudder, he flipped the Spitfire over on one wing and dropped into his dive. At 4,000 feet he released his bomb then levelled out climbing rapidly away. As the other Spitfires attacked he could see five bombs falling into the target area alongside a road while the remaining three bombs fell approximately 200 to 300 yards south-east of the target near a lake. Forming up on Drobinski, they turned towards the next leg of their journey. Ursel was in friendly hands and they landed there to re-fuel before continuing back to Coltishall. But on the way to Ursel, when they were fifteen to twenty miles from the Dutch Coast over water, Drobinski sighted a Big Ben contrail. Excitedly, he reported it immediately to Control saying that it was suspected to have come from the Hotel Promenade area. It was seen rising vertically, its trail rising from 10,000–30,000 feet, leaving a small cloud of dust on the ground below.

2 March 1945

A busy day for the Squadron. First flights were at 09:00hrs when F/Lt Rzyski led four Spitfire IXFs to the same target area as the bombing mission the previous day. The four Spitfires rolled down the runway and jumped into the morning air climbing to 10,000 feet. At the same height they crossed over land south of The Hague. Turning inland they began patrolling roads and railways in The Hague/Leiden/Harlen area, then west of Amsterdam and Ijmuiden. They saw nothing on the roads in these areas, no movement at all. Returning to the target, the four Spitfires attacked, strafing buildings and roads with cannon and machine-gun fire. Rolling into their dives Rzyski led the aircraft down, pulling out at 400 feet to pour shells into the target area. But they saw no activity and climbed back to 10,000 feet turning for base north of The Hague. They landed safely back at base at 10:45hrs. On their way to the target Rzyski spotted a Big Ben contrail and immediately reported it. From The Hague area it rose very rapidly climbing to 15,000 feet before the pilots lost sight of it.

While Rzyski and his section were patrolling, another armed recce, led by F/Lt Szelestowski, took off at 09:30hrs. Crossing the North Sea at 10,000 feet they flew direct to the target but found the area was obscured by cloud. Heading south they quickly discovered that the target at Ockenburg was also obscured by cloud. Without firing a shot in anger on that patrol, the four Spitfires returned to base, arriving at 11:15hrs. All aircraft were intact.

The third flight of the day was another armed recce over the Haagsche Bosch area, led by W/O Rutecki. Climbing to 10,000 feet, the four Spitfires headed for the continent. They reached land at Katwijk and flew straight to the target. Leading, Rutecki spotted the target area, radioed to the rest of his section then applied rudder and pulled on the control column, rolling the aircraft into the top of his dive. Height melted away as he bore down on the target coming in from the north-east, his engine roaring. Pressing the firing button his cannon and machine guns burst into life as he strafed the target with the rest of his section coming in one after the other north-east to south-west. Levelling out at 1,000 feet, Rutecki saw shells hit the target area. To avoid flak he pulled the control column climbing rapidly away from the carnage below. At 6,000 feet the section turned, heading along The Hague to Gouda road where they sighted a stationary train of three coaches. Two Spitfires suddenly peeled away from the others, rolled into their dives and peppered the train with cannon and machine-gun fire. Rutecki watched as his fellow pilots strafed the carriages leaving the middle one engulfed in flames. They turned again, searching for more targets. Moments later they spotted a building and what looked like a power generator. This time three of the four aircraft peeled off and strafed the structures. Rutecki could see strikes from their cannon on the buildings and the power generator. Light accurate flak came up quickly from the ground and Rutecki radioed for the rest of the flight to form up with him. The four Spitfires turned for home spotting stationary barges in Katwijk. Low on fuel the fighters left the barges behind without attacking and headed out over the North Sea. They landed safely back at Coltishall at 14:30hrs.

While Rutecki's section was on its way home, Coltishall launched another armed recce to the same location. Four Spitfire IXFs took off at 13:55hrs led by F/Lt Malarowski. This was Red Section and early in the sortie Red Two turned back due to technical problems. The remaining three Spitfires pressed on, climbing above the cloud to 8,000 feet. They reached land south of the Hook and turned north flying directly to the target area where they peeled off into their strafing dives, from

6,000–2,000 feet. They saw no movement of any kind. Climbing back to 8,000 feet they turned north again and then headed back to base leaving land at Zanvoort. They landed safely back at base.

The final flight of the day left Coltishall at 16:00hrs and was an armed recce led by F/Lt Franckiewicz. The Four Spitfire IXFs approached the Dutch coast at 16:30hrs and turned north along the coast crossing into land at Katwijk. They flew direct to the target area. Each Spitfire carried an additional fuel tank. Sighting the target, Franckiewicz ordered the section to attack. Jettisoning their tanks three Spitfires dropped to 8,000 feet then rolled into diving runs on the targets: some buildings in a wooded area. Yellow Four suddenly called on the radio. He was unable to jettison his tank and could only watch as shells from the rest of the section's guns tore into the structures. Two aircraft attacked a crossroads while another attacked a structure resembling a studio. Though no activity was seen, their attack had caused considerable damage. Satisfied, Franckiewicz ordered the section home. They turned towards the sea, leaving the land south of The Hague. They finally touched down at Coltishall at 17:30hrs.

3 March 1945

Only one flight took place. Visibility was twenty miles on this day with cloud at 7,000–8,000 feet. In the morning four Spitfire IXFs, led by F/O Maksymowicz, took off from Coltishall at 09:00hrs climbing to 10,000 feet. They formed up over the sea then turned towards Holland. Thirty-five minutes later the four Spitfires crossed from water to land between The Hague and Katwijk. Turning south they flew straight to the target. This flight was an armed recce to Staalduine Bosch. As they flew towards the target, they saw black smoke rising from buildings in the Haagsche Bosch area stretching as far as Rotterdam. Fires could be seen among the buildings as the smoke drifted high into the sky (as much as 8,000 feet according to the squadron's history). Seeing the target, buildings in a south-east corner of some woods, Maksymowicz called for the section to attack. Pushing the control column forward he dropped the aircraft to 6,000 feet then quickly brought one wing up and rolled into his attack dive, his machine guns and cannon spitting fire. Levelling out at 2,000 feet he could see his tracer and high explosive shells ripping into the buildings. Grey smoke began to pour from the structures as the aircraft attacked. One Spitfire raked the entire length of the woods with his guns as he tore over the targets. The flak that came up to meet them was inaccurate and nowhere near the target. Maksymowicz climbed to 4,000 feet, called for the others to form up on him over the North Sea, then turned towards the sea and for home. All four Spitfires formed up over the sea at 09:50hrs and headed back to Coltishall. They landed shortly after 10:00hrs.

The following day there was no operational flying for 303 Squadron.

The intelligence officer gave a lecture on aircraft recognition and tactics for Big Ben patrols to the pilots.

5 March 1945

The first two flights of the day were complete write-offs owing to technical problems with the Spitfires. Even the third armed recce, led by Maksymowicz, ran into trouble. The four Spitfires of Red Section climbed into the late morning sky at 11:05hrs heading for Duindigit. But before the flight reached the continent Red Four turned back with engine trouble with Red Three providing an escort home. The remaining two Spitfires pushed on, climbed to 9,000 feet, crossing in north of The Hague and flying straight to the target. Covered in a thin layer of cloud stretching from 4,000–35,000 feet, the target was difficult to see. But through the gaps in the cloud the two Spitfires attacked the buildings in the target area, strikes from their guns causing damage in several places. They saw no movement as they pulled out at 1,500 feet, but flak burst all around them. Maksymowicz realised the flak was accurate. Suddenly his No. 2 called that he'd been hit by flak but that he was still functioning. Breathing a sigh of relief Maksymowicz headed for the North Sea and home. Both aircraft landed safely at 12:40hrs.

Twenty minutes earlier, three Spitfire IXFs and one Spitfire XVI, with F/Lt Bartys leading, took off from Coltishall heading for Wassenaar/Rust en-Vreugd. Climbing to 6,000 feet they headed for Holland but didn't see landfall because of heavy cloud cover. They flew on for another ten minutes but couldn't see the target. Turning back for home they returned to base at 13:45hrs without firing a shot.

The next armed recce launched by 303 Squadron was aborted just as the Spitfires crossed the British coast. However, the final sortie of the day saw four Spitfire IXFs, led by F/Lt Malarowski, get airborne at 13:10hrs. The four fighters roared across the North Sea to the Dutch coast. Climbing to 10,500 feet they crossed the coast at Katwijk, flying east before turning towards the target area. Again, cloud totally obscured the targets. Wasting no more time Malarowski led the section towards the North Sea. All four aircraft landed back at base at 14:55hrs.

6 March 1945

The Squadron mounted several anti-midget submarine patrols but sighted nothing. Only White Section, led by F/Lt Szelestowski, saw anything of any significance. During their routine patrol Szelestowski sighted a V2 contrail at 08:30hrs from 10,000–30,000 feet, curving towards the British coast. They saw no sign of any submarines. For the next two days the Squadron did no operational flying. Practice bombing with 10 lb bombs was completed.

9 March 1945

An eventful day for 303 Squadron. Flying began with anti-midget submarine patrols just after dawn. A total of six aircraft in flights of two began their patrols at 08:35hrs. However, they sighted no submarines but a V2 contrail was sighted and appeared to have come from The Hague area. The last patrol ended at 09:00hrs.

Later in the morning, the Squadron mounted its first armed recce of the day. The target area was Duindigit and four Spitfires, with F/Lt Socha leading, climbed into the morning sky at 10:25hrs. Forty minutes later, the section reached the target. Dropping into their attack dives Socha led two Spitfires down on the target (a set of buildings in a wooded area) strafing with cannon and machine guns. Above, Blue One could only watch in despair as his drop tank wouldn't release. Climbing up to 10,000 feet, Socha reported a V2 contrail that appeared to have been fired from The Hague area. He lost sight of it at 30,000 feet when they were twenty miles off the Dutch coast. All aircraft landed safely back at Coltishall.

At 11:10hrs four Spitfires, led by F/O Zdanowski, took off and climbed to 9,000 feet before turning towards Holland. They made land fall at Den Helder then proceeded over land to The Hague where the target was pin-pointed as structures and vehicles in wooded areas. The four Spitfires strafed the targets and Zdanowski saw several hits as he levelled out from his dive at 4,000 feet. Light intense and accurate flak burst all around the agile aircraft as they climbed as fast as they could away from the targets after their attacks. Turning towards the North Sea they crossed out north of The Hague when glycol was seen streaming from Wing Commander Falkowski's aircraft. Over the radio Zdanowski heard the wing commander report that his temperature was 140 and climbing. A few moments later, the hood flew from the crippled Spitfire and Zdanowski watched as the pilot baled out at 2,500 feet. Seconds passed as the body rolled through the air then suddenly the white parachute deployed. But the three remaining Spitfires couldn't pin-point where the wing commander had landed because of the low cloud cover. His position was roughly three miles south of The Hague.

The following statement that appears in the Squadron History was by F/O Zdanowski, W/Os Rutecki and Sztuka. 'During an operational Jim Crow and armed recce flight on 9 March we approached the Dutch coast at Den Helder at an altitude of 8,000 feet. After searching for shipping in the peninsula we flew south to attack V2 sites on the north of The Hague, meeting over the left side of which I notified the section. After attacking we climbed to 6,000 feet. After a while the Wing Commander joined us. We approached the sea. Joined with us, the Wing Commander was flying as leader and I noticed that glycol was pouring from his starboard radiator leaving a long vapour trail. I said, "You've got a glycol leak and what temperature of glycol have you?" The Wing Commander replied, "140" and we immediately returned to land. We approached the coast south of The Hague at 3,000 feet, No. 4 was all the time giving the fix and No. 2 was fixing Belgium. We turned to the south and, when four miles from The Hague, and one mile inland, we noticed that the Wing Commander's aircraft caught fire leaving white and black smoke behind. At 2,500 feet the Wing Commander baled out and after two seconds his parachute opened and three seconds later we saw the aircraft explode amongst some greenhouses near a road. We could not stay longer and flew onto Ursel for re-fuelling.'

The remaining Spitfires landed back at base at 15:05hrs.

The next sortie of the day was at 14:30hrs by three Spitfires with F/O Gorecki leading. Unfortunately, they ended up attacking nothing as the target was completely obscured by clouds.

At 15:10hrs two Spitfires were scrambled to intercept an enemy aircraft, and after being vectored to different places by Control, they returned to base. Five minutes after the first two Spitfires were scrambled, another two were scrambled also to intercept an enemy aircraft. They too saw nothing but several Liberators. After being vectored from place to place by Control, they were eventually ordered back to base without firing a shot or seeing a single enemy sighting.

The last flight of the day for 303 Squadron was an air-sea rescue flight. Two Spitfires were vectored ten miles out to sea by Control where they saw one Catalina and an empty dinghy on the sea. They saw two Thunderbolts patrolling the same area. Vectored again by Control, the two Spitfires roared towards the Wash area in search of a buoy and a crashed four engined bomber. But, again they saw nothing and were finally ordered back to base.

NOTE

1 Please note that the detail of 303 Squadron flying Big Ben operations during October and November 1944 can be found in Chapter III.

Appendix B

124 Squadron History

The operation to destroy the Germans V2 rocket sites included several squadrons of dive-bombing Spitfires, 124 Squadron playing a significant part.

The following information was taken from the Squadron History and is a snapshot of their attacks on V2 sites. It does not cover a wide range of operations and dates but covers the significant period from the beginning of February to the end of March 1945, when the V2 threat on the UK was finally thwarted.

22 February 1945

Flying began at 08:30hrs with a flight of four Spitfire IX (HF)s with the E wing. Led by F/Lt Brooks, the four Spitfires climbed to 12,000 feet, formed up and headed out over the North Sea towards Holland. The target was the Haagsche Bosch area. They crossed in just north of The Hague and turned towards the target. Brooks pin-pointed the V2 site below, checked his instruments, and ordered the section to attack. From south to north the Spitfires dropped on the target. Brooks rolled into his dive at 12,000 feet followed by P/O Fallon, F/Lt Maltby and W/O James. They roared down on the target and Brooks released his bombs, pulling out at 6,000 feet. As he climbed away he watched the rest of the section release their bombs and pull out at the same altitude. One of the aircraft fired his cannon as he pulled out and Brooks could see strikes on the target area. All their bombs fell in the target area. They climbed as rapidly as they could, to avoid intense accurate flak coming from north of the target. Above 5,000 feet, and clear of the flak, the Spitfires turned for home, landing at base at 09:55hrs.

The next operation was much larger. F/Lt Fowler led a section of 12 Spitfires on a bombing mission against V2 sites in Ockenburg. They took off at 11:35hrs and headed for Holland after forming up over the North Sea. Climbing to 12,000 feet they crossed in north of the target area, then turned towards the north-east. Fowler could see the target below and he

139

prepared to attack. Giving the order over the R/T he rolled his aircraft into a dive and dropped on the target from 12,000 feet in a north-east direction. As the height wound down he could see the target getting larger. Fowler thumbed the firing button, still in his dive, firing a long burst of cannon fire. At 6,000 feet he released his bombs and pulled out of his dive, turning tightly and levelling out. The rest of the Spitfires attacked in the same way and all the bombs were seen to fall in the target area. The formation wheeled away and headed back to base where they landed at 12:50hrs.

The afternoon saw a flight of six Spitfires, again led by F/Lt Fowler, take off from Coltishall at 13:55hrs to attack sites in the Haagsche Bosch area. They climbed quickly to 12,000 feet and headed for Holland. Crossing land over The Hague, the section turned towards the target. They attacked from south to north diving 11,000–6,000 feet. All the bombs fell in the north-east corner of the target area. As Fowler led the section back home, they experienced some moderate light flak just as they crossed into the North Sea. They landed safely back at Coltishall at 15:15 hrs.

Another armed bombing recce took place at the same time. Led by W/O James, a section of Spitfires went back to Ockenburg where they dive-bombed the target in a north-east direction. There was no enemy reaction to this and the flight returned to base at 15:15 hrs.

23 February 1945

Activity for the Squadron began at first light when W/O Parker led the first section of Spitfires on anti-midget submarine patrol. Three sections of two aircraft were detailed to patrol for enemy midget submarines. The patrol was hampered by bad weather and was uneventful. They took off at 07:05hrs and landed back at base at 08:25hrs. The last section landed at 09:00hrs.

24 February 1945

Back on dive-bombing detail, the Squadron began operations mid-morning. At 11:00hrs F/Lt Brooks (in Spitfire TA 795) took off, leading three other aircraft to targets in the Haagsche Bosch area. Bad weather forced them back and they aborted the mission. The next two armed recces were aborted due to poor visibility over the target. Only the afternoon recce was successful.

At 16:50hrs F/Lt Lawrence, leading three other Spitfires, took off and headed for Holland. They formed up over the North Sea and climbed to 12,000 feet. The target was the Haagsche Bosch area where the aircraft bombed the Ockenburg wood with great results. They landed back at base at 18:10hrs.

25 February 1945

At 11:00hrs a section of twelve Spitfires carrying 250 lb bombs rose into the grey morning air. The weather had improved considerably over night and it was now possible to mount operations. As they formed up over the North Sea, F/Lt Fowler, leading the flight, turned towards Holland and they crossed over The Hague at 12,000 feet. The target was again the Haagsche Bosch area but the primary target area near The Hague was obscured by cloud so the flight attacked a railway junction four miles east of The Hague. Rolling into their dives, the Spitfires dropped on the target, releasing their bombs; as they pulled out of their dives, some strafed the junction with cannon fire. Only one bomb hit the embankment while the rest undershot. They next attacked a canal bridge and lock west of Rotterdam but all the remaining bombs overshot the target. They landed back at Coltishall at 12:35hrs having experienced only moderate flak from Rotterdam.

The afternoon's armed recce was successful despite the fact that the primary target was obscured by clouds. Again the target area was the Haagsche Bosch. W/O Parker led six aircraft on the operation (taking off at 15:00hrs). Instead of the primary target, the flight attacked the railway line south of Haarlem. One aircraft had a hang up with one bomb refusing to release during the dive. The pilot, F/Lt Phillips, managed to jettison the bomb at sea as the flight headed for home. They landed back at 16:25hrs.

26 February 1945

Flying this day began at 09:55hrs when F/Ldr Charlesworth led three other Spitfires to bomb targets in The Hague area. Three of the Spitfires from the section bombed the V2 sites in the Haagsche Bosch area while the fourth Spitfire attacked targets in the Ockenburg woods. Over the targets there was no flak at all, but as they formed up and headed back home, crossing out over The Hague, they encountered moderate and accurate flak.

F/Lt Fowler led the next armed recce to the Haagsche Bosch area taking off at 11:35hrs. The section of four aircraft dropped into their dives over the target area, releasing bombs that successfully hammered into it. On the way in and the way out they encountered no enemy activity at all. All four Spitfires landed back at Coltishall at 13:00hrs.

That afternoon, at 13:30hrs, six Spitfires rose into the sky to attack the same area. Led by F/Lt Brooks, they climbed to 10,000 feet and crossed in over The Hague and turned towards the target: rocket sites in the Haagsche Bosch area. Each aircraft rolled into a dive, attacking the target successfully, their bombs exploding in the target area. As they crossed out over The Hague, the fighters encountered inaccurate flak. They landed back at base at 15:00hrs.

Later, two Spitfires acted as escort for two Mustangs photographing targets in Holland. They took off at 12:10hrs and landed back at 14:10hrs with the Mustangs encountering light flak south of The Hague as they crossed out over the North Sea towards Coltishall.

The next operation was another armed recce of six Spitfires attacking sites in the Haagsche Bosch area. They were airborne at 15:35hrs and climbed to 10,000 feet. They crossed over land and headed towards the target area dropping into their dives and releasing their bombs where most fell in the target area but some overshot. As they formed up to go home a Big Ben contrail was seen ascending at an angle of approximately 85 degrees. The trail began at 15,000 feet and as it rose high into the sky, it assumed a horizontal position and headed west. They landed back at base at 16:55hrs.

The last flight of the day took place at 17:30hrs, with F/Lt Charlesworth leading a section of four aircraft. Unfortunately, they ran into very bad weather and poor visibility and had to turn back to base, landing at 18:40hrs.

27 February 1945

Though two armed recces were launched in the morning from Coltishall, bad weather with a low cloud base forced both flights to return to base.

28 February 1945

A busy day for 124 Squadron. Flying began at 10:30hrs when F/Lt Charlesworth (flying TA 811) led a section of four Spitfire IX (HF)s, F/Lt Maltby (flying PV 303), W/O Howard (flying RK 908) and P/O Andrews (flying RK 960) to the Haagsche Bosch area. Flying at the standard height of 10,000 feet, they headed for the target area but bad weather forced them to head for other targets. Charlesworth turned the section towards Oostburg where they attacked a railway line and a wooden bridge over a canal with bombs and machine-gun fire. There was no enemy reaction to this attack. As they headed home, some forty miles off the Dutch coast the pilots reported seeing four explosions on the water. They landed back at 12:15hrs.

The next operation of the day took place at 11:30hrs with F/Lt Fowler (flying PV 332) leading W/O Parker (flying BR 209), F/Lt Melia (flying TA 813) and P/O Travis (flying SM 515) to V2 sites in the Haagsche Bosch area. But poor weather stopped them from bombing the primary target, so they turned on Ockenburg where three of the aircraft put their bombs well into the target area. One aircraft could not release its bombs after the dive and had to jettison them at sea. They landed safely back at 13:00hrs.

As Fowler's flight was returning another armed recce had set off from

Coltishall a few minutes earlier. F/Lt Brooks, leading three other Spitfires, F/Lt James (flying RR 252), F/O Mallen (flying PV 299) and W/O Farquharson (flying PV344), climbed to height and turned for Holland. Roaring over the North Sea they crossed into enemy airspace and turned towards their target in the Haagsche Bosch area. Low cloud stopped them from attacking their primary targets so they attacked a railway bridge nearby. Rolling into their dives, they dropped their bombs at the bottom of their dives and strafed the line with cannon fire. There was no reaction from the Germans. They landed back at base at 15:00 hours.

Another armed recce was launched at 14:30hrs. This time F/Lt Lawrence (flying PV 305) led F/Lt Phillips (flying RR 209), F/Lt Forth (flying TA 813) and W/O Paterson (flying TA 811) to the primary target again in the Haagsche Bosch area. As on the earlier missions the primary target was covered in cloud so the flight hammered a railway line north of Leiden. All the bombs but two fell on the tracks destroying that section. They landed back at Coltishall at 16:15hrs.

Over the next two hours, two more armed recces were dispatched to attack the primary target, a V2 site in the Haagsche Bosch area, and each time low cloud obscured the target and stopped the Spitfires from rolling into their dives and releasing their bombs. Instead, a wooded area at Wassenaar/Rust-en-Vreugd was bombed with great success and the railway line north of Leiden was also attacked.

1 March 1945

Low cloud over the main target at Haagsche Bosch forced the first two recces of the day to return to base without dropping their bombs.

But at 14:30hrs F/Lt Fowler led six Spitfires to the same area that was now clear of cloud. They bombed and strafed with great success and encountered only moderate and inaccurate flak. All six Spitfires returned to base at 15:55hrs without any damage.

The last operation of the day, led by F/Lt Lawrence at 16:30hrs, was also a great success. Again it was to the same sites in the Haagsche Bosch area where all the bombs from the diving Spitfires landed in the target area, except one which overshot to the north-east of the target.

2 March 1945

Only one mission took place. Led by F/Lt Lawrence, eleven aircraft of 124 Squadron took off at 11:00hrs. Their targets were rocket sites in the Haagsche Bosch area. Four near misses were seen as the aircraft rolled into their dives and released their bombs. The aircraft landed at Ursel and were re-armed each with two 250 lb bombs and four with one 500 lb bomb each. Heading back to the target area to continue the bombing they found the area covered in cloud and were unable to attack. The Spitfires carrying 500 lb bombs jettisoned them in the sea as the flight headed back to Coltishall.

3 March 1945

There were several armed recces flown by 124 Squadron. The first saw F/Lt Charlesworth taking off with three other Spitfires at 09:30hrs. Climbing to height they formed up over the North Sea and roared towards Holland. Crossing over the Dutch coast they headed for the targets in the Haagsche Bosch area. Charlesworth rolled his Spitfire into a dive and released his bombs on the target area. All the bombs hit the target with one a direct hit on the aiming point. However, one aircraft had to land at Ursel due to engine trouble. The three remaining Spitfires returned to Coltishall at 10:50hrs.

F/Lt Fowler climbed into the morning sky with three other Spitfires for an attack on V2 sites in the Haagsche Bosch area. Unfortunately, their primary target was obscured by cloud, so they turned their attention to targets in Ockenburg. Fowler could see their bombs land on the southern corner of the aiming point while one bomb overshot and exploded in a wooded area to the south. They returned to Coltishall at 11:25hrs without encountering any opposition from the German gunners.

At 12:10hrs it was F/Lt Lawrence's turn to lead three other Spitfires towards the same area. This time, the cloud had gone and the Spitfires rolled into their dives, dropping their bombs on the aiming point of the target, hammering the site with their bombs. Pulling out of their dives, they raked the target with cannon fire before climbing quickly away and heading back to base where they landed at 13:35hrs. Again, the Nazis did not react.

More dive-bombing took place in the afternoon when four Spitfires, led by P/O Andrews, attacked the railway line near Alphen. Their primary target of V2 sites in the Haagsche Bosch area was obscured by cloud so this secondary target was attacked. Peeling off at height the Spitfires dived on the line, releasing their bombs just before pulling out. Levelling off, Andrews turned tightly to view the results of the bombing. Two landed directly on the track while the rest were near misses. They had taken off from Coltishall at 13:40hrs and arrived back at base at 15:05hrs encountering no opposition.

F/Lt Melia led the next armed recce to the same area. They took off at 14:05hrs and climbed rapidly away from Coltishall, heading out to sea towards the Dutch coast. Arriving over the target they found it clear of cloud. Giving the order to attack, Melia rolled his Spitfire into a dive, peeling away from the others and dropped on the target. As the ground rapidly loomed up in front of him, he checked his instruments. He kept the

144

Spitfire steady and released his bombs then quickly pulled out of the dive. The others did the same and four bombs from the flight hammered into the aiming point while two overshot and smashed into some nearby houses. This time some light flak came lazily up to them from the target area but missed the four Spitfires completely. They arrived back at base at 15:25hrs.

F/Lt Fowler led a section of four Spitfires to the Wassenaar area at 15:45hrs. By the time they reached the target it was obscured by cloud as was The Hague. Not wanting to return to base with his bombs, Fowler led the section to the secondary target, a railway line between Leiden and Voorhorst, but all their bombs fell wide of the track. They returned to base at 17:15hrs.

Finally, the last armed recce of the day left Coltishall at 16:45hrs, bombing the Staalduinsche Bosch area where all the bombs fell in a wooded area south of the aiming point. The four Spitfires landed at base at 17:25hrs.

4 March 1945

Three armed recces took place. The first was led by F/Lt Charlesworth taking off with three other Spitfires at 09:00hrs. They formed up over the North Sea and headed for Holland. This time the target was Wassenaar Rust-en-Vreugd. Each Spitfire tipped onto one wing and dropped into a dive releasing their bombs just before pulling out. Two fell on the northerly aiming point while the rest hammered the target area. What makes this flight remarkable, according to the Squadron diary, is what they saw on the way back. When twenty miles off the English coast an object was seen by pilots of the section to come down in the sea leaving a spiral trail and making a large splash. There is no indication in the diary as to what this object was (a faulty V2 or an aircraft?). They landed at 10:30hrs.

While F/Lt Charlesworth was leading his section of Spitfires, another four aircraft took off from Coltishall at 09:30hrs. This armed recce was led by F/Lt Fowler to the same area as the previous section.

When Fowler reached the target he led the three other Spitfires in dives on the target area. But as he pulled out of his dive he realised that a ground mist was rapidly moving in and any actual results of the bombing couldn't be assessed by the time the attack was over. The mist quickly obscured the target. The fourth aircraft could not dive on the target because of the ground mist so instead, the pilot, Sgt Lattimer, bombed a railway line near The Hague but low cloud made identifying the results difficult indeed. They landed back at Coltishall at 11:05hrs.

The next armed recce was launched later in the morning at 10:15hrs, with F/O Fallon leading three other Spitfire IXF aircraft back to Wassenaar. But by now the target was completely covered in mist and cloud and bombing couldn't be carried out. In the end the aircraft returned to base at 11:30hrs without forming any attack.

5 March 1945

The first flight of the day was an armed recce to Staalduinsche Bosch. Led by F/Lt Lawrence, the four Spitfires were airborne from Coltishall at 09:45hrs. Carrying two 250 lb bombs each, they climbed slowly into the morning air, formed up over the sea and turned towards Holland. However, once over the target, they encountered heavy flak and Lawrence could see the target area was completely covered by low cloud. The secondary target would have to do. Wheeling the section around Lawrence headed for a railway line near The Hague. The Spitfires dropped into their dives and two bombs hit the track with the rest near misses. They returned to base at 11:15hrs.

At 10:25hrs pilots of 124 Squadron tried again to bomb sites at Staalduinsche Bosch, this time with F/Lt Charlesworth leading, but it was still obscured by cloud and they returned to base with their bombs still attached.

The next flight was led by F/Lt Fowler leading four Spitfires to Ockenburg. They took off at 11:25hrs and reached the coast approximately half an hour later. But low cloud and mist obscured most of the target area and the four Spitfires flew up and down the coast as they waited for a clear patch. Finally, Fowler spotted a gap in the clouds and rolled his aircraft into a dive in the clear space. The other followed and as Fowler pulled out he could see his bombs hitting the target area. Orbitting for a few moments he saw all the bombs burst and a sudden red explosion leap into the air followed by thick black smoke. No flak came up to meet them and there was no enemy reaction at all. However, as they headed out to sea one of the Spitfires developed mechanical problems and landed at Ursel with an escort of another Spitfire. The rest of the flight landed back at Coltishall at 12:23hrs.

At 12:15hrs F/O Fallon was leading three other Spitfires of 124 Squadron back to Ockenburg. Spying a hole in the clouds the four Spitfires attacked a suspension bridge with bombs but were unable to see the results of their attacks because of very low cloud.

The last operation of the day was another armed recce but it was wholly unsuccessful as cloud as low as 1,500 feet covered the whole of the target area and the aircraft had to return to Coltishall with their bombs.

6 March 1945

Two armed weather recces took place this day and no attacks were made due to the very low cloud covering most of Holland.

9 March 1945

The weather cleared and several attacks were made on The Hague race course. S/Ldr Scott, in company with three other Spitfires, led the first attack. Though it is not specified in the Squadron's diary, the target must have been something to do with the V2 programme as it was attacked several times by the Squadron's Spitfires throughout the day.

At 07:15hrs four Spitfires took off, climbing into the morning sky, bombs slung under their wings. Over the North Sea they headed for the Dutch coast and their target, The Hague race course. Bracing moderate light flak as they crossed over the coast towards the target, Scott gave the order to attack over the R/T. Touching his rudder he brought one wing up and rolled the Spitfire over into a dive. Just before pulling out, he released his bombs to ensure they fell as close to the target as possible. Three aircraft managed to bomb the area with good results. The fourth aircraft, unable to jettison its drop tank, went into a shallow dive and bombed Wassenaar. The section landed safely back at Coltishall at 08:35hrs.

Four more Spitfires from 124 Squadron climbed slowly into the morning sky at 08:38hrs. Led by F/Lt Melia, the four aircraft carried two 250 lb bombs and a drop tank each as they headed towards their target, Wassenaar/Rust-en-Vreugd. But the target area was obscured by cloud so Melia turned his attention towards The Hague race course, which was clear. One by one the Spitfires rolled into their dives, braving accurate and intense flak. They released their bombs that all hammered the race course dead in the target area. Climbing quickly away the pilots strained to get their machines clear of the flak and they headed back to Coltishall, landing at 09:56hrs.

Next it was F/Lt Charelsworth leading a section of Spitfires towards the race course. They took off from Coltishall at 10:50hrs and headed directly for the target staying well above 6,000 feet where the flak was the most intense. By now, the German gunners had woken up and were peppering the sky with accurate bursts of anti-aircraft fire. The Spitfires stayed above it until they peeled off into their dives and bombed the target area. All the bombs fell accurately and not one of the aircraft was hit by flak. They returned to Coltishall at 11:55hrs.

At 12:20hrs F/Lt Fowler was again leading a section to The Hague race course where they bombed the target area but were unable to pin-point their results because of thick cloud. Landing at Ursel, the Spitfires re-bombed and took off again for the race course but they were unable to attack because the target was now completely covered in very low cloud. In the end, Fowler and his flight jettisoned their bombs in the sea and headed for home, landing at 13:45hrs.

Poor weather made the next two flights impossible to complete and they both returned to base.

11 March 1945

At 07:00hrs four Spitfires, led by F/Lt Charlesworth, took off from Coltishall on an armed weather recce. They headed for The Hague area and discovered thick low cloud between 3–4,000 feet. They returned to base at 08:00hrs. Two more armed recces were flown that day but in both cases the weather had deteriorated and made accurate bombing impossible.

12 March 1945

At 15:30hrs F/Lt Lawrence led a section of four Spitfires on an armed recce to Wassenaar Ravelijn. Reaching the target the four fighters dropped into their dives and one by one released their bombs. Most of them burst in the woods while two burst in the woods north-west of the target and two others weren't seen. As there was no enemy reaction to the raid, one Spitfire strafed the target area in a shallow dive at 4,500 feet. They arrived back at base at 17:15hrs.

A section led by F/Lt Charlesworth also dive-bombed the same target. They left Coltishall at 16:45hrs and arrived over the target after Lawrence's section had left. Peeling off from the formation, Charlesworth rolled into his dive and flicked the firing button, pumping cannon shells into the target on the way down. As he pulled out, he released his bombs and climbed away. Four bombs hit the target area and two were near misses. One pilot couldn't release his bombs and landed back at Coltishall with a full load.

While the Charlesworth section was on its way back to Coltishall, the last armed recce of the day took off at 17:25hrs. This time the target was the race course but only two aircraft were able to release their bombs on this target as they pulled out of their dives. Four hits were seen in the target area but the exact position could not be identified due to ground mist making observation difficult. A fifth aircraft attacked the railway line between Gouda and Woerdan scoring hits on the station and the track. Some flak was encountered but no aircraft was hit. They landed back at base at 18:55hrs.

Throughout this campaign there was no evidence of the Luftwaffe, which by now had been virtually grounded due to lack of fuel and pilots (or simply destroyed in battle). This gave the Allies air superiority and enabled the pilots to attack with virtual impunity. Flak, poor weather and mechanical troubles were their biggest headaches. Also, at this stage of the war, the liberation of Holland was not far away. And that is when ground troops marched into V2 areas and overcome any chance of continued usage. However, as we have discovered, the Spitfire missions had already done this.

13 March 1945

The first flight of the day was an armed recce of four spitfires led by F/Lt Brooks to the Duindigit race course. They took off at 09:45hrs and successfully bombed the target with six bombs hitting the ride through the woods and two landing directly on the race course track itself. They landed safely back at base at 11:00hrs having encountered no enemy anti-aircraft fire.

That mission paved the way for a much bigger attack on the race course. This time twelve Spitfires took off from Coltishall led by S/Ldr Scott (flying PV312). The Spitfires took off at 12:00hrs and formed up over the North Sea then headed for the Dutch coast. According to the Squadron diary, 'one aircraft returned early owing to mechanical trouble but the remaining 11 aircraft made a successful attack on the target area.' The aircraft were armed with one 500 lb bomb and two 250 lb airburst bombs.

'Excellent results were claimed,' wrote the Squadron's diarist. 'A large yellow orange explosion was seen in the wooded area to the south-west of the ride through the woods.'

Landing at Ursel to re-bomb and re-fuel, the pilots returned again to the race course on the way home and dive-bombed successfully with all the bombs pounding the wooded area. They landed back at Coltishall at 13:20hrs after braving intense and accurate flak crossing the coast.

The race course was attacked again that day by two more sections and all the bombs fell accurately in the target area. The intense, accurate flak experienced by the main flight earlier was now silent.

14 March 1945

The Hague became the prime target again. The first armed recce took off at 13:45hrs and was led by F/Lt Melia. The four Spitfires managed to bomb through ground mist but could see no results of their handiwork and returned to base at 15:00hrs.

The later armed recce of four Spitfires led by S/Ldr Scott had more success. They took off from Coltishall at 14:50hrs and arrived over the same target more than half an hour later. As they rolled into their dives there was no reaction from enemy anti-aircraft gunners and all their bombs smashed into the wooded area between the race course and the Leiden road.

A new target in Wassenaar Ravelijn was selected for the next armed recce led by W/O Parker. Leading four other Spitfires they took off at 15:50hrs, formed up over the North Sea and turned towards Holland. Over the target the Spitfires rolled into their dives and released their bombs. 'Four bombs were seen to burst in the south-east corner of the target area,' recorded the Squadron's diarist, 'followed by a cloud of yellow smoke. Three other bombs burst in the north-west corner of the wood.' One pilot could not release his bombs over the target area and managed to jettison them safely in the sea on the way home. But this time the gunners were awake and the four spitfires encountered accurate intense flak as they crossed over the coast. One aircraft was slightly damaged. They landed back at base at 17:25hrs.

That afternoon, Spitfires from 124 Squadron again attacked the race course at The Hague with all bombs dropping in the target area.

17 March 1945

The first mission of the day was railway interdiction near Woerden. Four Spitfires, led by F/Lt Fowler, attacked a railway bridge and had two direct hits on the track with the remainder near misses.

The rest of the day would be railway interdiction attacks that would stop the Germans moving much needed supplies to troops and V2 sites.

At 09:40hrs S/Ldr Scott led a section of four Spitfire IXFs on a railway junction assault at Vlakla. The section split in half with two aircraft going for the junction at Vlakla (where two bombs scored direct hits), and the other two attacking railway lines at Ouewulven. Pulling out of their dives the pilots did not see the results of their bombing. The four aircraft landed at Ursel to re-arm and re-fuel and on the way back to base attacked the railway at Gouda with no hits. They landed at 11:05hrs.

The next armed recce attacked the Gouda to Woerden railway line. Two direct hits were seen and the rest were near misses. This flight, led by F/Lt Charlesworth, took off at 10:45hrs and landed at Ursel to re-arm and re-fuel. On the return journey they attacked the railway lines at Oulemborg but achieved only near misses, with no direct hits.

That afternoon's armed recce was more successful. Taking off from Coltishall at 12:00hrs, the four Spitfire IXF, led by F/Lt Forth, attacked the Gouda to Woerden railway. 'Two bombs fell on the embankment and the others were near misses,' wrote the Squadron's diarist. Landing at Ursel to re-arm and re-fuel the Spitfires climbed into the sky at 15:25hrs. Minutes later they rolled into their dives, bombing the railway junction between Gouda and Woerden this time with direct hits and four near misses. They landed back at base at 16:55hrs. Flak throughout this flight had been moderate but totally inaccurate.

18 March 1945

The first armed recce of the day revisited the Gouda to Woerden railway line early in the morning but achieved no results whatsoever from their dive-bombing. One of the four Spitfires on that detail had mechanical trouble and had to turn back to base.

F/Lt Forth led four Spitfires on a dive-bombing mission on a railway bridge at The Hague to Gouda line and achieved some damage to the structure with several near misses.

That afternoon F/Lt Oakley led a formation of twelve Spitfires to attack the race course at Duindigit. They roared off the runway at 12:35hrs, formed up over the North Sea and turned towards the Dutch coast. Arriving over the target the formation split into three sections and four aircraft, led by Oakley, rolled into steep dives towards the race course. Pulling out of his dive, Oakley released his bombs and climbed rapidly away. He then watched the other three dive-bomb the target.

The remaining eight aircraft bombed suspected flak positions plastering the gun emplacements with bombs and cannon fire as they dropped in on the enemy. Landing at Ursel, the Spitfires re-armed and re-fuelled, taking off at 17:50hrs. Climbing rapidly they attacked The Hague to Gouda railway junction, pounding it with bombs. Only two were direct hits, the rest near misses. They landed back at base at 18:15hrs.

19 March 1945

The Squadron concentrated on dive-bombing the railway targets. The first railway strike took place at 09:05hrs with F/O Fallon leading four Spitfires. Instead of forming up into a loose formation of four aircraft they were separated in cloud and only three aircraft attacked the bridge over the railway line south-west of Woerden. 'One bomb burst below the bridge on the track and one on the track beyond the bridge,' wrote the Squadron's diarist. The rest were near misses. The section dive-bombed other targets, included a railway bridge near Alphen with no hits. They arrived back at base at 10:40hrs.

F/Lt Melia led the next section of Spitfires. They took off at 10:00hrs and climbed into the morning sky. Crossing over the Dutch coast Melia turned the section towards the target: the railway junction on the Utrecht to Amersfoort line. Peeling off, Melia rolled his Spitfire into a dive. The target loomed up at him as he released his bombs. He then quickly pulled out. Below he could see his bombs hitting the track. The rest of the bombs also hit the track destroying that section of the railway junction. They landed safely back at base at 11:40hrs.

The last mission of the 19th was led by F/Lt Charlesworth. His section dive-bombed The Hague to Gouda railway line. Two direct hits were seen and the rest were near misses. Throughout these three missions there was no enemy reaction at all.

20 March 1945

Charlesworth led a section of four Spitfires in an attack on the Gouda to Woerden railway line. They were airborne from base at 09:20hrs and on the outward journey achieved no results from their dive-bombing. They landed at Ursel to re-arm and re-fuel. Taking off at 12:00hrs they attacked The Hague to Rotterdam railway line. 'There were direct hits on the line and embankment and many near misses,' wrote the Squadron diarist. The line was cut and there was no enemy reaction. They landed at 13:15hrs.

The next section took off from Coltishall at 10:15hrs and attacked the railway junction at Alphen. Two direct hits were seen by the pilots and the rest were near misses. 'On the way to Ursel they attacked an M.T. vehicle and left it smoking,' wrote the Squadron diarist. On the return journey the section dive-bombed The Hague to Gouda line, achieving three direct hits.

In the late morning S/Ldr Scott's section dive-bombed the railway line near Voorhout and achieved one hit on the embankment and the rest near misses. On the return Scott's section achieved several direct hits on the track and a bridge near Gouda before returning to base.

The last railway interdiction mission of the day dive-bombed the bridge near Nromwijk scoring one direct hit on the bridge and the remainder clustered around it. On the return journey, after re-arming and re-fuelling at Ursel, they attacked the railway bridge near Gouda and scored several hits on the track.

At 16:20hrs F/Lt Melia led a section of four Spitfires on an armed recce to the storage sheds at Ypenburg. Only two aircraft achieved results scoring hits on the outhouses to the east of the target. The bombs from the other aircraft overshot the target, while two other aircraft aborted the mission due to mechanical problems. The section arrived back at base at 17:35hrs.

The final mission of the day was an armed recce back to Ypenburg. Three aircraft rolled into their dives and released their bombs over the target. Several strikes were seen on buildings in the target area while one aircraft could not bomb due to mechanical problems. They returned to base at 18:00hrs.

21 March 1945

By now they were encountering virtually no enemy opposition at all. Activity over the next few days would be very intense for 124 Squadron. It was now almost entirely railway and road interdiction strikes with the Spitfires dive-bombing targets and rail lines throughout the days and weeks ahead.

At 10:35hrs a section of Spitfires, led by W/O Parker, attacked the road and rail bridge on The Hague to Gouda line, achieving only one near miss. On their return, the pilots attacked the same bridge with two direct hits and several hits on the north and west of the bridge. Orbitting overhead, Parker watched the embankment collapse and could see the rails on the bridge were twisted. They landed at base at 14:40hrs.

At 11:35hrs P/O Andrews led a section of Spitfires to dive-bomb railway lines and a bridge at Kronwijk. There were two direct hits on the south-west part of the bridge and all the other bombs fell in a cluster around it. On the return, the sections attacked another rail bridge, this time at Voorburg, achieving six direct hits and the rest were near misses.

Later that same day, F/Lt Forth's section successfully attacked the Leiden to Haarlem railway where the road bridge crossing the track received three direct hits and there were several near misses including some bombs that landed on the road.

23 March 1945

The first two dive-bombing missions were on the Leiden to Haarlem railway line with mostly near misses. The flight took off from Coltishall at 11:00hrs, led by F/O Travis, who managed to hit the embankment of the railway. Farther down the line, two Spitfires dive-bombed a road bridge achieving three hits.

Later that day two Spitfires were dispatched to escort Mustangs photographing The Hague area. After that another dive-bombing raid was made on the Gouda to Utrecht railway line, with two direct hits on the embankment by a bridge over a canal and two direct hits on the track.

24 March 1945

The pace of the dive-bombing continued the next day with an early morning raid led by F/Lt Fowler leading four Spitfires on a mission to attack a road bridge over the Leiden to Haarlem railway line. Only two bombs exploded and they were both near misses.

F/Lt Fallon's section took off from Coltishall at 11:00hrs and dive-bombed a bridge on the Gouda to Alphen railway line. They scored one direct hit on the bridge and one on the track; others were near misses. When they landed at Ursel one of their aircraft had a taxiing accident so only three took off later for a return to base. On the way they bombed a bridge on The Hague to Gouda railway line scoring three direct hits and cutting the track in three places. The rest were near misses.

The armed bombing recce, led by F/Lt Lawrence, dive-bombed the Leiden to Alphen railway line on the way out and on the way back to base. They cut that section of track in several places before landing back at Coltishall.

The rest of the afternoon was taken up with patrolling and escorting returning bombers and was completely uneventful.

25 March 1945

The first flight at 09:45hrs was led by F/Lt Brooks. They dive-bombed a railway junction at Frenelen, achieving one direct hit that cut the line and several near misses. There was a sadness that clouded the day: when F/Lt Maltby dropped down to 200 feet and a bomb exploded directly beneath his aircraft he spun into the ground. Though the wreckage of the aircraft could be seen on the ground there was no sign of the pilot. The remaining three aircraft landed at Ursel, re-armed and re-fuelled and took off dive-bombing the same railway junction before breaking off to Woerden, which was covered in debris after the attack.

Later that morning, F/Lt Lawrence led a section of Spitfires that bombed the Arkncelen to Woerden railway line cutting it in three places with their dive-bombing efforts. The weather over the target area was reported as deteriorating so there was no flying for the rest of the day.

27 March 1945

The first flight of the day took place at 13:30hrs when F/Lt Fowler's section attacked the Woerden to Utrecht line with no results. That afternoon the squadron attacked another junction but achieved no hits. S/Ldr Scott dive-bombed a railway south-east of Amsterdam but there were no results. That afternoon, the tracks on the Woerden line were cut when a section of Spitfires, led by F/Lt Lawrence, attacked the Woerden to Amsterdam line cutting it where the bombs struck.

Later, another detail was sent to attack the same railway junction but they achieved only one direct hit on a truck and four near misses. In the last flight of the day, Spitfires, led by F/Lt Lawrence, dive-bombed the Woerden to Amsterdam line, cutting it in several places.

30 March 1945

Two dive-bombing Spitfires attacked The Hague to Rotterdam railway and put it out of action with one direct hit on the track. Another bridge closer to Rotterdam was also hit but the results were not seen due to worsening weather conditions. On the return flight one aircraft could not leave Ursel due to mechanical trouble, so the remaining three carried on. They attacked a road bridge near The Hague but did not know the results as the whole area was covered by major fog.

The afternoon's flight, led by F/O Fellan, ran into a thunderstorm just twenty miles from the English coast on their return from a bombing raid. Fierce rain and wind ensued and the engine of one aircraft cut out and F/Sgt Lett went missing, believed to have been killed. The remaining aircraft returned to base landing safely.

The last flight of the day was an air-sea rescue search for downed F/Sgt Lett. An ASR launch over the radio reported that they had found a body.

31 March 1945

At 13:15hrs dive-bombing began again with Fowler's section attacking along the Leiden/Haarlem railway line. They reported two hits on the road leading up to the bridge across the line. There were two other near misses and the rest were not seen.

A section of Spitfires, led by F/Lt Charlesworth, attacked The Hague to Gouda railway line achieving six direct hits.

Another raid, led by F/Lt Lawrence, took off at 14:40hrs, and struck the Woerden to Utrecht line with no direct hits, only near misses. Another aircraft bombed the Brenckelen to Woerdern line with near misses only.

At 16:55hrs a section of aircraft, led by S/Ldr Scott, took off from Coltishall and attacked the railway line south of Hardwijk with bombs hitting the side of the embankment south-west of Amsterdam.

The last flight of the day, a section of four Spitfires led by F/O Travis, took off from Coltishall at 17:25hrs. Two of them attacked the Leiden to Haarlem railway line, while the other two attacked a bridge on the same railway. One bomb damaged the bridge and one went right through to the canal below making a large hole in the line. They landed back at base at 18:50hrs.

Appendix C

229 Squadron History

From September 1944 to January 1945 229 Spitfire Squadron played a significant role in Big Ben operations. Like 303 Squadron, most of their work was hammering the supply lines of the Germans before attacking V2 sites themselves. Railway lines and shipping lanes were the major targets along with any troops and vehicle movements.

As the Germans increased their activity in the area, 229 Squadron, operating out of Coltishall, increased their attacks and reconnaissance patrols that would ultimately lead to the destruction of Hitler's V2 rocket programme. Not before many thousands had been killed, however.

What follows is, largely, 229 Squadron's official diary. In most cases, the targets are identified either as a wooded area near The Hague, or they are not identified at all. However, once 229 Squadron began carrying out armed bombing recces, dive-bombing targets, we can assume that those targets would have been V2 sites or targets related to the production of the V2 rockets.

The Squadron's contribution to the destruction of the V2 sites began in earnest in early September with patrols over the German supply lines from ships, to rail yards (as detailed in Chapter II). What follows is the rest of 229's contribution to Operation Big Ben, after a lay-off period at the end of September 1944.

1 December 1944

Whilst 602 and 453 Squadrons were laid on for a large dive-bombing campaign with twelve aircraft to bomb The Hague/Bosch and Hague Promenade areas, 229 and 303 Squadrons continued to carry out armed recce missions.

The first flight of 229 Squadron in December 1944 was a weather recce upon which the success of 602's and 453's bombing operation depended. At 09:00hrs F/Lt Rigler and F/Lt Welch took off heading across the North Sea to the Dutch coast. After flying south to the Hook they set course for base at 10:30hrs and landed at 11:10hrs.

With the weather deteriorating, an armed recce to Den Helder was launched by 229 Squadron. F/O Walker and F/O Hayes took off at 09:15hrs. They reached Den Helder forty minutes later and climbed to 9,000 feet but did not find targets to attack. They returned to base at 11:15hrs.

The bombing missions that day by 602 and 453 squadrons had been unsuccessful because the weather over the target prohibited them from attacking. Their fighters jettisoned their bombs in the sea and returned to base.

That afternoon, 229 Squadron was released from operations for the day. Their CO Major Harrison of the South African Air Force discovered he was to be posted to the Empire Central Flying School.

2 December 1944

The first flight of the day took off from Swannington at 08:20hrs but poor weather forced the Spitfires to turn back at 09:40hrs.

At 08:40hrs F/Lt Burrett and F/Lt Welch climbed into the grey morning sky for a Jim Crow mission to monitor shipping in the Den Helder area. They climbed below cloud base to 4,000 feet where they spotted two small vessels just north of the Den Helder harbour. They headed back to Swannington, landing at 10:10hrs.

Another weather recce took place later in the morning for a bombing mission by 602 and 453 Squadrons. At 11:15hrs W/O Cookson led two Spitfires away from Swannington across the North Sea towards Holland. They crossed land at Westhoofd and turned towards Katwijk before returning to base at 13:11hrs. The weather was so poor the bombing mission had to be cancelled.

That same day, 229 Squadron were told they were to move back to Coltishall and that the aircraft were to be ready to fly from there at 10:00hrs the following day. The Squadron by now had received new Spitfire XVIs, which were flown over to Coltishall with all the other aircraft (Spitfire IXs included). It was the first time the new Spitfires had been flown by the Squadron.

3 December 1944

Bad weather kept flying to a minimum, and although the Squadron declared itself operational at 10:00hrs they were ordered not to fly. The whole day was taken up organising the dispersal at Coltishall and the removing of aircraft and equipment from Swannington to Coltishall. By now 229 Squadron had twenty-three Spitfire IX aircraft, seventeen Spitfire XVI fighter bombers, a single Spitfire V and a Miles Magister trainer.

4 December 1944

Poor weather took its toll once again. P/O Doidge and W/O McKenzie were forty miles from the Dutch Coast when they were forced to abort the mission and return to base.

At 11:30hrs F/Lt Rigler led an Armed Recce to The Hague. However, the target was completely covered by cloud and the four Spitfires returned to base at 13:55hrs.

5 December 1944

The first flight of the day was a weather recce over The Hague; it reported that the weather was likely to take a turn for the worse. At 08:15hrs, F/Lt Patterson took off from Coltishall for a Jim Crow mission over Den Helder but sighted nothing and reported on the weather. Cloud covered everything at a height of 5,000 feet. The two Spitfires returned to base.

Due to poor weather conditions the next armed recce due to take off at 11:30hrs was cancelled. It was this armed recce the CO was hoping to lead in the Squadron's new Spitfires. It would be the first armed recce carrying two 250 lb bombs.

All was not lost. At 14:30hrs the CO took off leading a section of four Spitfire XVIs on the Squadron's first diving bombing operation in The Hague. But the weather thwarted them again preventing any accurate pin-pointing over the target. The four Spitfires landed back with bombs at 16:05hrs.

6 December 1944

The first flight of the day was a weather recce over Den Helder, which showed the cloud base to be at 1,500 feet with the top at 3,000 feet. But it was at 11:00hrs that the CO, Major Harrison, led four Spitfire XVIs on an armed recce to the Haagsche Bosch in The Hague. This time the weather was clear enough for them to dive-bomb onto the target. Harrison touched his rudder, rolling the fighter into a dive, his hand hovering over the bomb release. As the height wound down he watched the buildings coming closer and closer. Pulling the release, the two bombs fell from under his wings and he quickly pulled out of his dive, climbing rapidly away. Turning tightly he saw the two projectiles accurately pin-point the target. The next two bombs also hit the target very accurately. Two more landed within 200 yards of the target. Only the unfortunate W/O Hayes had his two bombs hung up and could not attack. He later managed to jettison them in the sea. After their first successful dive-bombing operation the four Spitfires wheeled away and headed back to base where they landed at 12:25hrs.

At 13:35hrs F/Lt Rigler led a bombing recce on the Wassenaar/ Langenhurst area but due to poor weather the results were never known. The four aircraft bombed through a gap in the clouds diving from 7,000 feet to 4,000 feet but the accuracy of the bombing could not be verified as the results were never seen by any of the pilots. F/Lt Rigler claimed to have seen clouds of smoke rising high into the sky which the other pilots claimed was simply shadow on the clouds. As they returned to base they sighted a large trail of black smoke going into the sea, which could have been an aircraft exploding in mid-air. The Spitfires did not investigate owing to their lack of fuel. They landed back at base at 15:30hrs.

7 December 1944

F/Lt Patterson led a flight of four Spitfire XVIs in very poor weather at 09:35hrs. At virtually zero feet, Patterson found heavy rain and thunder over the whole area. It was so dark only the flames from their exhaust could be seen as they roared across the North Sea towards Holland. But they couldn't see the coast at all and somewhere in the vicinity of Ijmuiden they turned back and headed for Coltishall where they landed at 11:05hrs. No bombs were dropped and they didn't cross into enemy territory.

The next flight that day was a weather recce at 12:30hrs led by F/Lt Kirkman. The four Spitfire IX fighters patrolled Texel, Egmund and the Amsterdam area. Throughout the patrol they encountered very poor weather with cloud layers at 1,500 feet and as high as 10,000 feet. That day F/Lt H J Burrett left the Squadron due to repatriation back to New Zealand.

8 December 1944

An interesting entry in the Squadron diary outlines the movement of experienced pilots and the poor training, in the eyes of the diarist, of the new pilots. He recorded: 'A proposed Ramrod of 6 Spitfire XVI from 229, 602 and 453 Squadrons to bomb The Hague was cancelled on account of very poor weather and no operational flying occurred. In the morning Group Captain Dunn, D.F.C. of Operations 12 Group visited the Squadron and flew a Spitfire XVI. The departure of F/Os Walker and Andrews and W/O Hayes was postponed till after a squadron presentation. Later, an aircraft recognition test, which showed the abilities of the new pilots to be well below standard.'

9 December 1944

Again, the weather forced the Squadron to remain inactive and no operational flying took place. Poor weather over The Hague ensured that no bombing or armed recces took place.

10 December 1944

In the early morning, P/O Doidge led three other Spitfire XVI fighters from Coltishall at 08:15hrs to attack a special target with bombs. The target was Leiden Main Station, which had been attacked by Typhoons earlier. The Spitfires were to observe the results from the previous Typhoon raid and complete the job. Just north of The Hague Doidge turned towards Leiden. Climbing to 11,000 feet they circled the town but below them the target was obscured by cloud. However, there were gaps in the cloud cover. Spying one, Doidge rolled into a dive, dropping from 11,000 feet to 4,000 feet where he released his bombs. Turning tightly he roared away as the rest of the section dropped their bombs. F/Sgts O'Reilly and Wheatley both reported seeing four bombs hit the station itself. The other four also hit the target.

At 10:30hrs F/Lt Kirkman led a flight of four Spitfires XVI carrying 250 lb bombs to Wassenaar/Langenhorst. They crossed over land at Westhoofd and bombed the targets from south-west to north-east. Kirkman rolled into his dive at 9,500 feet, his hand hovering near the bomb release as his altimeter wound down, the aircraft rapidly losing height. In his bomb sight he could see the target: a white and grey concrete building. He dive-bombed it. At 5,000 feet he released his bombs and pulled out of the dive. The rest of the section attacked and all eight bombs hammered the area striking successfully. Accurate and light flak followed them out of their dives but none of the aircraft were hit. They landed back at base at 11:20hrs. The Squadron diarist wrote: 'A possible show on a new target at the Hook, for which F/Lt Patterson and P/O Doidge were all keyed up with promise of bags of flak was cancelled at the last moment on account of weather. Pat was very disappointed but Bill who already visualised his name in headlines in the morning's papers was not feeling too well and was somewhat relieved.'

11 December 1944

The first operation of the day was a bombing mission in a heavily defended area of the Hook. Climbing into the morning sky at 10:01hrs, led by F/Lt Patterson, they headed for what was their most successful bombing recce to date: Westhoofd.

Rolling into a dive at 10,000 feet, Patterson dropped his bombs at 4,500 feet. All the bombs fell on the target-structures in a wooded area. P/O Doidge bombed a road while F/Sgt O'Reilly bombed a road junction. Light, intense and accurate flak came from a one-mile radius around the target that followed the Spitfires two to three miles out to sea. The aircraft landed safely back at Coltishall at 11:35hrs.

The afternoon bombing recce was led by F/Lt Rigler, leading a section of four Spitfire XVIs to The Hague/Voorde area. Taking off at 12:55hrs, they climbed to height and headed over the North Sea towards Holland.

Rigler could see the target was partially obscured by cloud. As a result they circled for fifteen minutes, then three aircraft bombed from north-east to south-west diving from 6,000–4,000 feet. The results weren't visible because of the cloud. P/O McConnochie bombed from south to north. He rolled into his dive seeing the horseshoe building rapidly growing in his sights. Levelling out, he released his bombs then climbed rapidly away turning tightly as he did. Below he could see his bombs hit the building. Forming up with the rest of the section, the four Spitfires ran into light flak as they crossed the Rotterdam Canal where W/O Beckwith received superficial damage to his radiator. They landed safely back at Coltishall at 13:45hrs.

This day was to prove to be one of their best. At 15:00hrs F/Lt Patterson led an armed recce with bombs to Wassenaar/Rust-en-Vreugd. Climbing up to 11,000 feet they headed for Holland, but found that the target was covered in mist. They waited for the mist to clear, then Patterson peeled off, rolling into his dive from 10,000 feet. The section bombed from north to west. Keeping the aircraft steady he could see the height pouring away as the Spitfire screamed down onto the target. Pulling out at 4,000 feet he released his bombs but they fell near a large five-storey building 100 yards from the pin-point position. The rest of the bombs fell on the target, which was slightly north and along the road.

Suddenly, flak poured up at them, the heaviest yet. Coming from some woods about a mile from the target the flak was so intense it was like a carpet of shells exploding around the aircraft. F/Sgt O'Reilly, flying No. 4 position and taking the brunt of the flak, decided to fly straight into it, strafing the flak positions with his cannon. Miraculously, none of the Spitfires were hit but the flak followed them as they headed back towards base. They landed back at Coltishall at 16:40hrs.

That evening, the Squadron said goodbye to Major Harrison at a dinner dance where the beer flowed freely and everyone crowded into the officers' mess, happy with their day's work.

12 December 1944

Bad weather kept the Squadron grounded. Major Harrison left the Squadron.

13 December 1944

No flying took place today either, as heavy mist ruined any chance of flying. F/Lt Patterson was promoted to S/Ldr and CO of the Squadron.

The next day the weather again made operational flying impossible.

15 December 1944

The weather again made armed recce flights very difficult. Early in the morning (08:25hrs), two Spitfires took off for a weather recce over Ijmuiden and reported the cloud was from 2,000–6,000 feet. No more flights took place that day.

16 December 1944

This was another day of bad weather, very heavy mists and rain. No operational flying took place. In fact, no operational flying took place until 23 December owing to terrible weather and extremely poor visibility.

23 December 1944

The weather had cleared enough for some flying to take place. The first sortie took off from Coltishall at 09:10hrs with a section of four Spitfire XVIs climbing into the morning sky. Twenty miles from the Dutch coast they spotted a V2 contrail, which appeared to be fired from well inland.

They crossed over Westhoofd flying at 12,000 feet and could barely see the town through a gap in the clouds. Thick cloud covered the whole area prohibiting any pin-point dive-bombing. They returned to Coltishall with empty drop tanks and their bombs still hanging from their wings.

24 December 1944

From the dispersal area in the morning the pilots and ground crew could see several V2 contrails. The sky was clear with hard frost on the ground. It was a perfect day for flying and would prove to be very busy.

At 10:10hrs eleven aircraft, all carrying one 500 lb bomb and two 250 lb bombs, took off from Coltishall, climbing slowly into the crisp morning sky. Preceding this formation, W/Cdr Fitzgerald with F/Lt Bob Sergeant headed towards the target. They carried two 250 lb bombs and a drop tank.

The target was a block of flats around a square courtyard, eighty yards by 100 yards, according to the Squadron diary. This target lay between Westhoofd and The Hague. The diarist states: '229 were the first on the target followed by 483 and 602 Squadrons at five minute intervals. At this rate the highlights of the V2 concern would be on the receiving end of 16 tons of well aimed High explosive for the target is the headquarters and billets of the "gas main" gun men.'

Suddenly, very shortly after take off, Bill Doidge's engine cut completely and he was forced to make a steep landing just outside the dispersal area on the extension strip. Everyone was outside watching the

Squadron form up when Doidge came in steep and fast. He struggled with the controls as the aircraft dropped quickly. Hitting the ground, his undercarriage buckled and collapsed dropping the aircraft onto its belly. It slid for 100 yards. As it did so, the 500 lb bomb came free and bounced along behind the Spitfire. One of the 250 lb bombs also fell away. The squadron diarist recorded: 'This was a signal for general panic among the onlookers. Most of the crowd ran away from the crash but the usual half dozen "mad types" ran to the rescue. Fortunately, the bombs remained silent and Bill Doidge emerged from the cockpit under his [own] volition. White and shaken but nevertheless he was the old Bill. Meanwhile, the armourers were removing the bits and pieces that make the bombs tick.'

The remainder of the aircraft crossed in north of Zendvoort at 10:55hrs. Flying at 10,000 feet over the Haarlem / The Hague main road they turned south towards the target. The sky was clear and visibility excellent, which meant it was no problem to the flight to identify the buildings. The W/Cdr and F/Lt Sergeant bombed first. They peeled off at 8,000 feet dropping into their dives. At 3,000 feet they levelled out, released their bombs then climbed away, orbiting the target to watch the main section do their work. At 11:00hrs the squadron began bombing the buildings. Red flashes where the bombs landed were seen in the south-west corner of the building as the bombs rained down from the diving Spitfires. Some of the fighters strafed with their cannon as they released their bombs and climbed away. Most of the bombs fell in a confined area from the south-west corner to the centre.

Smoke and dust shot up from the structures as the bombs exploded. Flames could be seen licking a small part of the building, emitting thick smoke. The Squadron climbed away heading for a prearranged landing ground at Ursel.

In the meantime, the W/Cdr and F/Lt Sergeant remained orbiting the area to watch the results from 453's bombing runs. Light and medium flak shot up to the aircraft from the target area. As the Spitfires attacked the flak followed them bursting all around them. Suddenly, one aircraft of 453 Squadron was hit by flak and crashed.

After ten minutes W/Cdr Fitzgerald and F/Lt Sergeant left the scene, heading towards an area north of The Hague where they crossed out over the North Sea and headed back towards Coltishall. The two Spitfires landed safely at 11:55hrs.

However, at Ursel the nine Spitfires of 229 Squadron prepared to re-arm and attack other targets on their return to Coltishall. The idea had been to 'bomb up' at Ursel and to attack three other targets on the way back. However, there were no bombs available so the Spitfires re-armed with cannon and machine-gun ammunition. The first section of three aircraft led by the CO, S/Ldr Patterson, took off from Ursel at 13:45hrs and flew straight towards their targets in The Hague/Langen area. At 14:10hrs

Patterson identified the target situated in a wooded area. Flying at 7,000 feet, Patterson peeled off, rolling into the top of a dive onto the target below. Thumbing the firing button he watched the height bleed away and pulled out at 2,500 feet when he fired his cannon. Shells poured from his guns and ripped into the wooded area. Strikes from his aircraft and from the others were seen in the woods but there were no spectacular results. They continued their dives heading out to sea, crossing out north of The Hague at 14:15hrs. They arrived back at Coltishall at 15:00hrs having fired 1,000 rounds of ammunition.

Another three aircraft took off from Ursel at 13:45hrs and flew straight for the target which was in the Wassenaar/Rust-en-Vreugt area. Led by F/Lt McAndrew, the Spitfires climbed to 10,000 feet then each rolled into its dive, cannon and machine guns spitting shells. The Spitfires strafed a wooded area and were greeted with intense but inaccurate flak. Once again strikes were seen on the target area without results. Pulling out at 3,000 feet the Spitfires climbed away towards an area south of Katwijk and headed out to sea towards England. They landed back at Coltishall at 15:00hrs.

The remaining three Spitfires took off from Ursel at 13:45hrs. Led by F/Lt Kirkman they flew straight to their targets in The Hague/Haagsche Bosch area. Kirkman kept his section in orbit over the target, a wooded area, flying at 12,000 feet. Then cried 'break' and rolled into his dive, thumbed the firing button and sent a hail of shells into the target area. Attacking from south-east to north-west the aircraft fired all they had at the structures and vehicles in the wooded area. Pulling out at 6,000 feet they turned and headed straight out to sea. The three aircraft landed back at Coltishall at 15:00hrs. It had been a long day.

25 December 1944

As the sun rose into a cloudless sky, the pilots waited for the call that would send them hurtling into the sky on operational flying. Visibility was one hundred percent, the sky was a brilliant blue and the Squadron was placed on readiness. While they waited for the first flights to be launched everyone had their fair share of the usual Christmas trimmings. They finished the day with not a single minute of flying.

26 December 1944

Unlike the previous day, visibility was very poor as fog covered the whole airfield and no flying took place. The same was true of the following day when bad weather and near zero visibility kept the Squadron on the ground. But by the 28th the weather cleared and operational flying took place.

28 December 1944

P/O McConnochie led the first bombing recce of the day. Leading a section of four Spitfires each carrying two 250 lb bombs, they took off from Coltishall at 10:10hrs and climbed steadily into the morning sky. The target was The Hague/Langenhorst area. The four Spitfires headed out across the North Sea, crossing into enemy airspace over Egmond at 10:45hrs. McConnochie turned the section to follow the Alkmaar/Haarlem/The Hague road roaring towards their target. Climbing to 8,000 feet, he spotted the target below, which included a railway line and a large white building along with other structures.

Quickly checking his instruments to make sure everything was all right, McConnochie peeled off, rolling into a dive. From south-east to north-west the aircraft attacked. As the target grew in his sights, he kept the Spitfire steady in the dive, released his bombs and pulled the stick back, levelling out at 3,000 feet. McConnochie thumbed the firing button expecting his guns to belch flame and shells but both cannon jammed almost immediately, and after a few short bursts so did his machine guns. Climbing away, he saw that his bombs had pounded the south corner of the white building. P/O Van Dyck's had also hit the same area.

But the bombs from F/Sgt Haupt and W/O Beckwith had hit the railway line in the south-west corner of the target, cutting the line. By now the gunners below had woken up and began to pump light flack into the sky to catch the Spitfires. Climbing away to the east, they left the target area smoking. At 7,000 feet they crossed out over Katwijk at 11:08hrs and landed back at Coltishall thirty-seven minutes later.

The next operation of the day was another bombing recce, led this time by P/O Bill Doidge. Flying the lead Spitfire in the section of four, Doidge climbed rapidly away from Coltishall at 12:25hrs. Forming up over the North Sea they set a course for Holland and ten minutes from the Dutch coast they altered course crossing over land south of Katwijk flying at 12,000 feet. Dead ahead, Doidge spotted a V2 contrail, well inland, rising rapidly. The target area was Wassenaar/Rust-en-Vreugd and Doidge brought the aircraft to 11,000 feet after sighting the target. Preparing to dive, he led the section in a quick orbit of the target, then peeled off, rolling the Spitfire into a dive. They attacked from south-east to north-east. Pulling out at 4,000 feet, Doidge fired his cannon, raking the area with shells. Turning, he climbed quickly, looking down at the target area and could see the last of his section pulling out of his dive. All eight bombs had hit the target yet there were no results just dust and debris. He could see light flak slowly clawing upwards to try to reach the fighters but it was inaccurate and too far away. Re-forming north-east of the target, Doidge led the section home, crossing out over the North Sea between The Hague and Katwijk. They landed back at Coltishall at 13:40hrs.

The entry in the Squadron History for this mission is an interesting one. 'This was one of the quickest bombing recces ever made with each aircraft taking 1 hour and 15 minutes,' wrote the Squadron diarist.

The third 'show' of the day began badly. Four Spitfires were to take off at 15:00hrs to attack The Hague/Hotel Promenade. Three aircraft led again by P/O McConnachie took off on time but the fourth piloted by F/O Sanderson was delayed by seven minutes having difficulty starting.

Sanderson roared away from Coltishall, his throttles open, hoping to catch up with the rest of the section now seven minutes ahead of him. Yet, all he could see in front of him was empty sky. For several minutes Sanderson strained to find his fellow pilots but was unsuccessful and reluctantly he turned back and landed at Coltishall. Somewhere over the North Sea the rest of the section roared on over the waves heading for the Dutch coast.

At 15:35hrs they crossed over land at Ijmuiden flying at 10,000 feet. Turning, McConnochie led the other two aircraft down the coast towards the target area. Changing course again, he dropped to 9,000 feet then rolled his aircraft over, dropping into a dive. Leading the attack in a south-west to north-easterly direction, McConnochie dropped his bombs and pulled out of his dive at 5,000 feet, strafing the target as he did so. Bombs hit a narrow stretch of wood, and several houses east of the pin-point area were hit with bombs from the Spitfires. They re-formed north of The Hague at 7,000 feet and headed for home. At 16:20hrs the three Spitfires landed back at Coltishall and taxied into dispersal. The three pilots were just in time to take an aircraft recognition test that had been going on throughout the day.

29 December 1944

'Fog again! Later the fog became mist and gradually blew away giving us an afternoon of brilliant sunshine,' recorded the diarist. But the weather over Holland was not so accommodating and the squadron remained on the ground in a state of readiness. To keep them busy, S/Ldr Patterson led a talk with all personnel attending to discuss a variety of engineering ideas. The diarist recorded: 'Among matters which were discussed, was a scheme for a quick transfer of overload tank to 500 lb bombs, the difficulties of starting the bowser tractors in the morning and counter-measures to be taken, the men's billets and other technical and welfare issues.'

Throughout the day the Squadron waited for a word from operations but they remained silent. 'In the evening, the long awaited dinner and dance in the Officers' mess took place at which the 229 Squadron officers behaved with surprisingly irreproachable decorum except for a few small incidents in the early hrs of the morning.'

30 December 1944

Though no operational flying took place on this day because of poor weather the Squadron was on practice flying. However, a sudden mist descended on the airfield with eight aircraft still in the air. Two managed to land while the remaining six landed at bases in the area including Wittering, King's Cliffe and Matlaske.

That night, following the 9 o'clock news, a commentary by F/Lt Rigler and F/Lt Welch about their experiences dive-bombing V2 sites in Holland was broadcast. Many pilots heard the broadcast and generally agreed it was very good. 'A camp concert of local talent was also employed in the evening at which F/Lt McAndrew's sister a member of the WAAF Gang Show gave an excellent display of ventriloquism in very short skirts,' recorded the Squadron diarist.

31 December 1944

Everyone awoke to a morning of hard frost. Roads in the area were treacherously icy but the sky was crystal clear and intensive air operations began. Information came through that 602 and 453 Squadrons would not be able to take off due to ice on the runways at Swannington. That left 229 Squadron to take on the mantle of operations for the day.

The first flight of the day was a Jim Crow shipping recce by F/Lt Sergeant and F/Lt Kirkman who changed course several times while flying over Holland to avoid snow and hail storms. They were in the air for an hour and forty minutes and sighted little shipping.

The first bombing recce took place at 09:35hrs when F/Lt Rigler leading three other Spitfires took off from Coltishall and climbed out over the North Sea towards Holland. The target was The Hague/Haagsche Bosch. Climbing above the cloud and snow storms to 10,000 feet they roared on. But before reaching the Dutch coast P/O Grant had to turn back due to engine failure. He was escorted by P/O McConnochie and that left two Spitfires to carry out the bombing run. The target was a wooded area where V2 sites were thought to be. It would be the usual sheds, vehicles and other equipment that the Spitfires would bomb. F/Lt Rigler and S/Ldr Donovan made landfall over Westhoofd climbed to 12,000 feet and headed west of Rotterdam where they orbited the target area. For ten minutes the two Spitfires orbited high overhead as S/Ldr Donovan tried to identify the objective. Visibility was very clear and they could see some of the lakes were frozen over. Finally, Donovan identified the target, rolled the aircraft over and dropped into a dive. From 9,000 feet the Spitfire dived straight and level towards the target. Donovan watched the ground grow quickly. The height wound down on the altimeter and at 4,000 feet he released his bombs and pulled out climbing rapidly away. All of their bombs hit the wooded area as they attacked from north-east to south-west. They encountered some light flak during this operation but it was neither intense nor accurate. Climbing up to 10,000 feet the two Spitfires headed for home and landed back at Coltishall at 11:40hrs.

The early afternoon operation was a big one. The target was The Hague/Haagsche Bosch storage site, which had been identified as having six V2 rockets. It was later confirmed that the storage facility had twelve rockets.

At 12:55hrs twelve Spitfire XVI fighter-bombers lifted off from Coltishall climbing slowly into the sky. Each aircraft carried one 500 lb bomb with a twenty-five second delayed fuse and two 250 lb general airburst bombs. Leading was S/Ldr Patterson. They formed up over the North Sea, then climbed to 10,000 feet setting a course for the Dutch coast. The Spitfires crossed over land at Katwijk and turned south towards the target.

Patterson pushed his stick forward, gently dropping the Spitfire to 8,500 feet. But he suddenly realised his R/T had failed making it difficult to lead the Squadron in the diving attack. It would have to be hand signals and a waggle of the wings. Motioning to the closest aircraft that he was about to dive, he peeled off, diving from the south to the north on the target. Releasing his bombs, Patterson pulled out of his dive at 3,500 feet and climbed, turning to watch the other aircraft attack the site below. All but one of the bombs fell on or around the storage site. The one that didn't fell short amongst some nearby houses.

Suddenly, there was a bright red flash in the woods, which some of the pilots believed was possibly a V2 that had been hit.

Throughout the attack the target area had been protected by intense and accurate flak. The last pilots on the operation dropped into their dives braving the flak. Luckily no one was lost to the anti-aircraft fire. However, some pilots of the last two sections dived on the target from too far away making the dive at too small an angle, which they rectified. S/Ldr Donovan's Spitfire was hit by flak in the spinner and sustained minor damage.

According to 229 Squadron's diary they crossed out over The Hague at heights 'varying from 3,000 feet to zero feet at 1340hrs.' They were encountering very heavy, intense and accurate flak from the coastal areas. F/Lt Kirkman reported seeing German troops running for their anti-aircraft guns while some of the others reported light flak guns on rooftops. The concentrated fire followed the pilots out to sea. F/Lt Sergeant had a bad time with flak all around him and in front of him. Three miles out to sea the squadron formed up and the intense flak followed them with F/Lt Sergeant having a bad time in front and behind him. The flak followed him persistently as he crossed out north-west of The Hague. Joining the others, they set a course for Ursel where they landed at 14:20hrs. All except P/O Van Dyck who climbed into the clouds to avoid the flak and emerged to find the Squadron gone. Setting a course for Ursel himself he managed to land later. But F/Sgt Wheatley promised to stay behind to report on the bombing results. Finding himself alone he contacted Control and asked for a vector growing more and more uneasy as he flew. In the end he was vectored to an emergency landing field at Le Zoote.

After re-fuelling at Ursel the squadron took off at 15:35hrs and landed back at Coltishall at 16:45hrs. While at Ursel, Patterson was told by the Dutch Liaison officer that the enemy were using the royal palace as a headquarters. All the pilots had been briefed to avoid it presumably so as not to upset the Dutch people.

In the month of December 229 Squadron had dropped a total of 44,500 lbs of bombs on enemy positions. They had flown a total of 202 hours and ten minutes, making the number of sorties 136. According to 229 Squadron's diary they dropped 136 250 lb bombs and a total of twenty-one 500 lb bombs.

1 January 1945

For the New Year the squadron was broken down into two flights, A Flight and B Flight. P/O Doidge of A Flight led the first operation of the New Year. It was a bombing run to The Hague/Langenhorst. The four Spitfires took off at 10:25hrs and were flying for just twenty minutes when they were recalled due to the probability of bad weather closing in on Coltishall before they landed.

But the weather cleared quite quickly and the second operation of the day began when four Spitfires, led again by P/O Doidge, took off at 12:25hrs. The target was The Hague/Haagsche Bosche area.

They climbed away from base forming up over the North Sea and then headed for Holland. They crossed in over Westhoofd flying at 11,000 feet. They turned north and headed for the target identified north of The Hague. It could be seen quite clearly. Doidge turned the section so they were ready to begin their dives and flicked on his R/T switch calling, 'Echelon Break!' Peeling away from the formation, he rolled into his dive at 10,000 feet, ready to release his bombs at the right moment. As he roared down on the target, another wooded area with storage facilities for the rockets hidden inside it, he waited for the right height to release his bombs. Finally, he reached the height he wanted, pulled the release lever and dropped his bombs then levelled out at 3,000 feet. They bombed from south to north.

As the aircraft dived on the target an intense curtain of flak was fired up at the Spitfires from enemy gunners below. Climbing rapidly away after pulling out of his dive, Doidge levelled off at 8,000 feet to watch the results of the bombing which were excellent. Four bombs fell on the targets in the woods while two others fell about 200 yards south and two more about 150 yards to the west. Not wanting to hang around, the flight quickly formed up and headed back to base, crossing out just north of The Hague at 8,000 feet. They crossed out over the sea only to be followed by flak in the coastal waters. The royal palace just to the north of the target was clearly to be seen as undamaged.

2 January 1945

No flying for 229 Squadron took place on this day, the weather being so poor. The Squadron's diarist, however, recorded this incident in the History. 'In the evening, S/Ldr Donovan set off to a New Year's party at Wattisham in the C.O.'s car and returned with quite a tale of woe. The car ran out of oil at Norwich and burst a tyre 15 miles from his objective at midnight on some lonely country lane. He reached his destination in the early morning, the party having ended and appears to have spent the remainder of the time getting back and borrowing a tyre and wheel.'

Flying the next day was also cancelled due to low cloud. However, pilots remained at dispersal all day and filled the time with talks from the CO on events to come and on night flying. In the afternoon, records 229 Squadron's diarist, the pilots watched combat films.

3 January 1945

Again, the weather was doubtful at the break of day for flying. However, a major operation was laid on that involved twelve aircraft from 229 Squadron, twelve from 602 Squadron and two Mustangs from 26 Squadron, which were to take photographs of the bombing. Both Mustangs were to be escorted by Spitfires of 303 Squadron. The target for this bombing operation was the tramway sheds at The Hague/ Loosduinen. Intelligence reports indicated that 4-ton tankers refilled at this site with liquid oxygen for despatch to V2 firing points.

The building, recorded 229's diarist, was built of brick and light metal with a glass roof. 'It is believed that the walls have probably been considerably strengthened as the oxygen must be produced under pressure. Consequently, heavy and accurate bombing was detailed to put the target out of action in one blow.'

Laid on for 12:00hrs that day, ground staff worked feverishly to arm the Spitfires. However, the ground crew were working on the normal schedule of arming four aircraft for an armed recce and not for twelve. They didn't have time to bomb up twelve aircraft, each with one 500 lb bomb with a twenty-five second delayed fuse and two 250 lb bombs with the same fusing. The diarist wrote: 'At 1100 hrs, the Armourers Sergeant, almost with tears in his eyes, begged the CO for more time and the show was delayed until 12:15hrs. But the aircraft were not ready by 12:10hrs and the show was cancelled to everyone's great dismay.'

Later that afternoon, the squadron was released from readiness and the pilots detailed to play football.

4 January 1945

The weather again played havoc with flying. High winds ripped across the airfield carrying rain and sleet interspersed with brilliant sunshine. The raid on the Tramsheds at The Hague/Loosduinen was set for 10:30hrs. But again the operation was cancelled and an armed recce took place instead. The Squadron diarist wrote: 'It is now known that the block of flats at Hague Narlot attacked on 24 December is definitely un-inhabitable and one of the combat films taken by F/Lt McAndrew shows very extensive damage to the clock tower and buildings and smoke pouring from the courtyard.'

The first operation of the day was an armed recce to The Hague/Haagsche Bosch, led by F/Lt Rigler. The four Spitfires took off from Coltishall at 11:25hrs and by late evening they had not returned. Later, when the pilots returned to Coltishall the story was told. Only one aircraft bombed the target while the rest experienced mechanical trouble. All the aircraft landed at various airfields in Belgium.

At 13:25hrs P/O Doidge led the day's second armed recce. The four Spitfires, carrying two 250 lb bombs each with twenty-five seconds delayed fuses climbed into the grey winter sky, heading for Holland. The target was The Hague/Voorde and the sky over it was clear, bright and sunny. Flying at 15,000 feet, they crossed land at Ijmuiden and Doidge, spotting the railway line that led towards the target, dropped the section to 10,000 feet following the railway.

There was no sign of enemy activity and the sky was clear of flak. Over the R/T Doidge heard F/Lt Sergeant express his uneasiness at the ominous quiet. Doidge spotted the target below, notified the rest of the section to attack and rolled into his dive. The four Spitfires attacked from south-west to north-east in dives from 10,000 feet to 3,500 feet. Doidge watched the altimeter spin as the height poured away; in his sights he could see the target area. Releasing his bombs he pulled out, turned and climbed away, watching the rest of the section attack. Bombs hammered the target all of them falling within 100 yards of the pinpoint. They climbed away flying north past The Hague and Leiden crossing out at Katwijk and headed over the North Sea to Coltishall. They landed back at base at 15:20hrs.

Later that afternoon the Squadron was notified that the operation to attack the tram sheds at The Hague/Loosduinen would be on for the next day at 10:00 hours. Unfortunately, the Squadron still had the four aircraft from the day's first armed recce sitting in Belgian airfields. 'The Engineering

Officer declared that since we had already four aircraft on the other side he could not possibly find the aircraft,' recorded 229 Squadron's diarist.

5 January 1945

Heavy snow and sleet, compounded by strong winds, marred the early morning activities making the Ramrod operation to the tram sheds doubtful indeed. Outside the dispersal area the Squadron's Spitfires were bogged down in the snow and mud. Only with all hands, aircrew and ground crew working together were they able to push the aircraft onto the perimeter track. To make up the twelve aircraft, two were borrowed from 453 Squadron but had great difficulty taking off from their base at Swannington. The airfield there was covered in ice and snow. Finally, the two Spitfires managed to take off and landed in time at Coltishall.

With engines ticking over, the pilots sat restlessly in their aircraft waiting for the signal that would send them into the cold morning air. At 10:20hrs they were told the operation would be postponed until 11:00hrs. But further bad news came less than thirty minutes later. 602 Squadron were to make up a wing with 229 Squadron, but they were unable to take off from the snow – and ice – covered tarmac at Swannington. At 11:00hrs the operation was postponed until 12:30hrs and at 12:10hrs it was cancelled. 'During the whole morning the weather had been terrible with snow, sleet and rain and no one really imagined the show would take place,' recorded 229 Squadron's diarist.

The pilots who had landed the day before in Belgium now returned to Coltishall. That section had been led by F/Lt Rigler. They made landfall on that mission over The Hague and were approaching the target when the leader's engine began running rough. Rather than abort the mission, Rigler decided to carry on, though he decided not to dive on the target because his engine was getting much worse. He turned out to sea, followed by W/O Nee and they both jettisoned their bombs in the water rather than over the built-up areas of The Hague. Over the target F/Lt Welsh and F/O Sanderson rolled into their dives from 8,000 feet down to 4,500 feet when they released their bombs but they saw no results and no explosions. After his dive, F/O Sanderson's engine began to fail as well. Detached from the rest of the section, Sanderson set a course for the closest friendly airfield, which was Maldegen in Belgium.

Over the R/T Rigler contacted the rest of the flight as they formed up on him, his engine still running rough and getting worse. They were three miles north-west of The Hague over water. The last thing he wanted was to ditch in the cold icy grey of the North Sea. Turning inland he decided the best course of action would be to land at Ursel also in Belgium. Setting a course he led the section to Ursel and they touched down at 12:55hrs. Three hours later, re-fuelled and with his engine purring smoothly, Rigler led the section to Maldegen to join F/O Sanderson. 'The engine trouble,' wrote 229 Squadron's diarist, 'was apparently caused by plugs. But it is believed that the pilots are somewhat prejudiced on account of them being a Packard Production.'

With Rigler, Sanderson, Welch and Nee safely back at Coltishall on the 5th and with the Ramrod operation to the tram sheds cancelled, the normal armed recces took place as the weather cleared in the afternoon.

At 13:35hrs four Spitfires took off from Coltishall heading towards Holland to attack The Hague/Ruis-en-Werve area. However, within twenty minutes P/O McConnochie experienced engine trouble and he turned back to base. The three remaining Spitfire XVIs continued on course, crossing land over Westhoofd. Turning towards the target, Kirkman spotted a V2 contrail shooting straight up coming from the Egmond/Haarlem area. He then spotted the target and gave the order to attack. Pushing the stick sideways, he touched his rudders and brought his wing up, rolling into a dive at 10,000 feet. Checking his instruments to make sure the aircraft was behaving properly, Kirkman rested his thumb on the firing button as the height flowed rapidly away. At 4,000 feet he released his bombs, pulled the stick back and climbed rapidly away. Turning tightly, Kirkman brought the aircraft around onto the target again and thumbed the firing button. His cannon burst into life as he strafed the target. There was no flak or activity from the enemy. Kirkman circled the target area, in formation with the other two Spitfires but by now a cloud had obscured the target and he could see no results from their bombing. They headed back to base.

7 January 1945

The Squadron's diarist recorded only one event on this day of any significance. At 14:30hrs six Spitfires were scrambled to intercept an unidentified aircraft, 'bogey' flying at 20,000 feet. They were scrambled in three sections of two aircraft and each section was given various vectors for interception and told to climb. The weather was so bad that most of the aircraft were airborne for only a few minutes before they were forced to return to base. Only F/Lt Welch made contact with the bogey, which turned out to be a friendly B17 Flying Fortress marked N.Z.Q with a C on its tail. Flying at 25,000 feet Welch was dressed only in his normal thin, threadbare battle dress, his Mae West over that and normal low shoes rather than flying boots. Tucking into formation with the B17, Welch checked to make sure everything was all right and flew with the bomber for forty-five minutes. The intense cold was seeping into his bones. Finally, the crew gave him the thumbs up and Welch peeled away, dropping rapidly to warmer temperatures. He landed back at base with his face, hands and feet numb.

The day's only armed recce took place in the afternoon. Led by F/Lt Rigler, the four Spitfires climbed slowly into the grey afternoon sky and headed out over the North Sea towards Holland. The target, The Hague/ Haagsche Bosch, was obscured completely by cloud so Rigler turned the section towards the secondary target, which was Rust-en-Vreugd. They attacked, dropping their bombs but could see no results from their efforts because of the clouds. Rigler spotted a four-ton vehicle on the Utrecht/ The Hague road and wheeled the section around to attack. One by one, the aircraft dropped on the vehicle raking it with machine-gun and cannon fire. Rigler's guns poured shells into the truck and he could see strikes hitting the vehicle and the road around it. They left the vehicle burning fiercely. The weather by now had worsened with poor visibility and cloud down to sea level and severe icing conditions. Rigler knew they had to get back as soon as they could before the weather got worse. He pushed the throttles open and tried to stay above the cloud for as long as possible. After several minutes over the North Sea the section dropped through the cloud and landed safely back at Coltishall at 16:30hrs.

8 January 1945

Heavy snow stopped all flying on this day. The Ramrod operation for attacking the tram sheds had been laid on for the morning again but was cancelled due to very poor weather. Instead of flying, the pilots listened to a representative from Rolls Royce talk about the Packard-built Merlin engines in the Spitfire XVI. The idea was to encourage the pilots to have faith in the American-built version of the magnificent Merlin. Whether he succeeded in giving the pilots the confidence they needed is not known. Only the amount of engine trouble they'd been experiencing with the new aircraft has been identified here.

9 January 1945

229 Squadron's diarist wrote: 'For some time now it has been known that 229 Squadron is to be disbanded (officially on 10 January 1945) and on return of 603 Squadron (Beaufighters) from the Middle East we should assume their title of 603 "City of Edinburgh" Squadron, it is not quite certain whether we shall absorb their personnel and remain doing exactly the same work with Spitfires or whether on the disbandment of 229, 603 Squadron will absorb our personnel. It now appears that we shall be known as 603 Squadron, and remain exactly as we are with the same pilots and commitments but will have the old 603 Echelon whilst the Squadron No. 229 will just disappear.'

This was the last entry in the official 229 Squadron History. They had played a major part in the dive-bombing campaign on the V2 sites in

Holland and would continue over the next few months to bomb and strafe the rocket sites until Allied ground forces overran them. But the pilots of 229 Squadron would be attacking as 603 Squadron. Their contribution to the success of the campaign can never be ignored.

Appendix D

603 Squadron History

To complete the additional Squadron Histories in these Appendices, some input from 603 City of Edinburgh Squadron is needed. 603 took a very active role during Operation Big Ben, but it was deemed necessary to only include a snapshot of their duties here, as too much repetition would be included (in comparison to the detailed transcript of 602 Squadron already presented):

23 January 1945

The aerodrome was still unusable owing to snow. During the morning two new pilots joined the Squadron, both Indians. It was noted that five more pilots would soon join the Squadron.

24 January 1945

After another night of hard frost, the snow still remained. Pilots stood by during the morning but were released at noon. In the afternoon photographs of the Squadron were taken by the photographic section.

In the evening 'A' Flight ground crew enjoyed a party put on for them by the pilots at a neighbouring hotel. The whole evening was very successful and thoroughly enjoyed by all in spite of a very cold ride through the snow and fog.

So far, the Squadron had been referred to in correspondence and communication as both 603 and 229 and for purposes of complete clarity as 603/229 or 229/603. In spite of repeated queries from various sources the adjutant, owing to lack of official information, was unable to answer enquiries as to what was really the correct squadron number. However, official word came through during the day that the Squadron would no longer be referred to as 229 Squadron but 603 City of Edinburgh Squadron.

26 January 1945

In spite of more snow falling during the night and throughout the morning, the first signs of a thaw appeared. In the morning, pilots attended a lecture on the mechanism and handling of Spitfire Mark XVIs (given by 303 Squadron), and primarily for the benefit of the 303 pilots who were shortly to convert from IXs to XVIs.

28 January 1945

A talk was given during the morning on Big Ben targets. Later, pilots were instructed in the cockpit layout and gyro sighting of the Spitfire XVI.

In the afternoon, Fitness Training (FT) was undertaken in the form of a snowball match between air and ground crew.

31 January 1945

Information came through that the body of F/Sgt Manley (the loss is recorded in Chapter II's 229s Squadron History) who was last seen on a Jim Crow on 15 September 1944, had been washed up on the Dutch coast.

Statistics for the month of January's flying were:

Total number of Operation sorties – 74
       ″   ″   ″   ″   hours – 96 hours, 20 minutes
       ″   ″   ″   ″   bombs dropped – 96x250 lbs

These figures were considerably lower than usual for any month but the aerodrome and weather had made flying impossible on no fewer than seventeen days.

Note: night flying tests in Mark V Spitfires were carried out by the Squadron on 17 January 1945.

3 February 1945

The day proved to be the best for several weeks, being warm and very sunny with clear blue skies. The aerodrome rapidly dried and became quite serviceable, so that even the new pilots were able to indulge in their first sector recce, but in Spitfire Vs (owing to the operational demands on the Spitfire XVIs).

An armed recce was led by F/Lt Batchelor to Staalduine Bosch at the Hook of Holland. The four aircraft went straight into bomb the target, which was very clearly seen in a shallow dive from south-east to north-west and from 10,000–4,000 feet. The bombing was very accurate indeed, and a cluster of five bombs fell right on the aiming point, which was a housing estate used as suspected billets and stores. This was very near three erections suspected to be flak positions. Black smoke was seen to rise. Two more bombs fell centrally on a large building with corrugated roofing.

As they turned to cross out west of Gravenzande at 7,000 feet at 15:35hrs, clouds of smoke were seen rising from the Loosduinen area where 602 and 453 Squadrons were attacking the tramway.

The flak from Staalduine Bosch Woods was very concentrated.

4 February 1945

A possible twelve aircraft show was in abeyance during the early morning on account of poor weather reports. But as the weather deteriorated – with low cloud and some drizzle – it was finally cancelled. There was then the possibility of an armed recce of eight aircraft taking off, but in view of the state of the drome and the high winds this was impracticable and could not materialise. Aircraft coming from the hangar could not taxi over the sodden turf and were forced to travel by the peritrack, sometimes taking nearly an hour to do so.

At 11:20hrs two of the readiness aircraft were scrambled for an x-ray at 22,000 feet but such was the state of the drome near the dispersal, one became bogged down and another took its place. F/Lt McAndrew and W/O Beckwith climbed to 4,000 feet and orbited about three miles east of base, but after a few minutes they were recalled and landed at 11:30hrs having seen nothing.[1]

6 February 1945

The weather was good for an early operation. A four aircraft show was arranged to bomb Target No. 1 (The Hague Loosduinen Oxygen Factory). It had been previously bombed on 3 February by 602 and 453 Squadrons. However, according to aerial photographs, the factory was still operational and a second attack was deemed necessary. This was cancelled due to poor weather conditions, but a successful attack was executed on The Hague.

8 February 1945

A day planned for armed recces and readiness, but that state of affairs did not remain long unaltered, and a show to attack The Hague to Loosduinen was laid on for 10:15hrs, later altered to 10:00hrs.

Before then, twelve aircraft, led by S/Ldr Rigler, took off on this attack and were to land and re-fuel at Ursel. They would then return to base after strafing transportation targets on the railways from Utrecht.

During the morning the other pilots were employed on the Link Trainer and at aircraft recognition in Dispersal.

The twelve aircraft on the show were airborne at 10:00hrs and flew into The Hague via The Hook of Holland at 9,000 feet. Sandwiched between thick cloud from deck to 1,000 feet and 10,000 feet upwards, they flew to Loosduinen hoping for a gap but finding none. They turned south and tried again. This time they were rewarded, a gap appearing over the storage and firing sites at Staalduine Bosch. All aircraft bombed and one strafed the target in dives from 10,000–4,000 feet, the leading four on a north-west/south-west course and the other section from north-east/south-west. Bombs were seen to fall well within the target area, mainly on the south-east corner, one building receiving a direct hit. The aircraft then made their way to Ursel where they landed at 11:30hrs.

Despite bad weather, the aircraft took off from Ursel again at 13:05hrs to strafe transportation targets on the main lines out of Utrecht but were ordered to return to base as the weather was still deteriorating. All aircraft landed at 14:05hrs having put in thirty operational hours. Four aircraft were then put on readiness and remained that way until dusk, but there were no untoward incidents.

9 February 1945

Four aircraft, led by F/Lt Batchelor, were airborne at 08:20hrs for an armed weather recce of The Hague area. For thirty miles out the weather was clear but then the cloud began from 3,000–4,000 feet, building up and consolidating in layers towards the east, but eventually the recce had to be terminated and the aircraft returned to base.

A second recce met a similar fate, but a third (at 12:30hrs) discovered that the cloud had moved significantly inland. The Spitfire XVIs quickly returned to base where a ramrod was laid on for 14:30hrs. Ten aircraft armed with one 500 lb bomb and two 250 lb bombs were airborne at 14:35hrs to attack The Hague/Loosduinen with the alternative of Staalduine Bosch. The aircraft set course and flew directly to The Hague, crossing over the Hook of Holland at 12,000 feet (15:00hrs). They then flew directly to Loosduinen, which was clearly visible, and at 15:02hrs in dives from 12,000–3,000 feet, bombed it on a course from east to west. The aircraft broke and climbed, and bursts were seen over the whole of the northern half of the target area.

One building was seen to be smoking badly, but after a second attack a large orange flash and a mushroom of orange smoke shot up from it. The aircraft then flew to Ursel, landing at 15:45hrs.

14 February 1945

At 09:25hrs twelve Spitfire XVIs, led by F/Lt Batchelor and each armed with a 1,000 lb bomb load, took off towards The Hague. Their mission was to attack storage sites. The formation flew straight to the target and dived from east to west from 10,500 feet to 4,000 feet. Bombs were seen to fall along the length of the road throughout the target area, but three sticks hit the target. Black 1 (F/Lt Welch) had a hang up caused by electrical failure and jettisoned his two 250 lb bombs at sea, taking his 500 lb bomb back to Ursel. The aircraft experienced moderate medium flak from the whole target area. However, at 12:10hrs, they were airborne again, attacking the liquid oxygen factory at Loosduinen, flying direct from Ursel to the target and attacking it from 10,000 feet in dives from 4,000 feet at 12:30hrs with cannon and machine-gun fire on an east/west course. The aircraft crossed out over The Hague and returned to base landing at 13:25hrs.

Immediately the aircraft were seized for re-fuelling and laid on for another show at 16:00hrs. However, while taxiing out F/O McConnochie had the misfortune to run into a tractor drawing a bomb trolley, which had remained in the peritrack despite the movement of aircraft. The bump was gentle and little damage seemed to have been done on cursory examination, and as the driver of the tractor baled out in time, no one was hurt. Only eleven aircraft took off on what was to be another successful mission on The Hague.

23 February 1945

Bad weather cancelled operations and the Squadron took the opportunity to move to their new home in Ludham.

28 February 1945

An extremely heavy programme was executed: thirty-six sorties were flown on ops and four non-ops, with a total of forty-seven hours and ten minutes operational flying and two hours thirty minutes non-ops flying.

The total operational sorties for February were 227; total operational hours 380 hours and fifteen minutes; total training sorties were 164; training hours 146 hours and forty minutes. 447 bombs were dropped on operational duties.

1 March 1945

V2 sites in The Hague were bombed by XVIs, led by F/Lt Bachelor, in dives from 10,000–2,000 feet.

2 March 1945

Four direct hits were again scored on a junction of roads believed to contain a V2 firing site, and two more on the main road running south.

F/Lt Welch led six XVIs at 14:25hrs in an effort to maintain the scale of attack before the weather began to close in. The policy was to completely destroy the Haagsche Bosch as a V2 firing site. At 15:08hrs the section dived from 7,000–3,000 feet along the main axis of the wood to score eight direct hits on the crossroads with four further hits on the road leading to it. Flak from this site had been getting less intense, and during this sortie no flak at all was experienced.

A total of 15,000 lbs of bombs were dropped by the Squadron during the day on the Haagsche Bosch and the standard of bombing was considered to be very high.

3 March 1945

After one sortie, aircraft were crossing out at Katwijk when at 7,000 feet they sighted a damaged Fortress, losing height at 140 mph. The inner starboard engine had been completely shot out. The Spitfires closed in and escorted the Fortress back to Woodbridge, where after giving the thumbs up sign, the pilot went in for a successful belly landing.

10 March 1945

603 Squadron, despite experiencing heavy cloud cover, managed to bomb V2 rocket sites. Forty-one sorties were flown, only one of which was abortive, thirty-two attacking their targets, the remaining eight forced to bomb railway lines.

14 March 1945

An armed recce of four aircraft was laid on for 08:45hrs, to be followed by a Squadron show in the early afternoon. However, low mist and thick haze out at sea postponed all operations and it was not until after 12:00hrs that any definite programme could be arranged. During the morning therefore, pilots spent time studying some new combat films. Ops then reported that the big show was off and that a programme of armed recces would be arranged. At 12:50hrs F/Lt Sergeant took off in a four-Spitfire XVI group with a 1,000 lb bomb load, specifically to bomb V2 sites. The pilots found the conditions quite good with no cloud but quite thick haze. At 13:30hrs they bombed their target, scoring four hits on the aiming point. No flak was encountered and the aircraft returned to base at 14:05hrs.

Just before they landed F/Lt Welch had taken off in a section of four more Spitfire XVIs, similarly armed to attack V2 sites at The Hague. They encountered light flak and returned safely to base at 15:50hrs.

29 March 1945

16:30hrs. An attack made on the V1 firing ramp at Ypenburg.[2]

Operational sorties for March totalled 626; operational hours 889 hours and twenty minutes; total number of bombs dropped: 1,385.

Note: Although 603 Squadron had some admin. problems (i.e. with their official name and relocating to be with 602 Squadron), they carried out many intense and accurate sorties during Operation Big Ben.

NOTES

1   It was deemed important to include this entry because it highlights the detail of the very poor weather conditions the Spitfires experienced during the winter of 1944/5.
2   A V1 target, but it must be stressed, this was unusual.

Appendix E

A Tribute to 453 Squadron

Due to repetition and space restrictions in this book, it was decided to showcase the work of 453 Squadron in one handy Appendix, which would highlight their contribution and pay tribute to the men who flew.

Under Article XV of the Empire Air Training Scheme, 453 Squadron came into being on 23 May 1941 at Bankstown in New South Wales. The Squadron's role would be to serve with the Royal Air Force overseas. The Squadron's first commanding officer, S/Ldr W H Harper, was an RAF officer and his pilots were made up mostly of Australian and New Zealand NCOs.

On 15 and 21 August 1941 the Squadron arrived in Singapore after departing Australia without aircraft. Here, the Squadron was equipped with the obsolete Brewster Buffalo fighter, which had proved to be no match for Germany's Luftwaffe. Indeed, the Buffaloes were shipped to Singapore under the assumption that Japanese aircraft would not be as good as the Germans' or the Allies'. That assumption proved to be wrong. As the Japanese swarmed through Malaya on 8 December 1941, the Squadron moved to a forward airfield in Ipoh to try to halt the invaders. Suffering heavy losses, the Squadron provided air cover for ground troops and attacked Japanese aircraft whenever they could and the unit met with success, destroying eight Japanese aircraft. The cost of this action was high as several Buffaloes were destroyed on the ground. The unit withdrew to Kuala Lumpur but lost more aircraft when the Japanese attacked with a large formation of bombers and fighters. The formation attacked 453's base and destroyed five Buffaloes further damaging another four aircraft. Vastly outnumbered, 453 pilots managed to shoot down four enemy aircraft during this action.

Left with only three serviceable aircraft, the squadron withdrew to Singapore on 24 December where it merged with RAF 251 Squadron. As the Japanese relentlessly advanced on the island, the squadron continued to fight against the invaders, hoping to stem their advance. Overwhelmed and outnumbered they continued to fight. On 26 January

1942 251 Squadron was evacuated from Singapore leaving 453 the only operational Squadron on the island to fight the Japanese. They fought on with six Buffalo aircraft until they were finally ordered to withdraw to Sumatra on 5 February 1942; the ground crew left by ship the next day. The remnant of 453 Squadron returned to Australia on 15 March 1942 and was immediately disbanded. But that was not the end of the story.

On 18 June 1942 at Drem, near Edinburgh, 453 was re-formed with new personnel and new aircraft, the Spitfire, and they soon joined Fighter Command operating from a series of airfields. With its new lease of life it did not take long for 453 Squadron to prove itself as a multi-role fighter squadron flying defensive patrols over England, escorting bombers over European skies as well as flying offensive roles across the North Sea on German targets.

By early 1944 their offensive patrols had been changed to defensive operations designed to keep German reconnaissance aircraft from detecting the build-up of shipping and materiel for the invasion of Europe. As Allied forces stormed the beaches of Normandy, overhead 453 Squadron's Spitfires flew combat patrols to keep the soldiers safe from enemy air attack. For the next three months of the war, the Squadron was involved in operations supporting the Allied advance into Europe from forward air bases on the continent now in Allied hands. Flying from these bases they could spend much more time operationally over the targets. But by September 1944, 453 Squadron had returned to England where its Spitfires turned their attention to attacking the V2 assembly, storage and launch sites in Holland. The last operational mission for 453 Squadron was escorting the aircraft that returned Queen Wilhelmina to the Netherlands, now liberated from German control, on 2 May 1945. The war in Europe ended six days later with Germany's surrender. On 29 August the Squadron moved from Britain to Germany to be part of a long-term Australian presence in Germany, but this never materialised and the Squadron disbanded at Wunsdorf on 21 January 1946.

Unlike the Allies, the Germans did not build large, four-engined bombers that could hit England from bases deep inside occupied Europe. At any rate, the chances of survival of enemy bombers over England after 1941 would have been slim indeed as the Royal Air Force continued to rebuild its forces after the Battle of Britain. At the same time the Americans were arriving, adding to the air power available. In the V2 rocket, however, the Germans had a potent weapon. Its range of 220 miles, extremely high speed, and one ton warhead gave the Germans their offensive arsenal.

The V2s now attacking England came from the area of Wassenaar, which was a region of pine woods and sand dunes near Leiden from the race course north of The Hague and from Walcheren Island. During late

September 1944 some V2s launched from Oudermirdum, north of Amsterdam, struck Norwich.

As we have already seen, the defence devised against this was to attack the launching sites, suspected supply routes and supply depots. One of the V2 storage sites for their liquid oxygen fuel was the 'House in the Wood', Huis-den-Bosch, in a wooded park in The Hague.

This historic structure had been built in 1645 and was very dear to the Dutch. It had originally been built for the Consort of the Prince of Orange and in 1899 hosted the first International Peace Conference. But now, the national Dutch treasure was being used for military purposes and posed a problem for the Allies. This prime target could only be attacked provided there was no destruction of Dutch property or any taking of Dutch lives.

Royal Australian Air Force 453 Squadron was the first squadron to make reconnaissance flights and the first attacks. Part of Number 12 Group of Fighter Command, 453 was stationed in the Coltishall sector with 229 and 602 Squadrons also tasked to attacking V2 sites. These three squadrons initially made up the anti-V2 wing.

At RAF Coltishall's satellite stripe Matlaske, 453 Squadron practised dive-bombing throughout October and November 1944 whilst continuing to fly reconnaissance flights to pin-point V2 sites. 453 also began re-equipping with the Spitfire XVI.

In November the Squadron moved to Swannington in Norfolk because the field at Matlaske had become waterlogged. From Swannington, 453 began their first attacks on the rocket sites in the wooded area around The Hague.

On 21 November four Spitfires climbed into the cold autumn air on their way to Holland. Led by S/Ldr Ern Esau DFC, the four fighters climbed to 10,000 feet as they headed towards rocket storage sites at Rust-en-Vreugd near The Hague. Over land, Esau led the flight down to 8,000 feet, then calling for the Squadron to attack over the R/T, he brought one wing up and rolled into his dive. Behind him the other three Spitfires did the same. At 4,000 feet, Esau released his bombs and pulled out of his dive, climbing quickly away to avoid flak. The other 453 pilots did the same. They could see that all the bombs had fallen in the target area. Turning the flight around on the target again, S/Ldr Esau dropped into a strafing run. Pressing the firing button he could see his shells ripping into buildings and vehicles before climbing hard. The flight formed up on him as they headed home.

Two hours later, F/Lt Bennett led another flight of Spitfires on a dive-bombing attack on rocket storage and firing site at Huis-te-Werve. Diving onto the buildings below, Bennett released his bombs and saw them fall into the target area as he pulled out of his dive. He could see the bombs from the rest of his flight also fall into the target area. On the way home, the Spitfires strafed what appeared to be a stationary V2 rocket. The same day another flight of Spitfires successfully attacked a rocket storage site at Waasenaar-Raaphorst.

Throughout November attacks on the V2 sites continued. On 1 December a planned combined strike with 602 Squadron on targets in the Haagsche Bosch had to be cancelled because of terrible weather. However, the mission was successfully carried out on 6 December 1944 when F/Lt Bennett led a flight of Spitfires to bomb targets near the Huis-den-Bosch. Checking his bank and indicator instruments, oil pressure and revs to see if all was well, he rolled into his dive, leading the flight down onto the target. One by one, the fighters released their bombs, which all landed in the target area with four hitting the pin-point site. The only damage done to the historic site was some broken glass in the windows.

Throughout December 1944 453 Squadron was very busy as the sorties mounted. The weapon load for the Spitfires was doubled on Christmas Eve with the aircraft now carrying two 250 lb bombs under the wings and one 500 lb bomb under the fuselage. The added weight cut down the Spitfire's range, forcing the squadrons using this new weapon-load to refuel at Ursel, a forward airfield in Belgium on the return journey.

On Christmas Eve 1944 thirty-three Spitfires from the anti-V2 wing mounted sorties for the heaviest attack to date on suspected sites carrying the additional bomb load. The first of these flights climbed away from Swannington in the morning. Roaring across the North Sea towards the Dutch coast they were headed for a new V2 target – a block of flats near Huis-den-Bosch at Hague Marlot that housed the troops used for launching the rockets. Twelve Spitfires from 453 took part in this raid, led by the CO S/Ldr Esau. Behind Esau, F/Lt Bennett's fighter was hit by flak and burst into flames. But before it disintegrated, Bennett managed to bale out around 1,000 feet landing between the target and the race course where he was taken prisoner and held as a POW until he was returned to 453 Squadron on 17 May.

Throughout January 1945, whenever weather permitted, the Squadron attacked targets in Huis-den-Bosch and Rust-en-Vreugd, but for most of that month the poor weather conditions made flying impossible. Three pilots from 453 Squadron were awarded the DFC in January: F/Lt Rusty Leith and F/Lt Pat McDade (who saw out the rest of the war as POWs) and F/O Fred Cowpe.

Some of 453 Squadron's pilots were on the receiving end of a V2 rocket attack when one crashed 150 yards from the hotel where P/O 'Froggie' Lyall and W/O Jack 'Stew' Stewart were staying while on leave in London.

With the bad weather of January behind them, 453 Squadron intensified their attacks throughout the month of February as improved conditions allowed the Squadron to fly 246 sorties. One of these targets was the liquid oxygen factory at Loosduinen that was surrounded by houses on three sides. It would prove to be a very difficult target to hit in order to avoid causing civilian casualties while destroying the factory's ability to function. Attacks were made from the fourth side and on 3 February 1945 S/Ldr Esau led twelve Spitfires into the target area in the early morning. He could see the installation below and ordered his flight to attack.

Checking his instruments, he touched the rudder, pulled the wing up and roared into a steep dive onto the target. One after the other, the remaining Spitfires followed, dropping their bombs with precision. Forming up over the target, Esau led the flight to Ursel where the Spitfires were re-fuelled and re-armed. A few hours later, they took off from Ursel and headed to the factory, again attacking it with bombs and cannon-fire before returning to England.

While attacks on the wooded areas of The Hague and Staalduine Bosch continued the squadron lost two aircraft. On 21 February W/O John Carmichael's Spitfire was hit by flak. He baled out north of Leyden and was hidden by Dutch farmers until liberated by Canadians on 11 May 1945. W/O Bill Gadd was shot down. Instead of baling out, he belly-landed at Rijswijk and was also hidden by the Dutch until the liberation of Holland.

Another 453 Squadron pilot was forced down on 18 March 1945 when F/O Ernest Tonkin force-landed, crashing into a ditch after attacking a rail junction at Gouda. His aircraft began emitting smoke as he pulled out of his dive. Struggling with his controls, he searched for an area to get his aircraft down safely. Hitting the ground he came to a dead stop in the ditch. Water started pouring into the cockpit as he struggled with his harness. After several anxious moments, he managed to climb out of the aircraft and head for cover. Later, he made contact with the Dutch underground and was hidden by them until the liberation.

W/Cdr Don Andrews was the Wing Leader for the anti-V2 wing based in the Coltishall area. Three days after Tonkin was shot down, Andrews' No. 2, F/O Marsh, was forced down, his engine having lost oil pressure after attacking rail targets near Noordwijk. Struggling to get his aircraft back home, he realised he wouldn't make England and he baled out near The Hague.

As he clinged to his dinghy in high seas, the Spitfires from his squadron circled above while a Catalina amphibious flying boat tried in vain because of high seas, to rescue him. Instead, a German Red Cross boat, just short of Ijmuiden harbour picked him up. Taken prisoner, his captivity lasted only a few weeks until Holland was liberated. He returned to his squadron on 16 May.

Pilots of 453 Squadron flew their last anti-V2 sortie on 30 March, attacking V2 transporters at Katwijk. The following day the Squadron attacked V2 railway trucks carrying rockets back to Germany.

Annexe A

602 City of Glasgow Squadron

RAF
S/Ldr R A Sutherland DFC
F/Lt H R P Pertwee
F/Lt J C R Waterhouse
F/Lt R H C Thomerson
F/Lt A C Pullman
F/Lt G D Stephenson
F/Lt J R Sutherland
F/Lt G G Lloyd
F/O R W Farfan
F/O D Hunnam
F/O R C Rudkin
F/O J W H Roberts
F/O R F Baxter
F/Lt J P Banton
W/O J Toone
W/O J Crosland
W/O S Sollitt
F/Sgt M V Francis
Sgt T L Love
Sgt S Gomm

Royal New Zealand Air Force
P/O H H M C Hardy NZ42707
W/O L T Menzies NZ411016
W/O H G Ellison NZ415304

Royal Canadian Air Force
F/O F J Farrell J44106

Royal Australian Air Force
W/O J P Ryan AUS410097
F/Sgt Zuber AUS424617

Polish Air Force
F/Lt Z Wroblewski

Late Arrivals
F/O W M Campbell
W/O J N Amies
W/O R M Baerlein
F/Lt J N Hubbard

Aircraft: Spitfire XVI, Spitfires VB, occasional use of Spitfire XIV and IX (Tiger Moth).

Other squadrons mentioned in Squadron History: 2nd Tactical Air Force, 603 Squadron and 124 Squadron, Intelligence 3F at Fighter Command, officers of the Allied Central Interpretation Unit at Medmenham (study of recon photos), 26 Squadron of Fighter Command.

Annexe B

List of Spitfires that flew with 602 Squadron

(When Squadron Histories were analysed, 602 Squadron and others did not identify serial number of aircraft to pilot. However, they have now been restored as much as was deemed relevant for this work.)

Spitfires Mark XVI SM (unless otherwise stated)

Serial number	History of aircraft

SM205 – dive-bombing prototype J Quill

Serial number	History of aircraft
SM234	602S 20-11-44
SM235	602S 20-11-44
SM254	602S 23-11-44
SM257	602S 27-11-44
SM287	602S 27-11-44
SM288	602S 27-11-44
SM296	602S 23-11-44
SM301	602S 23-11-44
SM307	602S 25-11-44
SM341	602S 23-11-44
SM342	602S 22-12-44
SM343	602S 23-11-44
SM350	602S 23-11-44
SM351	602S 23-11-44
SM352	602S 23-11-44
SM353	602S 23-11-44
SM358	602S 22-12-44
SM361	602S 23-11-44
SM388	602S 23-11-44
SM424	602S 23-11-44

Annexe C

603 City of Edinburgh Squadron

From 24 January 1945, 229 Squadron was renamed 603 City of Edinburgh Squadron, and its pilots for the months of February and March 1945 (during Operation Big Ben) are as follows:

S/ Ldr D F M Rigler
F/Lt Welch
F/Lt Kirkman
F/Lt Batchelor
F/Lt McAndrew
F/Lt Staniforth
P/O Doidge
F/Sgt O'Reilly
W/O Mee
W/O Cookson
W/O Beckwith
W/O Thomson
W/O Wheatley
F/O Machon

P/O McGinn
F/O Burrows
P/O Manivelu
F/O Richmond
F/Sgt Laffan
W/O Maslen
F/Sgt Webb
S/Ldr Donovan
W/O Haupt
P/O McConnachie
F/O Sanderson
F/Lt Sergeant
W/O Green
W/O Godfrey
W/O Beckwith

Annexe D

List of Spitfires that flew with 603 Squadron

Spitfire Mark XVI SM and TB

(Accuracy rather than uncheckable quantity has been the watchword of this Annexe.)

Serial number	Flight history
SM337	603S CACOPS 10-3-45
SM340	603S CACOPS 5-3-45
SM348	603S FAAC 14-2-45
SM357	603S 18-1-45
SM385	603S CACOPS 10-3-45
SM396	603S
SM405	603S 9-3-45
TB357	603S 9-2-45
TB376	603S 13-2-45

Annexe E

124 Baroda Squadron

Spitfire IX HF (E)
Note: In the Squadron History, some aircraft serial numbers are given for each pilot. Included in the following Annexe is one serial number per pilot. The reader will note some repetition in serial numbers. This is due to the same aircraft being flown by different pilots.

Pilot	*Serial Number*
F/L A Charlesworth	RK860
W/O J James	PV299
W/O G Beadle	PV434
W/O C Farquharson	PV318
S/L G Scott	PV312
F/O W Andrews	RR252
F/O R Johnson	PV344
F/L J Maltby	PV283
F/L F James	PV354
F/L B Brooks	TA795
W/O N Howard	PV299
W/O P Jones	PV354
F/L J Melia	SM515
W/O E Parker	TA811
F/L R Forth	TA813
F/L P Phillips	PV151
F/L K Lawrence	SM515
W/O G Peterson	TA811
W/O A Williams	TA811
F/O A Travis	TA811
W/O McCall	TA811
F/L M Lloyd	PV296
F/O H Fallen	PV344
F/S F Oakley	FV283
F/S C Lett	PV296

F/O D Roy	RK911
F/L Oakshott	TA804
F/L J Fowler	RK911
Sgt C Lattimer	FV151
F/L J Hackett	TA811
W/O F Kelman	TB550
F/L C Gray	PV303

Annexe F

List of Spitfires that flew with 124 Baroda Squadron

Duties of aircraft: recce, patrol, escort, standard bombing, dive-bombing during Operation Big Ben and an air-sea rescue search. Total tour duration: September 1944 to April 1945. For this Squadron, it was decided to include a more complete history of the aircraft to clearly show the amount of useage (outside Operation Big Ben) each aircraft endured.

Spitfire IX (HF) E (unless otherwise stated)

Serial number	History of aircraft
PL 249	M70 39MU 17-6-44 504S 15-7 DeH 18-8 124S 25-3-45 12Gp Com Flt 20-9 SOC scrap 16-10-47
PV 151	M70 33MU 23-11-44 124S 1-2-45 6MU 17-10-47 sold E Smelt 25-5-50
PV 212	M70 9MU 18-9-44 124S FACE 15-2-45 SOC 22-2
PV 283	M70 45MU 2-11-44 504S 9-12 124S 25-1-45 29 MU 4-9 sold VA 5-12-49
PV 296	M70 25-9-45 124S 7-2-46 29MU 25-9 RDAF 25-10-48 as 414
PV 299	M70 8MU 27-9-44 124S 5-2-45 GAAC 7-6 ROS 29MU 5-9 Farn 7-1-49 loaned as fus only for test SOC 11-8
PV 303	M70 BHM 24 45MU 3-10-44 504S 22-12 124S 25-1-45 29MU 5-9 RDAF 20-11-48 as 415
PV 312	M70 45MU 26-9-44 124S 26-10 ROS Hutton Cranswick 23-8-45 VA EA 25-4-46 recat E
PV 318	M70 8MU 27-9-44 124S 5-2-45 ROS VAOx 16-3 124S dvd i/grd from cloud CE Full Sutton Yorks 29-5 SOC 31-5
PV 343	M70 8MU 27-9-44 504S 3-12 124S 25-1-45 329S 20-9 FAAC 15-11 FAF 24-11
PV 344	BHM M70 9MU 2-10-44 124S 7-2-45 29MU 20-9 RDAF as 417 28-10-48

PV 354	M70 45MU 29-9-44 124S 5-2-45 ROS 23-3 595S 6-9 RDAF as 418 28-10-48
RK 811	M70 6MU 16-9-44 345S 15-10 340S 23-11 341S 15-2-45 329S 22-3 595S 16-8 287S 22-11 RDAF 22-9-48 as 419 cd nr Skrystrup 27-2-50
RK 860	M70 8MU 12-10-44 124S 30-1-45 CE ops 25-3 SOC 8-5
RK 908	M70 33MU 18-10-44 124S 24-1-45 ROS VA 12-3 sold H Bath 27-4-49
RK 911	HFIX M70 8MU 12-10-44 124S 3-2-45 29MU 4-9 RDAF as 419 23-3-48 cd nr Ikast 12-1-49
RR 209	M70 45MU 14-10-44 124S 5-2-45 FACB 7-6 ASTH RDAF as 421 28-10-48
RR 252	HFIXE as MM4113 M70 39MU 19-10-44 124S 8-2-45 29MU 13-9 RDAF as 422 12-3-48 scrapped 1-9-53
SM515	HFIXE M70 33MU 23-11-44 124S 23-1-45 ROS VAO sold E Smelt 8-6-50
TA 793	39MU 7-12-44 82MU 31-12 SS275 19-1-45 Hap 13-2*
TA 795	M70 39MU 11-12-44 124S 23-1-45 CAC ops 9-3 DeH recat E 30-7 SOC 18-8
TA 796	M70 39MU 12-12-44 124S 24-3-45 595S 6-9 130S 15-8-46 to 6139M 16-9
TA 800	M70 33MU 12-12-44 124S 16-3 329S 30-8 FAF 24-11 GC2/7
TA 804	M70 33MU 9-12-44 124S 25-3-45 FAAC 30-5 595S 2-9 130S 16-5-46 abs SOC 5-2-47
TA 811	M70 39MU 11-12-44 124S 23-1-45 sold VA 28-11-49
TA 813	M70 39MU 11-12-44 124S 23-1-45 FAAC 5-2 ROS sold RDAF as 424 20-11-48
TB 918	M70 6MU 28-2-45 124S CE ops 30-3-RNAF 1946

Annexe G

229 Squadron

The following listing for 229 Squadron was made in the Squadron History on New Year's Day 1945. Entries noted with '*', means that the name of the pilot in the Squadron History is in extremely light type and therefore some error is possible in the spelling of his name. Apologies for any possible flaw.

'A' Flight
P/O Doidge
F/Lt McAndrew
P/O Grant (Can)
F/Sgt O'Reilly
F/Sgt Thomson
F/Sgt Wheatley (Aus)
F/O Trail
F/Sgt Green (Aus)

'B' Flight
F/Lt Co T Rigler, DFM
F/Lt Welch, DFC
F/Lt Kirkham (Aus)
P/O McConnochie (NZ)
P/O Van Dyux (Belgium)
W/O Cookson
F/Sgt Haupt*
W/O Breckith
F/O Manderson*
W/O Mee*

Intelligence Officer P/O H Cooper ably assisted by Cpl Stammers.

*Engineering Officer F/O Stedman

Annexe H

V1, V2 Target Statistics

The last rocket fell in the UK on 27 March 1945. In total 1,115 rockets fell. Of these, a total of 518 rockets fell in the London Civil Defence Region (from 8 September 1944).[1]

The tendency to fire principally at night, which had been noticed towards the end of February (and which was an indication of the effectiveness of the counter-offensive) remained very marked: only 36 per cent of these rockets fell in daylight.

Casualties would have been light during the period compared to earlier weeks but for ill-fortune which saw the last rocket but one fall on a block of workers' flats (Hughes Mansions, in Stepney). The flats were hit at 07:21hrs on 27 March; 134 people were killed and forty-nine seriously injured. Casualties for the last fortnight totalled 308 killed and 604 seriously injured, compared to 394 killed and 763 seriously injured in the previous fortnight. These brought the total casualties from rockets for the whole period of attack to 2,511 killed and 5,869 seriously injured in London, and 213 killed and 598 seriously injured elsewhere.

NOTE

1 See *Air Defence of Great Britain RAF Narrative* Vol. 6 (formerly Vol. 7).

Source Material

602, 603, 229, 124 Squadron Histories; *Air Defence of Great Britain (Vol. 6 formerly Vol. 7)*; original log book of F/Lt Raymond Baxter and exclusive Operation Big Ben interviews with the pilot; *Field Marshal Alanbrooke's diaries, The Memoirs of Field Marshal Montgomery; The Memoirs of Lord Ismay; Fight for the Sky – The story of the Spitfire and the Hurricane* by Douglas Bader; *Spitfire – The History* by Eric B Morgan and Edward Shackley; *Jaguar Heritage* Magazine (issue two); the Imperial War Museum for plans and photographic reference.

Index